J.R.D. Heaton.

Received from World of Books.com on 23.7.2015.

PHILIP SNOWDEN: A BIOGRAPHY

To Jack Reynolds, who first provoked my
interest in Labour history

PHILIP SNOWDEN: A BIOGRAPHY

1864–1937

KEITH LAYBOURN

TEMPLE SMITH

Published by
Wildwood House Limited
Gower House
Croft Road
Aldershot
Hants GU11 3HR
England

and distributed by
Gower Publishing Company
Old Post Road
Brookfield
Vermont 05036
USA

British Library Cataloguing in Publication Data

Laybourn, Keith
Philip Snowden: a biography 1864–1937.
1. Great Britain. Politics. Snowden,
Philip - Biographies
I. Title
941.082′092′4

Library of Congress Cataloging-in-Publication Data

Laybourn, Keith.
Philip Snowden: a biography: 1864–1937/by Keith Laybourn.
p. cm.
Bibliography: p.
Includes index.
1. Snowden, Philip Snowden, Viscount, 1864–1946. 2. Politicians-Great Britain—Biography. 3. Socialists—Great Britain—Biography. 4. Great Britain—Politics and government—1901–1936. I. Title.
DA566.9.S55L39 1988
941.083′092′4—dc 19
[B] 87-36558
CIP

ISBN 0 566 07017 0

Printed and bound in Great Britain at
The University Press, Cambridge

Contents

List of Tables

Acknowledgements

This biography could not have been written without the help of many individuals and institutions. I owe a particular debt to David James, the Bradford Archivist, who has long sustained an interest in the Keighley Labour movement and Snowden. But my thanks extend to all those libraries and library staff who have helped in my research.

This topic has, of course, been motivated by discussions with many individuals. I would particularly like to thank Dr David Clark MP, who first drew my attention to Snowden's work in the Colne Valley, and Jack Reynolds, who has been a constant source of inspiration and advice over many years.

I would like to acknowledge that the MacDonald diaries were 'meant as notes to guide and revive memory as regards happenings and must on no account be published as they are'. In line with Ramsay MacDonald's wishes I have used only small parts of his diaries and not sought to publish it *extenso*.

Abbreviations

ASE	Amalgamated Society of Engineers
BSP	British Socialist Party
CVDLP	Colne Valley Divisional Labour Party
CVLL	Colne Valley Labour League
CVLU	Colne Valley Labour Union
CVSL	Colne Valley Socialist League
ILP	Independent Labour Party
LRC	Labour Representation Committee
NAC	National Administrative Council (of the ILP)
NEC	National Executive Committee (of the LRC and Labour Party)
SDF	Social Democratic Federation
SDP	Social Democratic Party

1 Introduction

Philip Snowden was a profoundly controversial figure in the early years of the British Labour movement. His name is closely associated with that of Ramsay MacDonald in the 'betrayal' of 1931, which saw the end of the second Labour Government. Although his involvement with MacDonald's National Government was brief and tenuous, an unforgiving Labour movement, stung by his reference to Labour's electoral programme for 1931 as 'Bolshevism run mad', was almost as obsessionally hostile to him as it was to MacDonald. But Snowden had often been at the centre of controversy within the Labour movement even before the events of 1931 cut him adrift. In the years before the First World War he had established himself as one of the 'Big Four' in the Independent Labour Party (ILP), alongside MacDonald, Glasier and Hardie and, with them, had resigned from the National Administrative Council of the ILP in 1909 when their authority was challenged by Victor Grayson and others. The First World War saw him deeply involved in organizing the ILP's peace campaign at a time when the majority of the Labour movement were actively involved in the war effort. During the 1920s he switched political allegiance, moving from the ILP to the Labour Party in an atmosphere of internecine conflict. He also extended his reputation for hostility to trade unionism and was suspected of taking preliminary soundings on the viability of a Lib–Lab alliance.

Such controversy fuelled the forthright manner in which Snowden pursued his political principles and priorities. Indeed, in later years it was often his approach rather than his policies which drew most adverse comment. Yet, in his early years, his determination, constancy and resilience were a boon to an embryonic ILP. He was proud of being a Yorkshireman and resolved to show his Yorkshire 'grit' at every opportunity. This helped him to carve out his political reputation in Keighley and the textile district of Yorkshire where the forces of Liberalism were so powerfully opposed to the political independence of the working class. He, and a small band of ILP members, helped to turn that district into a centre of independent labour activity. He became a firm believer in the moral rightness of socialism and was lionized as one of the great ethical socialists of the Labour movement. His sermons – the most famous being 'The Christ that is to be' – drew widely from his nonconformist upbringing and advocated that socialism was the true liberator of the people and the guarantor of democratic rights. He soon became recognized as one of the great advocates of what was referred to as the 'religion of socialism'. The power of his message must have surprised those who saw him for he was small, frail, white-faced, plainly dressed and crippled to the extent of having to use walking sticks.

Attuned to the environment of the northern industrial areas, raised as a Wesleyan Methodist and steeped in the political atmosphere of Liberal Radicalism, it is not surprising that Snowden should faithfully reflect the attitudes of his youth throughout his political career. He was a lifetime advocate of temperance, a faithful adherent of Gladstonian economics, totally committed to free trade and the gold standard, and staunchly Liberal Radical in his commitment to peace. What is more, he was absolutely convinced of the rightness of his own position and rather less loose-footed in his policies than many other prominent politicians. A. G. Gardiner, a friend from his Blackburn days, detected his resolute approach to politics well before the First World War. He wrote:

> Constancy is a rare virtue in politics. There are few men whom it would be safe to forecast their intellectual and political point of view ten years hence. But whatever happens, Philip Snowden will be where he stands to-day.[1]

Another writer added:

> To Mr. Gardiner, Mr. Snowden seemed the man of *idée fixe*, a Socialist *sans phrase*. . . . He was doctrinaire and academic in the extreme; but he fused his theories with an enthusiasm that burned at white heat. If ever there were a revolution in this country, Mr. Snowden would be 'Robespierre of the concentrated and remorseless purpose'.[2]

These comments captured the essence of Snowden's political character. He was always implacable in his approach and fixed in his ideas. These were qualities which proved useful in the hostile political environment of the Yorkshire and Lancashire textile districts in the 1890s, but they appeared harsh, grating and restrictive once the Labour Party began to make political ground after its parliamentary breakthrough in the 1906 General Election. His ascetic and puritanical Liberal Radical style was less relevant once the trade union movement nailed its flag to the Labour mast.

Nevertheless, Snowden rose swiftly in Labour politics and remained prominent until 1931. In 1898 he was returned to the National Administrative Council (NAC) of the ILP and from then onwards was rarely out of the political limelight: chairman of the ILP from 1903 to 1906 and again between 1917 and 1920: MP for Blackburn from 1906 to 1918 and MP for Colne Valley between 1922 and 1931, before being raised to the House of Lords; and, of course, Chancellor of the Exchequer of the first two Labour governments.

Considering Snowden's political importance surprisingly little has been produced on his career in comparison with other important figures of his generation. He provided his own pawky and partial account, *An Autobiography*, in 1934 but apart from this there have been only three full biographies of his life. Two were published in 1929 and 1930, before his political defection from the Labour Party, and both present rather rosy and uncritical assessments of his career. The most recent, the late Colin Cross's *Philip Snowden* (1966), is a respectful and gentle contribution which contrasts sharply with the more vitriolic personal attacks launched by Robert Skidelsky, in his *Politicians and the Slump* (1967).

Three sympathetic biographies, the last appearing twenty years ago, are a poor testimony to Snowden's contribution to the growth of the Labour Party. This examination of Snowden's life attempts to provide a more critical and up-to-date assessment of his contribution to the Labour movement and to illustrate the reason for his defection from Labour in 1931. Most readers will be attracted to the chapters which deal with the part he played in the notorious events which led to the end of the second Labour Government and the formation of the National Government. But in some senses, the whole book is built around this concern for it asks the reader to keep in mind two related questions. First, how far was Snowden's position on the events of 1931 consistent with his earlier life? Secondly, given his prominence in Labour circles, how typical was he of his generation of Labour politicians. Indeed, did 1931 see the end of the class of 1906 – the influence of Snowden and the other 29 Labour MPs who were returned to Parliament?

Whatever else emerges, it is clear that Snowden was typical of the Liberal Radical strand of Labour politicians which dominated the Labour Party leadership after 1906, although there was a second strand composed of trade union representatives in Parliament. For the first three decades of the twentieth century, these strands were always likely to clash and split the party. But largely because of the weakness of intellectual debate within the Labour Party, this split did not occur until 1931 when the defence of working-class interests dictated that a large proportion of the party, including the trade union section, found the consequences of Snowden's economic policies, which prescribed the cutting of unemployment benefits, unacceptable. It was Snowden's desire to maintain the principles and priorities of his youth, forged in the enervating environment of solid Liberal Radical nonconformity, that led him to support the MacDonald National Government in 1931. He thus became an isolated and hated ex-Labour leader – a once-revered figure who had helped to hand over power to Labour's political enemies.

Notes

1 W. W. Henderson, 'The Rt. Hon. Philip Snowden MP: Labour's First Chancellor of the Exchequer' in Herbert Tracey (ed.), *The Book of the Labour Party: Its History, Growth, Policy and Leaders* (Caxton, n.d.), p. 170.
2 Ibid.

2 Early Days in the Pennines

The experience of early life often shapes the man. In the case of Philip Snowden this adage was always evident in the beliefs and political style which he adopted throughout his career – though one should treat with care his description of himself as 'only a stolid, unimaginative, unpractical, truthful Yorkshireman'.[1]

Snowden was born on 18 July 1864 in the remote Pennine moorland parish of Cowling, near Keighley, in the West Riding of Yorkshire, the son of John and Martha, cotton and worsted weavers of Ickornshaw. It was in this small textile community, and its immediate vicinity, that he spent his early years.

The parish and township of Cowling covered an area of about 5,000 acres and was formed in December 1844 out of the old parish of Kildwick. It was spread across the natural divide of the Pennines and, despite being only five or six miles from Skipton, Keighley and Colne, was isolated by its terrain and limited transport facilities. Its bleak and harsh moorland environment meant that it was only really suitable for marginal pastoral agriculture, such as sheep rearing. Yet its economy had become more diversified in the eighteenth century when, faced with a general rising demand for textiles, many farmers and inhabitants turned to the domestic production of cotton and worsted pieces. John Snowden had in fact been a domestic weaver in his early years, though he must have been amongst the last generation so employed for the local handloom economy had disappeared by the time of Philip's birth, replaced by a small-scale factory production of textiles.

By the 1860s Cowling was in sharp economic decline. A combination of factors – the isolated nature of the area, the development of the nearby industrial centres of Keighley and Colne and the trade depressions of the 1850s and 1860s, caused by the interference of trade resulting from the Crimean War and the American Civil War – combined to depress its economy. As a result, the population, which had increased rapidly in the eighteenth century, began to drift away: decreasing from 2,247 in 1841 to 1,908 in 1871.

The community attracted few outsiders after the 1840s and this is clearly shown by the fact that, according to the 1871 census returns, more than 95 per cent of the population were born in Cowling. Those born outside the parish were usually professional people who had been specifically recruited to the area. They included George Bayldon, the vicar of Cowling, who was born in Barnsley, and Hannah Davy, the schoolmistress at Ickornshaw, born at Monkwearmouth, Durham.

The insularity of the community was further emphasized by the intermarriage of a relatively small number of families – such as the Snowdens, Binns, Gotts, Smiths, Emmotts, Nelsons and Whitakers. Philip was rather vague about his family pedigree, but it is clear that the Snowdens had intermarried with the Binns and Whitakers, old Cowling families, and that his mother, a Nelson, was descended from the Emmotts who had been farmers in the parish for several centuries. It is interesting to note that, in 1871, three of the 33 families living in the hamlet of Ickornshaw were named Snowden, that several others nearby shared the same name, and that James Whitaker farmed 60 acres of land at Ickornshaw. It is not too fanciful to suggest that they were all related.

Philip's parents had been born in Cowling – John in 1830 or 1831 and Martha in 1834.[2] They had three children – Mary Rebecca, born in the parish in 1858; Sarah, born at Haworth in 1861; and, of course, Philip, born at Middleton, a row of cottages on the hillside above the hamlet of Ickornshaw. From Philip's birth until 1879 his parents worked at a mill in Ickornshaw, most probably that of Phineas Snowden who employed 75 workers in 1871. At this time Ickornshaw was a small textile community of 160 people which, because it had schools, a chapel and a public house, as well as a medium-sized mill and two smaller outlying mills, acted as a focus of life for another 500 or so people who lived nearby.

Life for the Snowdens was probably no different from that of many other weaving families. In the 1860s and 1870s, West Riding weavers generally earned the paltry wage of 15 shillings per week, if they were men, and slightly less if they were women. Their wages were amongst the lowest in the textile trade and were subject to 'broken time', a form of unemployment between completing one piece and taking out an order, or ticket for another. Most weaving families were poor and usually only obtained a modest standard of living when all members were fully employed. In the case of the Snowdens, both parents worked and both daughters started as half-timers, dividing their time between school and factory when they reached the age of ten. Generally, they were fully employed, careful with their income and able to save in the Yorkshire Penny Bank. John Snowden must have been more assiduous and fortunate than many though, for Philip intimates that he had saved about £200 or £300 by the late 1870s, a fact which helps to explain why Philip was not forced to follow the usual course of entering the mill at the age of ten.

It was only through saving part of their small and fitful earnings that weaving families could expect to protect themselves against the vagaries of working-class life. Trade unionism was endemically weak amongst the West Riding textile workers and does not appear to have been an alternative available to the workers of Ickornshaw: local mill owners would have easily identified and 'blacked' anyone who challenged them in so small a community. But such action was not necessary, for the independent and assertive tendencies of workers were channelled into the more internalized practice of dissent and nonconformity.

The Church of England had opened a parish church for Cowling in 1845 and a Baptist Chapel had started in the hamlet of Cowling Hill in 1744, but the predominant religious faith of the area was Wesleyan Methodism, based upon Ickornshaw Chapel. The faith had been brought to the area in 1796 by Abram Binns who opened a chapel and a Sunday school. It expanded rapidly and a new chapel had to be opened in 1876. It was a plain and substantial building with accommodation for 500 attendants and contained a Sunday school, consisting of a hall and two classrooms, which could cater for up to 300 young children and their teachers.

The Snowdens' life revolved around the Wesleyan Chapel. John, who had received little formal education, was a regular chapel-goer and had attended the Sunday school as a boy. Indeed, by the 1870s he had become Superintendent of the Sunday school. Philip also attended both the chapel and the Sunday school, later recalling the 'hell-fire' lectures and the Revival sermons held there. Responding to his father's example and the dour tradition of the area, he took 'the pledge' to abstain from drink and was near to 'conversion' to Methodism. But he was not converted and explained this decision many years later, in 1898.

> I have still a very vivid recollection when a boy of eight, after a revival sermon in which the terrors of a burning hell had been depicted with rather more than usual realistic power, of 'going to the penitent form to get converted'. I struggled on my bended knees hard and long, my tears of penitence for my hell-deserving crime flowed copiously, but no relief could I get from the heavy burden of my sins. One after another my fellow-penitents jumped to their feet, shouted frantically, then sang vociferously. They had found Salvation. At last I was left alone, the one goat among the flock. This increased my desperation, for I remembered how my Sunday school teacher had often taught us that some would be taken and others would be left, and the preacher that night had told us that the Spirit of the Lord would not always strive with men. I began to think that because I had been such a hardened sinner (at eight) and refused to answer the pleadings of His Spirit, that the Lord had turned away from me in anger, and I was doomed to be eternally damned. A few earnest souls remained with me till very late. They prayed, they sang in major and minor, but their most powerful exhortations added to my

> pitiable penitence, could effect no change in my feelings. I passed a sleepless night. Towards morning the reaction came. I became reconciled to the prospect of an eternity in hell. It is surprising what consolation resignation to fate can give. As soon as I made up my mind that there was to be no salvation for me, the prospect of a burning bottomless pit ceased to have any terrors whatever. I began to rebel against a fate which had shut me out of heaven at eight years of age . . .; my sentence was not just, so my spirit asserted itself, and I determined that I would ask no longer for pardon from such a hard and unjust judge. This juvenile experience was very valuable, for it settled the hell and damnation question once and for all. From that day I could listen with grim pleasure to the blackest sermon ever preached and I could snap my fingers in the face of a vindictive monster who could have prepared such a punishment even for the deepest sinner.[3]

Though the precise nature of Philip's youthful rebellion may be questioned in the light of his self-justifying stance of the late 1890s, it is clear that he was not converted though he continued to attend both chapel and Sunday school. He may have been raised as a Methodist and in a religious atmosphere but his mind remained open to other forms of salvation.

To this may be added the educational opportunities which came Philip's way. His father, a fervent Radical Liberal committed to progress and self-help, was clearly ambitious for his son and permitted him to stay at school beyond the normal cut-off point of ten when he would normally have gone to the mill. Philip was also fortunate that educational horizons were being widened for working-class children. The 1870 Education Act had permitted school boards to be set up in areas of educational deficiency in order to supplement the existing private and Church school provision. Cowling formed such a board and Philip, having attended a Church school from 1869 to 1874, transferred to the Board school in 1874. He flourished in this new educational environment and was appointed pupil teacher by the Board in 1877; this meant that he had to take charge of a class throughout the school hours and to attend school every morning at 7.00 am for instruction from the headmaster. At this stage, Philip was set fair to be a schoolmaster.

As an exceptionally able child, Philip read more widely than most of his school friends. He read a variety of penny story books based on the adventures of Dick Turpin and, when W. Stead, editor of *Review of Reviews*, enquired into the reading of the newly-returned Labour MPs in 1906, Ethel, Philip's wife, wrote that 'The novels of Scott, Dickens, Thackeray and Eliot were the delight of his boyhood days'.[4] Other sources suggest that he read some of the work of Carlyle and Ruskin and other literary works typical of late Victorian Radicalism. He was nearly thirty before he began to read socialist literature. Ethel also added:

> But men have taught him more things than books, and a close observation of the minds and manners of the people amongst whom he lived has taught him more than the library of 2,000 volumes he has accumulated.[5]

In something as nebulous as a man's ideas it is perhaps fair to accept Ethel's point. Certainly Philip's thinking owed something to the isolated, independent, nonconformist and Radical environment of Ickornshaw.

Yet that influence must not be exaggerated. Whilst Snowden's advocacy of temperance and the missionary style of his oratory were based upon his early experiences, he was clearly denying some of his cultural environment. Also, he was of a new working-class generation who perceived increasing opportunities for lower-middle-class status beckoning with the extension of education and the vigorous emergence of a tertiary service and administrative sector in the British economy. This may well provide the clue to Snowden's early ambition and the attitudes which he later held in the Labour Party. He owed little to traditional working-class institutions, such as trade unions, and much to his educational upbringing. Aspiring to the non-industrial employment of the lower middle class, he saw himself as the impartial adviser whose decisions would be based upon soundness of principle rather than empathy with, or loyalty to, a particular social class. Indeed, in later political life he shared with MacDonald, and other Labour leaders, the vision of a Labour Party which drew support from all classes. This was, perhaps, based upon the fact that both eschewed the normal pattern of working-class life. Education and aspiration helped to make Snowden an outsider.

Snowden's career opportunities widened substantially in 1879 when the weaving mill at Cowling went out of business, throwing his family out of work. As a result they moved to nearby Nelson, in Lancashire, and Philip found employment as a clerk in an Insurance office at Burnley, a post which he kept until 1886.

The time he spent in Nelson was crucial to his political development. During these years he became increasingly aware of Radical politics and was closely involved in the agitation which surrounded the introduction of the 1884 Reform Bill, which extended the parliamentary vote to more working men. He recalled that

> Although still in my teens, I never missed a meeting in the district. I remember, when the House of Lords suppressed the County Franchise Bill, walking in a procession holding aloft a banner with the words: 'Down with the House of Lords' inscribed upon it.[6]

Religious nonconformity was powerful in the area and throughout the 1880s the Nelson Liberation Society mounted a strong campaign to disestablish the Church of England. Although Snowden's nonconformity was now cooler than it had previously been, he was deeply involved in the work of the Liberation Society: 'The Liberation Society held many meetings in the district, and they aroused intense interest. I never missed one of them.'[7]

A political attachment to Liberal organization now complemented Snowden's Radical Liberal sentiments. Indeed, he was to remain a firm supporter of the Liberal Party until the mid-1890s, and to retain a faith in the economic principles of Gladstonian Liberalism – particularly the need for free trade and balanced budgets – until his death in 1937. His commitment to free trade was indeed strengthened when he encountered the National Fair Trade League in the early 1880s. This was an organization which, whilst it demanded reciprocity in international trade, was advocating the introduction of protective tariffs for British goods. It was led by two manufacturers who were associated with the Bradford textile trade – W. Farrer Ecroyd, a manufacturer in the Bradford light dress trade and MP for Preston, and Samuel Cunliffe Lister, owner of Manningham Mills. It was a lecture by Ecroyd, delivered in Nelson, which convinced Snowden that protectionists were simply concerned with obtaining higher profits for British manufacturers.

He was also captivated by the lectures of ex-Chartist leaders. He listened to George Lomax, a Manchester Temperance and Radical speaker and to Thomas Cooper. By the 1880s most of the old Chartist activists had been absorbed by the Liberal Party and the message they offered to the young Snowden was the need to channel youthful energies into the Liberal Party. At this stage Snowden was an unquestioning adherent to the view that Liberalism paved the way to progress. Indeed, it appears that he was totally unaware of socialism, despite the fact that the Social Democratic Federation (SDF) had begun to make some inroads into Lancashire politics. In many respects Liberal Nelson proved almost as insular as nonconformist Cowling.

The social, geographical and, ultimately, the political horizons of Snowden's life were substantially widened when he joined the civil service in October 1886. He had entered the Open Competition for entry, passed with honours, and was appointed as a junior exciseman at Liverpool. He started on a salary of £50 per annum, which though small was far in excess of his father's annual income and rose to £80 per annum in October 1889 and allowed him to enjoy the more varied cultural life of Liverpool, with its music halls and theatres. From Liverpool he was sent to the Orkneys, where he gained a reputation as an able amateur actor, then to Aberdeen, where he first encountered socialists and listened to lectures by Prince Kropotkin, the anarchist, and Henry George, who was conducting a lecture tour of Scotland outlining the single land tax proposals which he had advocated in his book *Progress and Poverty*.

Snowden was not unduly influenced by the Aberdeen socialists and, in any case, was transferred to Plymouth in 1890. He was doing well in the civil service and had good prospects of promotion. But in 1891 he sustained a back injury, that he usually ascribed to a cycling accident, though it has been suggested that it was in fact spinal tuberculosis. This eventually forced his official discharge from the civil service in November 1893 and left him requiring walking sticks for the rest of his life.

Although the precise detail is scant, it is clear that he returned to Ickornshaw in the autumn of 1891, to be nursed by his mother who had left Nelson on the death of his father in 1889. This was clearly a decisive period in Philip's life. During a year of inactivity it became obvious to him that one institutionalized avenue for his individual mobility was now blocked. This must have been a shattering experience and he appears to have passed the time and dulled his frustration by reading widely. At this stage he sold 200 volumes from his library and bought a variety of books on socialism. He read Kirkup's *Inquiry into Socialism*, which helped to explain to him what socialism was about. He also read H. M. Hyndman's *England for All* and his *Historical Basis of Socialism*. The first of these books was produced for the Radically-orientated Democratic Federation and explained how social and economic change could occur without revolution whilst the second, based upon Marx's *Das Kapital*, attempted to explain the reasons for, and the solutions to, economic inequality. Even at this stage, Hyndman's views never appealed to Snowden, and he later admitted that he had never read any of the works of Karl Marx. He was more attracted by the *Fabian Essays in Socialism*, the Fabian Tracts, the poems of William Morris and a variety of publications by Edward Carpenter, including *England's Ideal* and *Civilisation, its Causes and Cure*. It was the spiritually uplifting type of socialist literature, rather than that which attempted to explain economic inequality, which attracted him. Indeed, it suited the moral approach which he adopted on most questions. But he was still not a socialist. His mind and emotions were still being moulded and, as he recovered from his illness, he increasingly associated himself with the local Liberal club and the Wesleyan Mutual Improvement Society. However in challenging socialism through these organizations he became attracted to it as a philosophy capable of tackling the social and economic problems of society.

Notes

1 'Ephesian' (C. E. Bechofer Roberts), *Philip Snowden: An Impartial Portrait* (London, 1929), p. 1.
2 The 1871 census enumerator sheets indicate that John Snowden was 40 in 1871.

Philip, in his *An Autobiography* (London, 1934), p. 51, suggests that his father was born in 1829.
3 *Labour Prophet*, April 1898.
4 *Review of Reviews*, vol. XXXIII, January–June 1906, p. 580.
5 Ibid.
6 Viscount P. Snowden, *An Autobiography*, vol. 1, 1864–1919 (London, 1934), p. 4.
7 Ibid., p. 4.

3 The Labour Movement in the West Riding of Yorkshire During the 1890s

Philip had returned to a region which had seen many changes since he had first left it for Nelson and the wider world in 1879. The atmosphere and mood of the area remained redolent with nonconformity and Liberalism. On the surface, little had changed and working-class life remained one of long hours, poor pay and the constant struggle against poverty. But he had returned to Cowling at a crucial moment in the growth of socialist and Labour protest movements in the region and was quickly sucked into the new movements because of the temperamental affinity which he felt with some of their aims, especially for those of the socialist and labour movements which emerged in nearby Keighley and its immediate surrounding area. Yet the movement he was about to join revealed many strands, some of which were never likely to captivate Snowden in his future career as a socialist agitator and key political figure in the early years of the Labour Party.

The Labour movement in the Yorkshire textile district *c.* 1884–1900

One strand of socialism, which was always anathema to Snowden, was the quasi-Marxist attitudes of class conflict offered by the Social Democratic Federation. But this organization had never had much of a presence in the West Riding of Yorkshire. There had been meetings by groups of socialists in the 1870s but the first major thread of revolutionary socialist activity in the area came when William Morris[1] – writer, designer and socialist – lectured in February 1884 at the Temperance Hall, Bradford on 'Useful Work and Useless Toil'. Morris spoke for the SDF but was disappointed at his reception, and later wrote that the Bradford workers were 'a sad set of Philistines'.[2] However Fred Jowett, George Minty, and several other men who became prominent socialists, attended and were stimulated to take up the cause of the SDF. Their efforts led to a meeting in June 1884, anticipating the future formation of an SDF branch in Bradford.[3] It is unclear whether or not this branch was ever formed, though an SDF branch was certainly opened in Leeds, where there were about 25 members actively supporting Tom Maguire's socialist efforts. But even this merged into the Socialist League and the SDF, as such, survived largely in the form of a scattering of individual members rather than branches in the Yorkshire textile district before 1895.

It was not until August 1895 that the SDF managed to make much impact upon Bradford, the real locus of independent Labour activity before the First World War, and even then its activities were swamped by the much larger Independent Labour Party. At that time a small branch of the SDF was formed with a mere six members.[4] After about six months the branch was declared to have 28 members and to have some influence through the support of Mrs. Nott, who was a Labour member of the Board of Guardians. Such limited success was short-lived and the branch appears to have expired towards the end of 1897, not to be revived until 1902.

Elsewhere in the textile district, the Armley branch of the SDF, in Leeds, seems to have continued through the 1890s.[5] Apart from this the only other significant area of SDF support occurred in Dewsbury where, though it rarely had more than 30 members, the movement was powerfully represented by the ILP's appointment of a local agent, an SDF supporter from Lancashire, who gradually forced the local ILP to form a Socialist Society, part of which was to be an SDF branch. It was this situation which ultimately led to the SDF and ILP conflict in Dewsbury over the candidature of H. Quelch, of the SDF, for the Dewsbury by-election of January 1902.[6]

Though the SDF's influence was limited in the Yorkshire textile district it could, nevertheless, claim to have helped sensitize some sections of the working class to their economic exploitation. Apart from Morris's own efforts, other SDF lecturers also toured the district. In the first half of 1893, A. G. Wolfe, SDF organizer in Burnley, conducted 27 meetings in Yorkshire and visited Bradford and Huddersfield.[7] H. M. Hyndman, the leading figure in the SDF, visited Bradford in February 1896 and again in October of that year. Chatterton, the SDF's national organizer, also visited Bradford on two occasions in 1896. J. Hunter Watts also lectured in Bradford market place, in July 1896, on 'How the Workers are Robbed' and 'The Duty of Revolt'.[8]

Despite such campaigning, it is clear that the SDF did not capture popular political support in the Yorkshire textile district. There have been many explanations offered for this failure. It may well have been the case that it simply failed to provide resources, finance and speakers on the scale that it had done in Lancashire, where it was far more successful. Hyndman's antipathy towards trade unionism, despite some contrary views held by other members of the SDF, might well have discouraged trade-union support. It could also be that the constant reference to class conflict was not in tune with the views of the working class in the district who were much more attuned to the Liberal and nonconformist message of progress through self-improvement . In any case, the SDF was quickly overtaken by other socialist groups who were more amenable to the various cultural and social strands which dominated the life of the local working classes.

Initially, the most influential of these groups was the Socialist League, formed by Morris and his supporters at the end of 1884 in opposition to Hyndman's domination of the SDF. It was Morris and the Socialist League who inspired many of the early Labour leaders whom Snowden was to work alongside in his early years as a socialist. Those who had intended to form a Bradford branch of the SDF in 1884 eventually formed a branch of the Socialist League in 1886. Apart from Fred Jowett, this small band of twelve socialists included several men who were prominent in the Bradford ILP in its early years – most notably Jesse Mitchell, George Minty, Paul Bland and Fred Pickles. Minty has been described as being of the William Morris type of socialist, 'with the heart of a child and the feelings of a poet'.[9] Jowett later wrote of Mitchell, Pickles, Bland and Minty that 'All four of them of blessed memory to me – they were really the earliest Bradfordian advocates of modern socialism'.[10]

Tom Maguire, Tom Paylor and J. L. Mahon fulfilled a similar role in Leeds. Indeed it was the branch of the Socialist League which they formed, rather than the Bradford branch, which helped to propagandize workers through the 1880s and took a lead in organizing the activities of gasworkers and general labourers who fought for wage increases in Leeds, Halifax and other West Riding towns in 1889 and 1890.

The Socialist League revealed a willingness to organize trade unions at a time when even in the Yorkshire textile district, notorious for the weakness of trade unionism, there were moves to improve the organization of the working class. In addition, William Morris, its leading light, had ensured that the League would be imbued with the commitment to brotherhood and the religion of socialism. The League's manifesto, written by Morris, was introduced by the peroration

> Let us all strive, then, towards this end of realising the change towards social order, the only cause worthy the attention of the workers of all that are proffered to them: let us work in that cause patiently, yet hopefully, and not shrink from making sacrifices to it. Industry in learning its principles, industry in teaching them, are most necessary to our progress, but to these we must add, if we wish to avoid speedy failure, frankness and fraternal trust in each other, and single-hearted devotion to the religion of Socialism, the only religion which the Socialist League professes.[11]

This type of socialism, with its commitment to brotherhood, living the life of a socialist, and stressing the almost religious commitment to the movement captured the moral sense of outrage which Snowden, and others, later evinced and touched the mood of many socialist activists in the textile district, and particularly those who were active in the Keighley ILP in the mid-1890s. It was this ethical type of socialism which appealed more than the SDF's emphasis upon class conflict.

The fact is that it was the ILP, rather than the Socialist League, which offered both a commitment to trade unions and ethical socialism, throughout the 1890s. It benefited also from the disintegration of the Socialist League in the late 1880s and early 1890s, following Morris's conflict with the anarchists and his subsequent withdrawal from the League. Also, the anti-parliamentarian attitude of Morris did not square with a Yorkshire electorate which was trained to view parliamentary and local politics as the routeway to gradual change.

The ideological conflict between Morris and some of his Yorkshire supporters had first become evident in 1887 when J. L. Mahon, representing Leeds, had put forward a resolution to the annual conference of the Socialist League asking that:

> every effort be made to penetrate the existing political organisations with Socialism, that all possible help be given to such movements as trades unionism, co-operation, national and international labour federations etc. by which the working classes are trying to better their conditions; that Parliament, municipal and other local-government bodies, and the contests for the elections of members to them, be taken advantage of for spreading the principle of Socialism and organising the people into a Socialist Labour Party ... tho' complete emancipation can only be achieved by the transformation of society into a co-op commonwealth.[12]

The anti-parliamentarians defeated the resolution. Nevertheless, it embodied the sort of policy which the Leeds and Bradford branches of the Socialist League were to pursue as they embraced the challenge of uniting political and industrial forces in the cause of Labour. Ultimately these activists moved outside the Socialist League, and into the ILP to mount their challenge.

Nevertheless, there was something of a hiatus between the collapse of the branches of the Socialist League and the emergence of the embryonic ILP. In the case of Bradford, the Socialist League appears to have expired in 1889 and Jowett, and the others, appear to have transferred their support to the Bradford Labour Electoral Association, which had been formed in 1887 as part of the attempt to increase the number of working men on public bodies.[13] Jowett and James Bartley, a typographer and briefly editor of a socialist paper known as *Demos*, hoped to shape this body into an independent Labour Party but it was not until 1891 that they were able to do so – and then only as a result of the infamous Manningham Mills strike.

The Yorkshire textile district had always been badly organized as far as trade unionism was concerned. The woollen and worsted workers were almost endemically weak, and those unions which existed were invariably small combinations of skilled men which exhibited a propensity to collapse when employers applied the least pressure. There were, indeed, only two woollen and worsted textile unions worthy of note. One was a regional weavers' and spinners' union which acted as the centripetal force for the development of textile trade unionism. Its roots lay in a weavers' organization formed at Dewsbury in 1875 and a similar body established at Huddersfield in 1881. It was founded in 1883 and was known as the West Riding Power-Loom Weavers' Association until 1900, when it became the General Union of Textile Workers. Although membership fluctuated considerably, it had only 4,000 members in the early 1890s, about two per cent of its potential membership. The other prominent textile union was the Amalgamated Society of Dyers, which had emerged in Bradford during the 1870s. Starting with a few hundred members it expanded to 3,600 in 1894, about half of its potential membership.

The great difficulty which these unions faced was that the diversity of the woollen and worsted industry made organization difficult. Some areas produced woollen dress fabrics whilst others concentrated upon worsted coatings. Dewsbury produced a 'shoddy cloth' from the wool recovered from used garments. Industrial diversity, local customs and the power and independent initiatives of many employers who wished to determine wage rates directly with their workers made it difficult for textile trade unions to attract wider support. Industrial practice and wages varied so much that it was not until 1913 and 1914, respectively, that the woollen and worsted industries established basic wage rates. Even then, many firms did not pay them, and the General Union was too weak to enforce these agreements on all but a minority of employers.

The endemic weakness of Yorkshire textile trade unionism was most apparent in 1890 and 1891, when Samuel Cunliffe Lister, and his board of directors, imposed wage reductions of up to 25 per cent on some of the workforce at Manningham Mills. A strike occurred and, with the lock-out of some workers, most of the 5,000 workforce at the mills were eventually embroiled in the dispute.[14]

In the event, the strike and lock-out lasted nineteen weeks between 17 December 1890 and 27 April 1891, and the workers were defeated. But the events of the dispute were divisive and, according to E. P. Thompson, in his essay 'Homage to Tom Maguire', proved the impetus for the growth of a more substantial independent Labour movement.[15] Thompson argues that the defeat of the Manningham workers proved vital to the political ambitions of the working class and raised discontent sufficient to raise the efforts of a few socialists into a viable Labour movement. Contemporaries were also aware of the political importance of the dispute. In October 1892, Fred Jowett, contesting the Manningham ward at the municipal elections for the Bradford Trades Council and the embryonic ILP stated that

> In the Lister strike, the people of Bradford saw plainly, as they had never seen before, that whether their rulers are Liberal or Tory they are capitalists first and politicians afterwards.[16]

The fact is that the Liberal-dominated Watch Committee of the town had attempted to prevent the public meetings of the strikers and had forced a confrontation which led to the reading of the Riot Act and public demonstrations of 13 April 1891. W. H. Drew, a member of the weavers' union and the strike leader, declared that all knew

> perfectly well that to a great extent the sympathies of the wealthier Bradford citizens were not with the workpeople in the struggle to obtain what they believed to be their rights. There were of course a few exceptions, and to these people every honour was due.[17]

The defeat of the strike did not, therefore, stem the tide of worker agitation. If they were unable to succeed through industrial action some, at least, were determined to bring about change through political agitation. The Manningham Mills dispute, by its very failure, incensed workers to such an extent that it prepared the pathway to political independence.

Announcing the end of the strike the *Yorkshire Factory Times* made the prophetic statement that 'Labour has so associated itself that even defeat must be victory'.[18] And, indeed, it would appear that the dispute did bring together trade unionists and workers of various persuasions and unite them on one platform. Committed socialists, such as Fred Jowett, Ben Turner and W. H. Drew, joined with Liberals and neutrals in condemning the Watch Committee. This criticism seemed to undermine the confidence that working men had placed in the impartiality of the local authorities and gave them a determination to seek municipal, parliamentary and school board representation for themselves. This frustration was perhaps best expressed in the words of Charlie Glyde when he stated that 'We have had two parties in the past, the can'ts and the won'ts, and it is time that we had a party that will'.[19]

The 'party that will' was formed officially about six weeks later at a meeting of the Firth's Temperance Hotel in East Parade, the former

Laycock's temperance hotel. A meeting was called by notice for Thursday 30 April 1891. Although very few attended, those present included Drew, Bartley, Edward Roche, Edwin Halford, Edwin Tolsen and Minty. A small committee was set up to continue the battle and another meeting was organized for 28 May. At that meeting the Bradford and District Labour Union was officially formed. Its intentions were defined in the following terms:

> Its object shall be to promote the interests of the working men in whatever way it may from time to time be thought advisable and to further the course of direct Labour representation on Local Bodies and in Parliament. Its operation shall be carried out irrespective of the convenience of any political party. Persons holding official positions in connection with political organisations shall not be eligible for membership and members of the Labour Union accepting official positions in any political organisation shall thereby forfeit their membership.[20]

A section of the politically active working class had taken the decision to abandon any direct association with the other major political parties.

The example of Bradford proved almost infectious as similar bodies were formed throughout the textile district. The ColneValley Labour Union was formed 21 July 1891, and similar organizations were formed at Huddersfield in September 1891, Halifax in July 1892, Keighley on 3 October 1892 and at Leeds in November 1892.[21] In most of these cases, as in Bradford, there had been preliminary soundings before the Labour Union/ILP was formed, but it was the Manningham Mills strike which seemed to act as a catalyst, reviving and giving more permanent form to the political as well as industrial frustrations of working men.

There was a flowering of working-class and Radical discontent at this time and it is clear that, in these early days, the independent Labour movement of the West Riding of Yorkshire was an eclectic movement. In some areas, like Bradford and Halifax, the trade union movement gave it much support. In others, like Colne Valley and Keighley, where trade unionism was much weaker, it was club life, the Labour Church or the Clarion movement which sustained the movement. However all areas displayed the full range of factors which were responsible for the growth of the ILP – the frustration of trade unionists, the ethical side of the movement, anti-Liberalism and a modicum of religious support.

Trade unionism was relatively weak in the Yorkshire textile district but remained, everywhere, a potent factor behind the emergence of Labour unions. In Bradford, the Trades Council was won over to the ILP when it had to choose between supporting Ben Tillett or the Liberal candidate, Alfred Illingworth, in the Bradford West parliamentary election. Against the wishes of Samuel Shaftoe, a Liberal and secretary of the Trades Council since the 1870s, it voted in favour of Tillett.[22] In

Halifax it was the victimization of two trade unionists and socialists, James Beever and James Tattersall, which led the Trades Council to form a Labour Union with the help of the Fabians.[23] Elsewhere, there was significant trade union support. The Keighley Trades Council was not a powerful body in the 1890s, and rarely had more than 1,500 members, but it did give fitful support to the Keighley Labour Union.[24] Even in Colne Valley, a geographically large agricultural and textile constituency stretching over the Pennines between Huddersfield and Oldham, trade unionism did help to contribute to the eventual political success of the Labour Union despite the fact that there were only about 1,500 trade unionists in 1895 out of a population of about 60,000.[25] Most of those who formed the Colne Valley Labour Union, with three obvious exceptions, were trade unionists. They included George Garside, the president, who was an engineer and W. H. Barker, Joseph Baxter, Saville Hirst, Walter May, Ephraim Sykes and Sam Eastwood, who joined soon after its formation and were all textile workers connected with the weavers' union.[26]

This association of trade unionism with the early ILP was, as E. P. Thompson suggests, the product of a number of factors; the reluctance of local Liberal parties to take notice of the wishes of the weak trade unionism of the area, the frustration of the Manningham Mills dispute and, above all, the fact that trade councils, apart from those at Leeds and Bradford, had generally emerged in the late 1880s and early 1890s without any type of traditional attachment to the Liberal Party. It was these trades councils which were quickly won to the cause of independent Labour.

It seems doubtful, given Snowden's lifelong disdain of trade unionism, whether he would have been attracted to the ILP if it had simply been a collectivist movement based upon trade unionism. What appealed to Snowden was the individual and ethical approach of the ILP in the Yorkshire textile district, for here was a movement which offered a more democratic and moral way of life to those who wished to redistribute wealth in order that all could enjoy a healthy life free from poverty. There were many other individuals who were similarly drawn by such ethical motives. John Lister, a substantial landowner and the owner of the Shibden Hall estates in Halifax, had been influenced by the teachings of William Morris and appalled at the environmental pollution of Halifax. He joined the Halifax ILP and became its main benefactor throughout the 1890s. It was Charles Worsnop, a businessman with Radical views, who decided to form the Fabian society in Halifax.[27] In Bradford, a number of businessmen joined the movement. One of the most prominent was Willie Leach who was in the woollen and worsted trade and who employed Fred Jowett in his early years. Leach was later to become a friend of Ramsay MacDonald and to receive junior ministerial positions in the first two Labour governments. The richest was undoubtedly Arthur Priestman who, with his brother H. B. Priestman, shared the substantial textile business left by his father in 1889. In Colne Valley there were several businessmen in the movement, most notably G. W. Haigh, France Littlewood, who became treasurer of the ILP, Ben Shaw 'the son of the great master cotton spinner of Milnsbridge', and James Iredale Swallow who was a commission spinner operating in a mill at Leymoor, Golcar.[28]

The movement also attracted some religious support. Although it is often assumed that Methodism was an important influence upon the Yorkshire Labour movement, because of the upbringing of people like Snowden, it is evident that little direct support came from that direction in Yorkshire. It was a small number of Congregationalists and Anglicans who offered direct and indirect support. Rev. R. Roberts, a Bradford Congregational minister, actually joined the Bradford ILP and sat on the School Board alongside Margaret McMillan from 1897. The Rev. Bryan Dale, a Halifax Congregational minister, was president of the Halifax Fabian Society and the Rev. F. R. Swan, Congregational Minister at Marsden in the Colne Valley, retired from his ministry in 1907 to become a full-time speaker for the Colne Valley Labour Union, followed by another three months as a full-time registration agent in Colne Valley and then on to the *Worker* in Huddersfield.[29]

Anglican support was also strongly evident. The Community of the Resurrection, an Anglican order based at Mirfield, presided over the formation of a movement called the Socialists of the West Riding. Rev. J. W. Moore, Rector of Kirkheaton, and Rev. W. B. Graham, curate of Thongsbridge in 1907, and formerly of Bradford, were also prominent in Victor Grayson's parliamentary by-election contest at Colne Valley in 1907. Graham was described by Blatchford as 'six foot a Socialist and five inch a parson'.[30]

Religious support was also strongly evident in the Keighley district. It was said of Canon F. D. Cremer, Rector of Keighley, that 'Christian Socialism ... pervaded his sermons'.[31] The nonconformist Rev. S. J. C. Goldsack, who formed a Union of Socialists, was forced to resign his pastorate. The Rev. J. Stansfield, Vicar of St. Peters, who married Mary Jane Dixon, a member of the local ILP, also gave support to the independent Labour movement and was an ally on the School Board.[32] Indeed it was Stansfield who captured something of the spirit of the Keighley ILP, which Snowden entered, when he expressed his view that social change would come through Christian religion and man's goodness, rather than Marxism or the bureaucracy of the Fabians:

> It is fiction to say that religion has nothing to do with a man's material progress and worldly success.... The Christian faith has not want of sympathy with that which even dreamers hope for in a regenerated society, and a better world for the present life.[33]

The collective trade-union strand and the moral and religious aspects of the movement were underpinned by the tendency of most areas of strong Labour support to build up their own alternative socialist culture – based upon club life, the Labour Church, Socialist Sunday schools and the Clarion movement. In times of limited electoral success it was often the cultural aspect of the movement which kept the hard-core of the local ILP branches together, and kept alive the vision of the regenerated society to which Stansfield referred and which Snowden wanted.

During the 1890s the ILP clubs proved to be one of the most vibrant forces of political independence in the Yorkshire textile district. In Colne Valley it appears that it was these clubs which kept the ILP alive in the difficult years of ILP activity between 1895 and 1905. According to one authority,

> It was the clubs which sustained the movement especially in the years around the turn of the century even though at times they seemed to opt out of political activity and concentrated upon social intercourse.... The strength gained from having a Labour club was not merely that it provided opportunities for political meetings or discussion which were alternatives to the village Liberal or Conservative clubs, but they provided a centre for the whole family.[34]

A similar observation could be made of the Bradford ILP clubs. During the 1890s these clubs, according to the *Bradford Labour Echo*, had 'awakened and developed the self-governing powers of the members'.[35] Club activities were regarded as 'a way of life'. Most clubs ran Sunday lectures and classes in singing, dancing, elocution and political economy. The North Ward Club entertained its members with the Garrick Orchestral Band in 1895 and subsequently arranged an outing to 'Grassington and Kilnsey Craggs to which they rode from Skipton railway station in wagonettes'.[36] The Eccleshill Labour Club held regular Labour church services on Sunday evenings throughout 1898, and attracted speakers such as W. Obank, who gave a lecture on 'The Religion of Socialism'.[37]

Despite such enthusiasm, there were many problems. The Colne Valley clubs led a precarious existence, as did some of the Bradford clubs. There were disputes about the selling of intoxicating drinks which led to one club, Great Horton, to lose more than 20 members who formed the rival Tillett Club.[38] Others such as the Bradford Central ILP Club, faced acute financial difficulties and decided to give up its premises and meet as a Central Group in the rooms of the Labour Institute in Peckover Street. It justified its action in terms of the need for political work because it was felt that

> as the belief spreads that its attention is almost wholly occupied in billiards and socials and gossip over the cup that cheers, the enemy becomes quite indifferent to its existence.... Now here is a chance for a new group which shall have no social side to monopolise its energies.[39]

Nevertheless, despite such doubts about the direction of club life, it revealed a remarkable resilience which kept the ILP together as a political force through the difficult years which followed the ILP's political failures in the 1895 General Election. In Colne Valley the rump membership of the Labour clubs was in the region of 200 and 250. In Bradford at the same time, there were at least 14 clubs and 1,000 members – a substantial movement even though the movement had contracted from its peak of 1892 when it had 21 clubs and about 2,000 members.[40] Club life played an equally important role in other Labour centres such as Huddersfield, Leeds, Batley and Dewsbury.

Imposed upon this base was the more fragmented, but important, Labour Church movement. This had been formed by John Trevor and Robert Blatchford in the Manchester area in 1891–92 and, though it barely lasted a decade as a meaningful national movement, it spread throughout the Yorkshire textile district in the 1890s. There were Labour churches in Huddersfield, Halifax, Bradford, Leeds, Batley, Keighley, and several smaller communities, by the mid-1890s. Although they varied in their style of procedure, some like Keighley evoking a religious framework whilst others were secular, they were all committed to 'Socialism as an ethical gospel' and 'the realization of the kingdom of heaven'.[41] The format of their meetings varied enormously, though most offered Labour hymns to old chapel tunes and focused their activities on the weekly lecture delivered, on Sunday afternoon or evening, by some prominent national or local speaker. Indeed, it was said of the Bradford Labour Church that

> The work done by the Labour Church is of the most invaluable kind. As an educational institution its influence cannot be overstated. Sunday after Sunday it brings to the town speakers of the first rank, and in many ways helps to keep the good work going.[42]

The membership of these Labour churches, and the audiences, often extended beyond the official membership of the ILP and their clubs. The Bradford Labour Church was said to have a paid-up membership of 2,000 in 1893, although this was said to have fallen to 300 by 1896.[43] Notwithstanding this apparent decline it was still attracting audiences of 1,000 or more for some of its Sunday meetings. The Leeds Labour Church was also said to have a large membership in the early 1890s though, like Bradford, its membership appears to have fallen to about 300 by the mid-1890s. In Keighley, though the ILP never had more than about 120 members in the 1890s, the Labour Church attendances were normally 400 or 500, and even higher when Philip addressed them.

The general object of the Labour Church movement was 'The Realisation of Heaven in this Life by the establishment of a state founded upon Justice and Love to thy Neighbour'.[44] It demonstrated its veracity by spawning a number of related organizations and activities, the most important of which was the creation of Socialist Sunday schools. In Yorkshire, unlike many in Lancashire, these schools often emerged from the activities of the Labour Church and were committed to shaping the minds of the young towards socialism, in line with the views expressed by James Keir Hardie in 1895. Growth was slow at first, although schools opened in Bradford, Huddersfield and Leeds in the late 1890s. By 1899, however, there were sufficient schools to form the Yorkshire Socialist Sunday School Union.[45]

The normal Socialist Sunday School meeting took place between 2 pm and 3 pm, in a board school, and commenced with the children singing socialist hymns, followed by group discussion, a further hymn and the reading of the 'Socialist Ten Commandments', which would have been attached to the wall throughout the proceedings. The group discussion consisted mainly of moral instructions drawn from a variety of texts. At East Bowling, Bradford, in 1906, J. D. Gould's *The Child's Book of Moral Lessons* was used.[46] The adult classes, usually held at the same time as those of the children, were based largely on a variety of lectures, such as George H. Froggett's 'Labour Attitude towards Religion' delivered at East Bowling in 1906.

The interlinking activities of clubs, the Labour Church and Socialist Sunday schools provided the emergent ILP with a viable and thriving alternative to capitalist culture and helped to create a socialist state in miniature. But for many, what completed this joyous alternative was the Clarion movement, which gained its name from the *Clarion* newspaper, presided over by Robert Blatchford, which adopted the message of encouraging brotherhood, fellowship and the making of socialists which had been advocated by William Morris in the 1880s. The Clarion movement contained fellowship groups, glee clubs, vocal unions, scouts and cycling clubs. There was also a Clarion Van movement, which aimed to provide lectures on socialism and to distribute socialist literature, which was organized for many years by Edward Robertshaw Hartley, a Bradford butcher who became a socialist in 1895.[47]

It was with some nostalgia that Snowden reflected upon the early years of the ILP in his *An Autobiography*, emphasizing his real interest in the ethical side of the movement.

> The Party quickly developed a large number of local speakers. Many young men who were Nonconformist local preachers were attracted to

> the movement by the ethical appeal of Socialism. Their experience in speaking was a great help to the Party propaganda. Working men who had toiled all day at arduous work went out at nights into the streets to preach in their simple way the new gospel of emancipation. Men who had never before attempted public speaking were given courage and the gift of effective oratory by the new passion for social justice which consumed them. The movement was something new in politics. It was politics inspired by idealism and religious fervour. Vocal unions were formed which accompanied cycling corps into the country at weekends, and audiences were gathered on village greens by the singing of the choirs; then short and simple addresses on Socialism were given. On their country jaunts the cyclists distributed leaflets and pasted slips on gates, and sometimes stuck them on cows, bearing such slogans as 'Socialism the Hope of the World', 'Workers of the World Unite'. Sometimes processions were organised in connection with a meeting of more than usual importance addressed by some national speaker. I remember one such procession where the small children were on a horse-drawn lorry, and stretched across the wagon over their heads was a banner bearing the Socialist slogan 'Production for Us and not for Profit'.[48]

It was this enthusiasm and the feeling of mission which the new independent Labour movement transmitted to Snowden. It converted him to the cause of socialism and appealed to his progressive Liberal and nonconformist instincts and offered a view of society and Labour which transcended class.

The impact of Labour

The various strands of the independent Labour movement came together to form the national ILP at Bradford in January 1893. From the start of that conference two points became clear. The first was that, despite its commitment to securing the 'collective ownership of the means of production, distribution and exchange', the new party was going to appeal to the broadest audience by not including socialist in its title. The second, and more pertinent, point was that it was obvious that the new organization was a provincial party very much based upon Yorkshire and Lancashire. Of the 120 delegates present, 48 came from Yorkshire, mainly from the textile district. Bradford sent 20, Leeds three, Batley one and Huddersfield six. The Colne Valley Labour Union sent no official delegate but were effectively represented by Edward Hoskins of Slaithwaite Labour Club, and France Littlewood.[49]

The prominence of the Yorkshire textile district is further demonstrated by the national figures of branch affiliation. In 1895, for instance, 102 of the 305 ILP branches were to be found in Yorkshire, compared with 73 in Lancashire and Cheshire, 41 in Scotland, 29 in London, 23 in the Midlands, 18 in the North East, eight in Kent, four in the Eastern Counties, three in Ireland, three in Southern England and one in Wales.[50] Although many branches collapsed over the next five years it is clear that the Yorkshire textile district was ILP heartland. It is hardly surprising then that W. H. Drew, a member of the Bradford ILP and secretary of the Bradford Trades Council, stressed to Ramsay MacDonald, on the eve of the Labour Representation Committee Conference held at Bradford in 1904, that Bradford was the 'Birthplace of the political Labour movement'.[51] What was true of Bradford was also generally true of the Yorkshire textile region.

Indeed, it is hardly surprising that the ILP was able to mount a serious political challenge against the Liberals and the Conservatives before the First World War. Even within the 1890s this challenge was becoming most obvious in both parliamentary and local elections. It had begun to win a toehold in politics, even though its political support remained patchy. And, indeed, Keighley, the area where Snowden first operated for the Labour movement, did, under his tutelage, become one of the ILP's major centres in the West Riding before 1900.

The Keighley Labour movement

The Keighley branch of the ILP was already well established by the time Snowden joined in 1895. It had been formed on 3 October 1892 as a result of the frustrations of the local Trades Council and political activists, who maintained that the working class and the Liberal Party 'have now arrived at the parting of the ways'.[54] Working men were 'at

Table 3.1 Parliamentary contests fought by the ILP in the textile district of the West Rising of Yorkshire, 1892–5

Constituency	Date	ILP candidate	Votes	Labour % of poll
Bradford West	1892	B. Tillett	2,749	30.2
Halifax	1893	J. Lister	3,028	25.4
Bradford West	1895	B. Tillett	2,264	23.4
Colne Valley	1895	T. Mann	1,245	13.4
Dewsbury	1895	E. R. Hartley	1,080	10.5
Halifax	1895	J. Lister	3,818	20.5
Huddersfield	1895	H. R. Smart	1,594	11.2
Leeds South	1895	A. Shaw	622	6.4

Table 3.2 Municipal successes of the ILP in four West Riding textile towns, 1891–1900[52]

Year	Bradford	Halifax	Huddersfield	Keighley	Total
1891	2	–	–	–	2
1892	2	3	1	–	6
1893	4	3	1	–	8
1894	4	1	1	1	7
1895	6	0	1	1	8
1896	4	0	1	1	6
1897	5	1	1	2	9
1898	5	1	1	4	11
1899	5	2	1	5	13
1900	6	2	1	5	14

Table 3.3 The number of ILP representatives in West Yorkshire, 1891–1900[53]

Year	Municipal	CC, UDC, RDC, PC, LB*	Board of guardians	School board	Total
1891	4	–	–	2	6
1892	7	2	–	4	13
1893	10	2	–	4	16
1894	10	2	–	5	17
1895	12	2	–	7	21
1896	11	2	–	7	20
1897	14	10	–	11	35
1898	15	9	3	15	42
1899	19	10	3	18	50
1900	19	10	3	21	53

* County Council, Urban-district council, Rural-district council, Parish Council, Local Board.

last sufficiently enlightened to carve out an independent pathway for themselves'. The precise process by which this had occurred is not known, but it is clear that several factors were involved. In the first place, there was some resentment that the paternalistic employers of the town – the Cloughs and the Briggs – were not sufficiently advanced to allow the views of working men to emerge either in the local Liberal association or the Town Council.[55] Secondly, it may well be, as Patrick Joyce has observed, that the paternalism of the large employers was breaking down in the face of the greater mobility of the workforce and the continuance of the independent Radical tradition in Yorkshire.[56] But such an assessment of events for Keighley is yet awaited. More likely, the breakdown of political consensus in Keighley began with the industrial conflict of the late 1880s. The most celebrated event was the engineers' strike of August 1889. Although the issue at stake was the wages and hours of the skilled and semi-skilled workers, comparisons were made with the London dock strike which was occurring at the same time. In contrast, the employers referred to the interference of trade union outsiders and appealed to the loyalty of their employees. Indeed, a representative of the engineering firm of Butterfield reflected this tendency beautifully when he remarked that

> some of their employees had grown up with the firm, and were really satisfied with the positions they held in the workshop, and all with the exception of the riff raff would willingly return to work were they not afraid of being jeered at and called 'black sheep' by their fellow workmen in the town.[57]

The strike was finally settled by wage concessions from the employers, but good relations between masters and men were not re-established and the industrial consensus was damaged if not broken. From now on the workers moved towards organizing on a wider front and formed the Trades Council in February 1890. Yet though this became the focus of industrial organization amongst the workers, trade unionism was never to be a potent factor in the activities of the emergent Labour Party – for it had neither the numbers (rarely more than 1,500), nor the intense and unbroken commitment to the ILP which similar organizations had shown in Bradford and Halifax.

Instead other factors contributed to the early growth of the Keighley Labour Union/ILP. The most obvious was the presence of a number of able agitators who were determined to offer an alternative to the industrial and political domination of the nonconformist industrialists in the town. The most obvious and prominent of these was Herbert Horner, a teacher who founded a local branch of the National Union of Teachers. It was he, with his brother Edward and several others, who formed the Keighley Labour Union and prompted it to pass a resolution condemning the fact that 'Mr. Holden [Keighley Liberal MP] had been rather indifferent of late in his conduct to the labouring portion of his constituents'.[58]

The Labour Union/ILP was always an impecunious organization and its members, if they were not self-employed, were likely to be victimized because of their political views. One notorious case was that of

G. J. Wardle, who edited the *Keighley Labour Union Journal* until 1898, when Snowden took over. He was employed by the Midland Railway Company who forced him to sign an 'agreement not to take part in any public meeting belonging to the Independent Labour Party'.[59]

For obvious reasons then the Labour Union/ILP was dominated by the self-employed and those in safe jobs during its early years. Apart from the Horners, there was W. F. Hardy, an engineer who opened a newspaper shop and became a sub-postmaster; Alfred Burrows, another engineer who set up a fish shop; Wilson Roper who ran a clothes shop and William Bannister from Howarth who became a hairdresser.

It quickly secured a small, but significant, presence in local politics. Its membership increased from about 30 in 1982 to 120 in 1900 and it was becoming increasingly influential in local politics. By January 1899 it had contested 16 local elections and won eight. Herbert Horner became its first councillor in 1894, becoming Alderman in 1898. And by 1899 there were also four ILP councillors – James Teal, William Prosser, W. F. Hardy and, of course, Philip Snowden. Mary Jane Dixon, the wife of Rev. J. Stansfield, was returned to the School Board in 1896 and was joined by Charles Whitehead and Philip Snowden in 1899. By the late 1890s the Party, with the help of Snowden, had made significant impact upon local political life and it was optimistically noted that 'Our victories were without adequate financial resources against wealthy and disciplined opponents are but a faint promise of whatever can be done with the proper equipment'.[60]

With limited trade union support the movement had depended upon the action of financially independent radicals, who in turn derived some of their support from the cultural activities which they encouraged. The fact is that the Keighley ILP was emphatically an ethical movement which owed as much to the progressive politics of nonconformist Liberalism as it did to the inspiration of William Morris's 'Religion of Socialism'. It was committed to creating a movement which would cut across class divisions and to working within the existing system. It was socialism which was to be based upon justice, freedom, equality and brotherhood.

The movement created its own version of the socialist state through club life and the Clarion movement. There was a Clarion Vocal Union, led by W. S. Wilkinson, which helped to extend fellowship and brotherhood through a regular programme of rambles and outdoor singing. A Clarion Scouts organization was formed in 1894 and, in 1897, a Clarion Cycling Club was established. In addition there were numerous dances and teas. At one such meeting in 1894 it was noted that

> The gathering was bright and happy and everybody enjoyed themselves. A varied programme of Songs, Recitations and Glees were given. . . . H.

Horner presided at the piano. The proceedings closed with the singing of Auld Lang Syne in the good old style.[61]

A Labour Church was formed because, as Herbert Horner stressed:

In too many cases a Nonconformist minister must preach what suits the wealthy manufacturer or those golden pillars of the Church will find means to get someone who will. They are so used to subservient acquiescence in their employees in the shop and factory that they expect the same from their spiritual employees on Sunday.[62]

Naturally there was some hostility to the creation of the Labour Church in October 1892. Nevertheless, the Labour Union bought 180 Labour hymn books, hired the Primitive Old Chapel from the Co-op for 8s. every Sunday, between 6.15 and 8.15, and began business.[63] By the end of 1894 the Labour Union/ILP had come to recognize the Labour Church as a vital part of its propaganda, noting that:

our most successful work has been the Sunday Service and the crowded audiences who have listened to the new Gospel and drunk with avidity the teaching put forth by the various speakers will no doubt furnish many recruits and staunch adherents.[64]

The Labour Church brought to the town some of the great names of the Labour movement. Margaret McMillan, Fred Brocklehurst, Enid Stacy, Caroline Martyn and others addressed the congregation alongside local speakers such as Snowden. The topics were varied, ranging from the history of trade unions to Philip's 'Religion of Socialism'.

Undoubtedly, the most popular lectures were those which evoked the religious sentiments of the audiences and combined them with a vision of a new, and better, society based upon justice and equality. The *Keighley Labour Journal*, summed up this association when it stated that its objectives, and that of the Labour Church, was an 'attempt ... to bring all those lofty principles contained in Christian ethics into practical realisation in our every day life.... "The Kingdom of Heaven on Earth". This is its religion and these are its politics.'[65]

By the mid-1890s the independent Labour movement in Keighley was well entrenched. It had a hard-core of supporters, was generally supported by the trade unions, but, above all, had created a vibrant and lively cultural life from which it was able to mount some successful local election campaigns. It was, however, like most independent Labour organizations, partly deflated by the ILP's poor performance in the 1895 General Election. But rather than lose members and support, as occurred briefly in Bradford and Halifax, the movement went forward. Part of the reason for this resilience was the fact that Philip Snowden joined the Keighley ILP in 1895 and, through his organizational skills, independence and oratory raised it to a new level of political achievement. His evangelical and missionary style struck the right chord in this nonconformist community and made him a popular and respected local figure. Yet, though he shaped the fortunes of the Keighley ILP for more than five years, there is no doubting the influence of Keighley Labour politics upon Snowden – for it galvanized many of the attitudes he had gained in youth and redefined them within a Labour, rather than Liberal, party framework.

Notes

1 E. P. Thompson, *William Morris: Romantic to Revolutionary* (Merlin Press, London, 1977 edition).
2 William Morris, *The Letters of William Morris to his Family and Friends*, P. Henderson (ed.) (London, 1950), letter dated 25 February 1884.
3 *Clarion*, 15 June 1901.
4 *Justice*, 7 September 1895; *Bradford Labour Echo*, 5 October 1895.
5 *Justice*, 11 September 1897.
6 K. Laybourn and J. Reynolds, *Liberalism and the Rise of Labour 1890–1918* (Croom Helm, London, 1984), pp. 125–7.
7 *Justice*, 12 August 1893.
8 Ibid., 11 July 1896.
9 F. Brockway, *Socialism over Sixty Years: The Life of Jowett of Bradford 1864–1944* (George Allen and Unwin, London, 1946), p. 30.
10 Ibid., p. 30.
11 Thompson, *William Morris*, p. 737.
12 Ibid., p. 452.
13 Brockway, op. cit., pp. 31–2.
14 K. Laybourn, 'The Manningham Mills Strike: Its importance in Bradford History', *The Bradford Antiquary*, New Series, Part XLVI, 1976.
15 E. P. Thompson, 'Homage to Tom Maguire', A. Briggs and J. Saville (eds), *Essays in Labour History* (Macmillan, London, 1960).
16 *Labour Journal*, 7 October 1892.
17 *Bradford Observer*, 2 January 1891.
18 *Yorkshire Factory Times*, 1 May 1891.
19 *Bradford Observer Budget*, April 1891.
20 *Yorkshire Factory Times*, 29 May 1891.
21 Laybourn and Reynolds, op. cit., p. 43.
22 J. Reynolds and K. Laybourn, 'The Emergence of the Independent Labour Party in Bradford', *International Review of Social History*, XX (1975), Part 3, pp. 331–5.
23 J. Lister, 'The Early History of the ILP Movement in Halifax', unpublished, Halifax Archives Library.
24 D. James, 'The Keighley Independent Labour Party 1892–1900: "Realising the Kingdom of Heaven"', in J. A. Jowitt and R. K. S. Taylor, *Bradford 1890–1914: The Cradle of the Independent Labour Party*, (University of Leeds, Bradford, 1980), pp. 57–61.
25 D. Clark, *Colne Valley: Radicalism to Socialism* (Longman, London, 1981), pp. 4, 89.
26 Ibid., p. 19.
27 J. Lister, 'Who are the Fabians?', *Halifax Courier*, 24 October 1891.

28 Clark, op. cit., p 19.
29 Ibid., p. 148.
30 Ibid., p. 149.
31 James, op. cit., p. 67.
32 Ibid., p. 59.
33 *Keighley News*, 24 October 1889.
34 Clark, op. cit., p. 126.
35 *Bradford Labour Echo*, 1 January 1898.
36 Ibid., 15 August 1896.
37 Ibid., 9 November 1895.
38 Ibid., 11 December 1897.
39 Ibid., 29 February 1896.
40 K. Laybourn, 'The Trade Unions and the ILP: The Manningham Experience', in J. A. Jowitt and R. K. S. Taylor, *The Cradle of the Independent Labour Party* (University of Leeds, Bradford, 1980), p. 36.
41 Brockway, op. cit., p. 41.
42 *Bradford Labour Echo*, 1 February 1896.
43 *Clarion*, 18 November 1893; *The Labour Annual*, 1897.
44 *Bradford Labour Echo*, 20 March 1897.
45 Ibid., 24 June 1899.
46 *Forward*, 27 October 1906.
47 H. Pelling, *The Origins of the Labour Party* (Macmillan, London, 1954), p. 142. The bearded figure seated on the Caroline Martyn van is E. R. Hartley.
48 P. Snowden, *An Autobiography* (Ivor Nicholson and Watson, London, 1934), vol. 1, p. 71.
49 Laybourn and Reynolds, *Liberalism and the Rise of Labour*, p. 43.
50 Ibid., p. 43.
51 Labour Party Archives, Labour Representation Committee, 11/69.
52 Laybourn and Reynolds, *Liberalism and the Rise of Labour*, p. 65.
53 Ibid., p. 65.
54 *Keighley News*, 23 July 1892.
55 Keighley Divisional Party, Minutes; Keighley County Liberal Association, Minutes. Both deposits are located in the West Yorkshire Archives, Bradford.
56 P. Joyce, *Work, Society and Politics: The Culture of the Factory in Later Victorian England* (Harvester Press, Brighton, 1980).
57 *Keighley News*, 31 August 1889.
58 Keighley Independent Labour Party, Minutes, 3 October 1892. Quoted in James, op. cit., p. 61.
59 *Keighley Labour Journal*, 26 March 1898.
60 Ibid., 31 December 1898.
61 Ibid., 25 March 1894.
62 Ibid., 14 May 1898.
63 Keighley Independent Labour Party, Minutes, 9 May 1893. Quoted in James, op. cit., p. 68.
64 *Keighley Labour Journal*, 30 December 1894.
65 Ibid., 16 December 1894.

4 'The Realising of the Kingdom of Heaven upon Earth': Philip Snowden and the Keighley ILP

Snowden was in the eye of the political storm when the ILP was challenging the Liberal Party's hold on the working-class vote. Nevertheless, initially he remained a Liberal by temperament and association. Indeed, he later reflected that he was 'cradled ... in Liberalism, and I gave a passionate adherence to my party which the most earnest Liberal could hardly hope to excel. Nothing but the deepest conviction could have induced me to desert the Liberal Party. . . .'[1] But desert it he did. Faced with a burgeoning independent Labour movement, Snowden felt obliged to steep himself further in socialist writings. Though his initial intention was to face up to the socialist challenge he was soon drawn to the new movement. In November 1893 he spoke glowingly of the socialist belief in service to others before the Craven Liberal Club, adding quotations from Jesus Christ in support. He subsequently met Enid Stacy, a prominent socialist lecturer, who visited Cowling in 1894 to lecture on the relationship between temperance and prosperity. Indeed, it was she who shaped the thinking behind his first writings on the matter in January 1895. On 19 June 1894 he heard a lecture given by E. R. Hartley, a Bradford butcher and later the secretary of the Clarion Van movement, on 'The Need for a Labour Party'. By the beginning of 1895 he was a socialist and had joined the Keighley branch of the ILP.

The move from the Liberal Party to the ILP took Snowden three years and it is important to see it as a break with the Liberal Party and not with Liberalism; for he always sustained a belief in the old progressive Liberal ideas and was always loyal to the Gladstonian economics of his upbringing, with their emphasis upon the need for balanced budgets. Nevertheless, socialism offered him a way forward for he believed that the collective ownership of the means of production was essential to avoid conflict and to remove inequality. But the view of state socialism which he countenanced was never precisely spelt out. He certainly felt, like MacDonald and the Fabians, that industry and services should be run by the state through impartial administrators. He appears to have shared their faith in the organic growth of society leading to the extension of state control. But he was also attracted by some of the ideas of William Morris and, on many occasions, announced his belief in a cooperative form of life based upon brotherhood. He also shared with Morris the belief that socialism should allow for the individual development of all, and considered this to be one of its central objectives. This conviction appeared in his famous published lecture *The Individual under Socialism* and was elaborated further in 'The Two Salvations', an article published in the *Labour Prophet*.[2] In the latter he asserted that there were two salvations, an individual salvation and a social salvation. The Christian religions had emphasized the first, demanding conversion in order to seek salvation from hell because of original sin. Although he felt that such views would be swept away by a better-educated public he also believed that the individual should strive for moral and intellectual improvement, with or without religion. But no amount of individual improvement could adequately deal with society's social problems.

> To change these conditions, which are preventing the individual regeneration of the masses, is the social salvation which is necessary to preach and put into practice as the complement to the preaching of individual salvation.[3]

It was socialism alone which could tackle the social problems which imposed limitations upon the ability of individuals to develop. Socialism would guarantee individual freedom and not, as some critics argued, threaten it with state bureaucracy.

It is easy to see why this blend of ethical and administrative socialism should appeal to Snowden. It met his concern for self-help and improvement; it evoked his experience in the civil service and fitted neatly with his attitudes on a number of issues of personal interest. It was, for instance, sufficiently flexible for him to fudge the apparent contradictions in his argument on the drink question. He was able both to attack the resort to alcohol as a personal failing, which added to poverty, and yet to suggest that no amount of temperance alone would eradicate poverty. Individual regeneration obviously required the social salvation which only socialism could provide.

This faith in ethical socialism eschewed economic explanations of inequality; they were not needed by the converted. But what was to be the agency of change? How was socialism to come about? To Snowden, it would come through the growth of capitalism rather than its collapse. As industry expanded it would require legislative control and from then it was only a short step to state control. To this Fabian perspective of the inevitability of socialism, Snowden added the ballot box. Much missionary work, stressing the moral justice of socialism, had to be undertaken in order to widen the appeal of socialism, to increase its electoral power and, ultimately to bring about the formation of a socialist Labour Government. To Snowden, there was no inconsistency between establishing a socialist faith and seeking electoral success. He was adamant that socialism would be achieved through parliamentary success rather than through class conflict. He could not conceive how class conflict could benefit the working class, believed that socialism was above mere class interests and doubted the wisdom of socialists depending upon the sectional interests of trade unions.

There was no obvious coherence or perfection in Snowden's socialist ideas. They were a mixture of influences and lacked intellectual rigour. An undercurrent of Liberal ideas to his views led him to hold a somewhat myopic attitude to events, never perceiving that capitalism might be hostile to the 'inexorable' growth of socialism. Yet these views were not untypical of many other socialist converts from Radical Liberalism. The trappings of Liberalism might have been removed but many Radical Liberal views remained. This is illustrated most notably in Snowden's faith in progress, which underpinned his belief in the inevitable growth of socialism.

The most obvious deficiency of this blend of ideas was its failure to explain the stages by which capitalism would move to socialism. There was a vague assumption that there would be a gradual and inevitable move towards state control but there was little evidence of how this would evolve from the Gladstonian economic philosophy which he advocated. As will be emphasized later, the economic views he proferred in the 1920s relied upon the success of the private sector: his desire to pay off the National Debt arose from a belief that it would force interest rates down and permit private industry to be competitive and successful in a free-world economy. But how was state control to emerge and why did he not prepare for it whilst in office? It is perhaps indicative of the confused state of Labour ideology between the 1890s and the 1930s that Snowden's static economic views were rarely challenged by the Labour Party faithful.

Snowden's rise in local politics was swift. He wrote a letter to the *Keighley News*, which appeared on 12 January 1895, complaining that wages had been halved in Cowling since 1880, that seven out of every ten women and nine out of every ten children over 11 had to work. He argued that the Cowling community was temperate and thrifty, and had an average of £10 per head saved in the Yorkshire Penny Bank, 'but this was all they had to show for their labour, the degradation of their women and withholding their children of advantage'. In February 1895 he gave a lecture on 'Socialism' and it was recorded that

> Mr. Snowden pointed out that Socialists were not bloody revolutionaries or dreamers, but a body of earnest men who were seeking to replace our present anarchical commercialism, our industrial struggle for existence, our system of profit-mongering and labour exploitation, by the collective ownership and management of all means of production of each and all alike.

But socialism had to be more than a mere economic transference of industrial control from a few individuals to the community. To be of value it had to improve the opportunities and capacities of mankind. With a true William Morris type of flourish, Snowden continued:

> Yet Socialism aimed at something beyond mere restricted demand for higher wages; its object was to realise those aspiring mutterings which had been faintly heard for ages, and to establish for the workers a true life – the development of the whole of man's capacities, the expanding of affections and the co-operating with Divine Order of the universe. Socialism did not claim to establish any new principle of morality or religion but it did claim to understand the moral law more clearly and perfectly than current philosophy or religion.... It was a religion that believed, with Ruskin that whether there was one God, whether there were three gods, or 10,000 gods, little children should have their bellies filled and their bodies kept warm. It was a religion which judged men not by creeds, but by deeds (hear, hear).

On 17 February 1895, he lectured to the Keighley Labour Church on 'The Religion of Socialism', and exactly a month later was addressing a public meeting at the Queen's Theatre, under the auspices of the Keighley Labour Union, on 'The Cry of the Children'.[4]

This local popularity may well have had something to do with a continuity of idiom and style. Snowden's audiences were accustomed to nonconformist revivalism and probably appreciated the elective affinity of his approach. He certainly employed the ranting and rhetorical type of lecture to good effect. Within a few months 'he was crowding the largest public hall in the town by his great powers of eloquence – powers utterly unsuspected a few months before either by himself or by his friends'.[5] Indeed, he presented an unusual spectacle at public meetings. Frail, white-faced and plainly dressed, he must have struck his audience as the unhealthy clerk he had once been. This impression contrasted sharply with the fire of his message and the missionary zeal with which it was delivered. The *Keighley Labour Journal* referred to his 'impassioned eloquence' and the 'nameless power which seizes the hearts and consciences of men'.[6] The final passage from one of his most famous lectures, 'The Christ that is to be', captures the religiosity of his style.

> But the only way to regain the earthly paradise is by the old, hard-road to Calvary – through persecution, through poverty, through temptation, by agony and bloody sweat, by the crown of thorns, by the agonising death. And then the resurrection to the New Humanity – purified by suffering, triumphant through sacrifice.[7]

This inspirational and religious approach contrasts sharply with the more factual style which he adopted for the discussion of industrial and financial matters – though he kept in tune with the Radical sympathies of his audience. Typical of this latter genre is *The Industrial Muddle and the Way Out*, a pamphlet based upon two lectures delivered to the Yeadon, Guiseley and District Workers' Union in March 1901. These examined the high levels of unemployment amongst skilled machine-shop workers in Keighley and suggested that the solution to unemployment was the raising of incomes in line with production.

> Machine invention would go on, and productive capacity would increase, and every such increase in the productive capacity of the people which was not met by an increase in the power of purchase would make the period of good trade shorter, and the period of trade depression longer.[8]

'The Way Out' of this economic depression appeared to be to lighten the economic burden of British industry by between 20 and 50 per cent by reducing the burden imposed by the high rents which accrued to land ownership. This was, of course, a Radical Liberal solution which suggested that capitalism, as such, was not the problem and that profits were not in themselves to blame for the reduction of workers' wages – a view which seems to have underpinned much of his later economic approach.

Between Snowden's fustian rhetoric and his heavily statistical lectures lay a gap, for he failed to explain how society would move from capitalism to socialism. The more general message he offered was the need for individual conversion to socialism combined with the belief that social reform and nationalization could only come through income produced by a prosperous capitalist economy.

Snowden rose quickly in Keighley politics. In 1894 he became clerk to the newly-formed Cowling Parish Council and in 1895 was returned to the Cowling School Board. He quickly attracted the attention of Herbert Horner and joined the Keighley ILP where 'within two or three months he was crowding the largest public hall in the town by his great powers of eloquence – powers utterly unsuspected a few months before either by himself or his friends'.[9]

His rise was swift and almost immediately he was asked to stand as the ILP candidate for Keighley in the 1895 General Election, though he withdrew from the contest when the Keighley ILP ran out of funds; but not before he had accused the Liberal Party 'big-wigs' of being 'parasites, bloodsuckers, hypocrites' and as men who 'fatten upon the blood and sweat of labour and their bondslaves'.[10] His particular attack was directed at the Briggs family, the paternalistic employers of political bosses of Keighley, though his criticism could be more broadly applied to numerous other Liberal mill owners in Keighley and the West Riding, who expected deference from their workforce, opposed trade unionism and considered themselves the true representatives of the working class.

In 1899 Snowden was returned to both Keighley Town Council and Keighley School Board. However, it is interesting to note that his local successes owed little to his involvement with the Keighley Labour Union – indeed, much the opposite. He was rarely involved in branch activity, barely ever attended meetings and never became an official. Instead his reputation rested upon his oratory and journalism. In 1898, he became editor of the *Keighley Labour Journal*, organ of the Keighley Labour Union/ILP, and wrote much of the paper himself under the bye-lines of 'Robin Redbreast' and 'A Mere Outsider'. Very quickly the circulation rose to 5,000 and revived the flagging interest in both the political and cultural aspects of the local Labour movement.

Snowden used the *Keighley Labour Journal* as an effective propaganda sheet against the Liberals exposing their failings in public affairs. Through its pages, he attacked the decision to raise the salaries of highly-paid public officials and objected to the extravagant expenses claimed by councillors and officials. Even at this stage, Snowden was revealing the parsimony for which he became famous later in his career.

The political temper of the Keighley parliamentary constituency suited Snowden's style. It was an area comprising isolated farming and weaving communities on the one hand and of a bustling textile and engineering centre on the other. Trade unionism was weak, the local Trades Council not having been formed until 1890. It was a Radical Liberal community, even if constrained by the more conservative Liberalism of particular employers such as the Cloughs and the Briggs. An optimistic independent Labour movement had to be aware of these facts and it is thus not surprising that the embryonic ILP should work through the moral appeal of ethical socialism rather than the sectional simplicity of class trade unionism. Snowden was at home in this atmosphere and flourished in the essentially nonconformist environment of Keighley. Here was a community which understood and appreciated the meaning of 'Brotherhood', where Labour supporters attended the Labour Church and participated in the Clarion movement. There was, indeed, a decent-sized activist minority in the Keighley area to which Snowden could easily relate.

It was in this political and social environment that Snowden obtained his political training in electioneering and administration. As unpaid clerk to the Cowling Parish Council he had tried, generally unsuccessfully, to make it a tool of effective and reforming administration, advocating that the Council should take over the community's water supply and later organizing a referendum on the street lighting. He sensitized Keighley Borough Council and Keighley School Board to their duties, and even John Clough, one of Keighley's leading Liberals, remarked that 'With Mr. Snowden on the School Board he was sure debates would be more interesting'.[11] On the Borough Council he exposed a blunder by which the Council proposed to buy land it already owned. The *Keighley Labour Journal* reflected that 'Mr. Snowden's exposure of what it really meant amazed the Council, and induced some members who seldom speak to utter an indignant protest...'.[12]

Many early socialists were of the opinion that municipal socialism had sharp limits defined by the existing law. They saw no way in which they could widen its application beyond those boundaries accepted by advanced Liberal town councils such as Huddersfield, which had municipalized tramways as early as 1882. Snowden was of a similar opinion: 'the fact is that Keighley Corporation had municipalised everything which can be done in the present state of law...'.[13] He felt that he had contributed towards this process in a positive manner and, in 1902, when he was more or less completing his withdrawal from Keighley politics he reflected that

> I had the satisfaction of knowing that during my two years of active work a very considerable part of the programme on which I had been elected had been carried out, or advanced as far as it is possible for the Corporation to go without additional parliamentary powers.... Most of the reforms I advocated which the Corporation themselves could carry out with their present powers are today accomplished facts....[14]

Snowden's early political experiences were enervating in the sense that they offered a limited Radical and socialist perspective. The range of Liberal–Radical impulses was powerful but inadequate to the needs of a new socialist state. Yet there was little to encourage Snowden to make a firm break with the past.

Notwithstanding its restrictive nature, Keighley politics did provide Snowden with the local political reputation which was necessary to bring him to the attention of the national leaders of the ILP. In December 1896, J. Bruce Glasier noted, in his Diary, 'Meet Philip Snowden & his mother ... Philip seems the best material. His lower limbs are paralyzed & he walks with crutches'.[15] His political talents were also quickly recognized by others and in July 1898, on the withdrawal of Pete Curran, he joined the National Administrative Council of the ILP. Glasier optimistically forecast that 'Snowden should be very useful – a real orator – and earnest thinker'.[16]

These comments speak volumes about the state of the ILP at this time. First, it was in poor political shape and clutching at any political talent which came its way. The political defeats experienced in the 1895 General Election and in subsequent by-elections, most notably Keir Hardie's defeat at Bradford East in 1896 and Pete Curran's failure at Barnsley in 1897, had done much to undermine the enthusiasm of its early supporters. Secondly, it was attracting a lower-middle-class type of leadership. Apart from Hardie, none of the other three leaders of the 'Big Four' – Ramsay MacDonald who had joined the NAC in 1896, Bruce Glasier, who had joined in 1897 and, of course, Snowden – had been employed in industry. All, including Hardie, gained part of their income from journalism.

The 'Big Four' all shared a common approach to socialism, despite the bitter and spiteful personal differences which developed among some of them. They emphasized the moral approach, were disdainful of change being accomplished by violent class warfare and generally perceived socialism as coming through the success and growth of capitalism. Their precise views often varied but there was a cogency and congruence in their economic and political thought.

As the newest member to the leadership, Snowden's first task was to establish his personal relations with the other members of the 'Big Four'. It is clear that from the start he identified most closely with Glasier. He never became a close friend to Keir Hardie, largely due to the fact that Glasier and Hardie were often at odds over the running of the *Labour Leader*, the organ of the ILP, and partly due to the idiosyncratic style of Hardie's leadership. He had already seen how Hardie could misjudge the local situation by the way in which he had intervened on the side of John Lister, treasurer of the ILP, in his 1894/5 conflict with the Halifax Labour Union over his right to individual freedom of action and thought. Throughout Yorkshire ILP activists had been offended by Hardie's interference.

As far as MacDonald was concerned, though Glasier moved towards him, Snowden remained distant and hostile – 'spiteful' to use MacDonald's own description. This antipathy appears to have been based upon an initial personal dislike to which political rivalry was added in later years. Snowden was prone to making astringent comments about MacDonald in private correspondence and conversation. On one occasion, he advised John Penny, Secretary of the ILP, not to send MacDonald to an Education Conference called to oppose the Conservative's Education Bill of 1901:

> I certainly think that the I.L.P. should be represented but for Heaven's sake don't send MacDonald. He doesn't know anything about this

> question. Better send Sam Hobson. But after all I am not sure if we should not be deploying a lack of the sense of humour to treat Gorst's Bill Abortion seriously.[17]

That comment was, of course, unfair. It was Snowden, not MacDonald, who lacked a sense of humour.

As the newest member of the 'Big Four', Snowden initially felt his way, agreeing with NAC decisions rather than shaping them. He also came in at the end of a debate about the future of the ILP which was to be crucial to the development of a Labour Party and could do little more than endorse the NAC line.

The general election defeats of 1895 had threatened the very survival of the ILP, leading many of its members to demand socialist unity, which effectively meant uniting with the Social Democratic Federation (SDF). This policy was discussed by ILP conferences and balloted upon, between 1896 and 1898. The issue was complex, confused and subject to numerous twists and turns, but what was clear throughout is that Hardie, strongly supported by Glasier and MacDonald, firmly resisted fusion with the SDF. At first they stalled efforts to establish socialist unity but when the crunch came in 1898, they openly opposed such a move on the grounds that it would be destructive to the ILP's hopes of winning support from the trade union and cooperative movements, as well as from Radical opinion. Hardie and the NAC opposed fusion at the ILP Conference and secured a branch vote on the issue of fusion or federation with the SDF. When the results of the ballot were made known towards the end of July 1898, it was evident that, in a small vote, there was a clear majority in favour of federation. This was put to the SDF Executive and the matter rested since their mandate was for fusion.

Snowden expressed no particular feeling about the socialist unity debate. His Keighley branch had actually voted 18 to one in favour of fusion when the matter was discussed in December 1897,[18] albeit with the proviso that such action should not interfere with ILP principles. But Snowden appears to have remained equivocal on the issue, was barely influenced by the activities of the Keighley branch and was possibly more supportive of Glasier and the NAC, if for no other reason than that he had little regard for the SDF.

With the socialist unity debate out of the way, Hardie pressed forward with the demand for a Labour Alliance aimed at uniting socialists and trade unionists in a non-socialist independent Labour Party. The idea had been floated in 1896 and was further discussed at the 1899 TUC Conference. Eventually in February 1900, the Labour Representation Committee (LRC) was formed. As far as one can judge, Snowden approved of this dramatic decision which was ultimately to pave the way for the emergence of the modern Labour Party. He appears to have been committed to the Labour Alliance, despite the fact that it was not an overtly socialist organization. Like other ILP leaders, he must have hoped that, by establishing an independent Labour Party, the trade unions who joined would gradually be forced to sever their links with official Liberalism and Conservatism and would gradually identify with the ILP's socialist viewpoint. What he grew to regret was the increasing domination of trade unionism which the formation of the LRC brought to Labour politics.

The ILP was essentially a provincial organization. It is thus hardly surprising that its leadership was assumed by young men who, by and large, were drawn from the regions and reflected the views and influences of their origins. Philip Snowden was such a man. He had not grown up in the cosmopolitan spaciousness of London politics but within the restrictive bounds of a nonconformist community on the edge of the Pennines. His was an isolated childhood, subjected to the horror of 'hell-fire' and damnation, and cultivated by the tradition of self-help and Radical Liberalism. He rose quickly in Keighley's Labour circles: 'the mighty Snowden rears his stately crest in the vicinity of Keighley'.[19] At his meetings he was usually introduced as 'Brother Philip Snowden of Keighley'. To many, Snowden was Keighley politics writ large. Though he eventually escaped his geographical and parochial bonds he could not outgrow many of the ideas which they had imposed. More to the point, the Radical–Liberal attitudes Keighley had nurtured were to be reinforced by the new company that he kept. Glasier, MacDonald and Hardie all shared views and experiences to which Snowden could relate. His belief in progress, his view that socialism was inevitable and that parliamentary reform was the agency of change were massaged by those around him. He shared their religious upbringing and their almost religious faith in the rectitude of socialism. But political success brought its own problems. Between 1900 and 1914 Snowden was faced with transmitting the 'religion of socialism' into electoral success and, though at first optimistic, he ultimately realized the difficulty of extending his own brand of socialism through the increasingly trade union-dominated LRC/Labour Party.

Notes

1 'Ephesian', op. cit., p. 6.
2 Loc. cit., April 1898. Also look at document section, items 2, 3.
3 Ibid., p. 5.
4 *Keighley News*, 27 April 1895.
5 *Labour Leader*, 12 September 1903.
6 *Keighley Labour Journal*, 10 November 1895.
7 P. Snowden, *The Christ that is to be* (ILP, London, 1903).
8 P. Snowden, *The Industrial Muddle and the Way Out* (Yeadon, 1901), p. 5.

9 *Labour Leader*, 12 September 1903.
10 *Keighley News*, 27 April 1895.
11 *Keighley Labour Journal*, 18 March 1899.
12 Ibid., 14 April 1900.
13 Ibid., 26 September 1902.
14 Ibid.
15 Glasier Diary, 16 December 1896. Deposited in the Archives Collection, University of Liverpool Library.
16 Ibid., 23 July 1898.
17 Archives of the ILP (Francis Johnson Collection), 1901/20 B. Published in microform by Harvester.
18 Keighley ILP, Minutes, December 1897.
19 *Labour Leader*, 27 February 1897.

5 Philip Snowden and the Blackburn Experience *c.* 1900–1914

> We expect to rely upon the support of the radical rank and file [of the Liberal Party] who are anxious for reform. (Blackburn Independent Labour Party, *Blackburn Labour Journal*, October 1900)

In the early years of the Labour Party, Snowden was the quintessence of Liberal Radicalism. His upbringing in Keighley and Nelson had prepared him to act as a spokesman for this brand of Labour opinion, but it was his experiences of Blackburn politics which helped to firm up his commitment to old Liberal views. The moment he agreed to contest Blackburn for the ILP and the SDF in the 1900 General Election he was thrown into a new political and industrial environment which sharply contrasted with that of Keighley politics. For one thing, the Blackburn cotton unions were far better organized and more politically influential with the Liberal Party than their Keighley counterparts. The Blackburn Liberal Party was also much less effective and far more fragmented than the Liberal millocracy which ran Keighley politics. It became almost axiomatic that parliamentary success for Snowden in Blackburn could only be achieved with the help of trade unionism and by some type of arrangement with the local Liberal Party. At the very least, as the Blackburn ILP acknowledged in 1900, the Liberal rank and file would have to be won over: a point which Snowden quickly appreciated. This basic essential of Blackburn politics coloured his attitude towards his whole political conduct which, perhaps more than any other Labour politician of national stature, had hitherto been marked by Edwardian politics. Blackburn was crucial to Snowden's political training.

In 1900, Blackburn was a town of about 130,000 people dominated by a cotton industry which directly employed 40,000 operatives. There were about 100 cotton firms in the town and about three-quarters of them were engaged in weaving alone. The largest of these firms were able to exert some paternal control over their workforce.

Blackburn was also a two-member constituency which had been a bastion of 'clog Toryism' in the late nineteenth century, a place where Liberal self-help ideals had withered before the appeals of the pub and the football club – patronized by the Tories. This Tory–working class alliance rested upon the economic and social relationship set up by the large Tory employers. Their paternal control, and the deferential relationship it elicited, was best reflected by the Hornby family, landowning industrialists who represented the borough at Westminster for a considerable part of the nineteenth century. Snowden was quick to appreciate their power and appeal, noting that 'Toryism has become Hornbyism'.[1] At the turn of the century, it was Sir Harry Hornby, representing Blackburn between 1886 and 1910, who symbolized the family's political influence in the town. Though he never spoke in the House of Commons, he was a much respected townsman, Churchman and free trader.

By 1900 the old political control of the Hornbys and their like was beginning to break down. The greater mobility of labour, the diversification of housing patterns and the gradual decline of the old family dynasties were beginning to disturb the established political patterns. The closeness of the factory communities, which had formerly provided the old Tory masters with votes, was being undermined. Hornby's personal reputation sustained the ailing Conservative Party, whose decline was being delayed by the weakness and the fragmentation of its political opponents. The Blackburn Liberal Party was still ineffective, actually refusing to put forward municipal candidates against the Tories in 1897, and the Labour movement was only just beginning to emerge as a political force. Nevertheless, changes were afoot.

A local branch of the SDF had been formed in 1883 and remained active into the twentieth century, inspired by Tom Hurley, a locally-born Catholic Irishman. Its success seems to have been the result of the local willingness to go its separate way from the national organization, and Hurley complained that 'the articles which appeared in *Justice* were sometimes beyond the understanding of Young Socialists who had just come into the movement'.[2] Nevertheless, local support seems to have transcended such difficulties and Hurley topped the School Board poll in 1895 and was returned to the Town Council in 1898. The Blackburn Fabian Society was formed in 1892, though it quickly dissolved into the ILP in 1893. By 1897 the local Labour movement was producing the *Blackburn Labour Journal*, which brought together the SDF and ILP supporters under one umbrella. Yet the number of Labour supporters remained small and their potential ally, the Blackburn Trades Council, was asserting its own political independence by putting forward its own candidates for local public office. However, fragmented as these forces were, a broad understanding did develop and the Labour movement was, by 1900, mounting a serious challenge to the Tories with four Trades Council, two SDF and two ILP councillors, with one ILP member and one member of the SDF on the Blackburn Guardians. As Jeffrey Hill has commented, the SDF's triangular alliance with the Trades Council and the ILP had, by 1900,

> out-stripped the Liberals as the chief opponent of a very powerful brand of local Toryism; it laid the basis for Philip Snowden's spectacular LRC campaign of 1900 and 1906 which finally broke the Tories' long-standing monopoly of parliamentary representation in the borough.[3]

Despite such reflections it is clear that Blackburn politics was in a flux. A declining Tory Party, largely dependent upon the personal appeal of Hornby, was met by division amongst the progressive parties. A broad alliance brought the three Labour organizations together but it was obvious that an even broader arrangement between the progressive forces was necessary to secure parliamentary success.

None of Snowden's early political experiences had prepared him for such an unstable political environment. Keighley politics had been dominated by an intransigent group of Liberal employers who brooked little opposition from their workers and who were prone to victimize those who joined the ILP or similar political parties. Blackburn was entirely different. A weak Liberal Party was prepared to be more considerate in its relations to Labour's political representatives. As a result, between 1900 and 1910, an emollient Snowden moved towards a Lib–Lab alliance as he became increasingly aware of its electoral advantages.

This softening of Snowden's political attitudes was partly a product of the importance of Blackburn trade unionism. The woollen and worsted industries of the West Riding of Yorkshire had always been badly organized and the Keighley Trades and Labour Council had struggled to sustain a membership of between 1,000 and 1,500 in the 1890s. Blackburn trade unionism was, by any standards, more impressive. The Weavers' Association was powerfully organized in north Lancashire and more than 12,000 of the 20,000 trade unionists affiliated to the Blackburn Trades Council were members of that union. Even a sceptic like Snowden had to acknowledge the importance of the Blackburn Weavers and pay due homage to the wishes of David Shackleton, their national leader. At the very least, he had to pose as a man in tune with local trade union interests – even if his speeches were full of empty rhetoric.

There was also another aspect of Blackburn trade unionism that he could not easily ignore the presence of a substantial female membership within the Weavers' Association. In 1900, about 16,000 women worked in the Blackburn cotton mills and many were members of the union. They had been actively involved in the militant activities of the weavers' unions in the area, had resisted the attempts of employers to reduce the wages of weavers by 10 per cent in the 1878 textile strike, and held considerable sway in the decisions of local branches of the Association. At the very moment Snowden sought parliamentary honours in Blackburn for the first time, the female textile workers were becoming sensitized to the need for female suffrage.

Snowden contested the Blackburn constituency at every general election from 1900 to 1918. In 1918 he was defeated very largely as a result of his opposition to the First World War. On the previous four occasions – in 1900 – when he was defeated, and in 1906 and the two elections in 1910, when he was successful – the breadth of his programme revealed his concern to take advantage of the uncertain and changing nature of Blackburn politics. His strategy was unambiguous: he attempted to attract both working-class Tories, by offering a distinctively Labour element in his campaigns, and Liberal supporters by advocating a Radical programme. His early campaigns touched upon the issues of adult suffrage, land nationalization, shorter Parliaments, the payment of MPs and the ending of the hereditary House of Lords. He presented the ILP as a neutral meeting ground for Liberal and Tory working men, and, in 1900, assured the Blackburn electorate that 'Socialism is not merely for the poor widow, it was the cause of the small capitalist, the struggling professional man, and the poor shopkeeper'.[4] His 'socialist' policies were to be seen as all-embracing and representative of the interests of all classes and most political viewpoints.

The buckshot nature of this political approach was difficult to sustain. Snowden's political Radicalism soon deflected him towards the Liberal Party. Although he initially denied that he was forging a Lib-Lab alliance it is clear that between 1900 and 1910 he moved inexorably in that direction. But why, having so recently cut himself off from the Liberal Party, did he move back towards the party of his youth?

There are many obvious reasons for this – most of them grounded in Blackburn politics. The constituency returned two MPs and was ideal for an arrangement whereby one Labour and one Liberal could stand against two Conservatives. It also appeared that the Conservative Party was beginning to lose political support and that an alliance of the progressive forces could prevail. In addition, a variety of specific factors emerged at each general election which pushed Snowden towards an electoral understanding with Liberalism.

In 1900 Snowden stood alone against the Conservative candidates, Hornby and Coddington, and was effectively a Radical candidate. Liberal voters were attracted to him because of his advocacy of temperance and his condemnation of the British involvement in the Boer War 'which could add nothing to the prestige of a great Empire'.[5] In Blackburn, unlike Preston which was fought by Keir Hardie, the Liberal Party was largely opposed to the war. In addition, Snowden offered a 'programme of advanced reform ... which in all its practical aspects is Radicalism pure and simple'.[6] Indeed he informed the *Lancashire Daily Post* that

> My platform will be a labour programme and the question I shall put pre-eminent will be the land question. Then will follow industrial monopolies, nationalisation of mines and railways, old age pensions, the reform of taxation in the direction of graduated income tax and death duties, a shorter working day, and similar measures.[7]

Although Snowden made no real concessions to the Liberals a section of the local Liberal Party, led by T. P. Ritzema, proprietor of the *Blackburn Weekly Telegraph*, gave him their support. This was not sufficient to return Snowden as one of Blackburn's two MPs, though enough to urge him to thank Ritzema for 'yeoman service'.[8] The result and the pattern of 'split' voting suggests that Snowden, despite some Liberal abstentions, picked up about three times as many votes from Liberals as he did from Conservatives. This ratio increased greatly at successive general elections before the First World War.

In the intervening years between the 1900 and 1906 General Elections, Snowden's Liberal credentials were strengthened. He fought a by-election at Wakefield in March 1902 and this campaign marked him out as a Radical. *Justice*, the journal of the SDF, noted: 'there is nothing of his election address to even suggest that he is a Socialist'.[9] However, it did not prevent his defeat by 2,960 votes to 1,979. In November 1902 the Blackburn Liberal Association also obtained national financial support for a candidate to be run 'with Snowden but

Table 5.1 Analysis of the Blackburn Poll, 1900

		Coddington (Con.)	Hornby (Con.)	Snowden (ILP)
Coddington	87	87	—	—
Hornby	280	—	280	—
Snowden	5,335	—	—	5,335
Coddington–Hornby	9,267	9,267	9,267	—
Coddington–Snowden	61	61	—	61
Hornby–Snowden	1,700	—	1,700	1,700
Totals	16,730	9,415	11,247	7,096
Turnout 85.8 per cent				

independent of him'.[10] When Edward Hamer came forward as the Liberal candidate for Blackburn in October 1903 he stressed his willingness to work within the framework of a Lib–Lab alliance.

It is true that Snowden gave no advice to his supporters to vote Liberal in the 1906 General Election but this was more than offset by David Shackleton's encouragement to all Blackburn trade unionists to support 'both Progressive candidates'.[11] In addition, Snowden's policies stamped him firmly as an old progressive Liberal. The national campaign in the 1906 General Election had been dominated by the issue of free trade versus protection. This was also the case in Blackburn, although all four candidates – two Conservatives, one Liberal and Snowden – claimed to be free traders. Nevertheless, Snowden drew a distinction between the commitments of progressive and of Conservative candidates, particularly doubting the political veracity of Sir Harry Hornby. He maintained that Hornby's advocacy of free trade would evaporate when he was faced with a question of loyalty to a party which was becoming dominated by protectionists. His analysis proved wrong but was sufficient to make free trade a distinguishing issue between the Conservative and the progressive candidates. The analysis of the poll also suggests that Snowden was benefiting from the Lib–Lab alliance. That vote, topped up by Labour plumpers and a number of Hornby–Snowden splits, almost entirely drawn from the Conservative working-class voters, proved sufficient to return Snowden to Parliament as Blackburn's first Labour MP.

Table 5.2 Analysis of the Blackburn Poll, 1906

		Drage (Con.)	Hamer (Lib.)	Hornby (Con.)	Snowden (ILP)
Drage	10	10	—	—	—
Hamer	311	—	311	—	—
Hornby	94	—	—	94	—
Snowden	1,504	—	—	—	1,504
Drage–Hamer	86	86	86	—	—
Drage–Hornby	8,751	8,751	—	8,751	—
Drage–Snowden	85	85	—	—	85
Hamer–Hornby	624	—	624	624	—
Hamer–Snowden	7,871	—	7,871	—	7,871
Hornby–Snowden	822	—	—	822	822
Totals	20,158	8,932	8,892	10,291	10,282
Turnout 94.9 per cent					

Despite some disquiet within Liberal ranks at the fact that more than 1,500 voters had plumped for Snowden and ignored the progressive alliance, the next four years saw the flourishing of that accord in Blackburn. The major reason for this was Snowden's more open relationship with the Liberal Party. At first it appeared that Snowden was going to alienate the Liberal Party in Parliament but by 1908 he was sensitive to Liberal feelings. He produced a book on the vital importance of drink to the social question, offered a *Socialist Budget* along the lines being taken up by David Lloyd George in 1909, and was working with Liberals on a variety of issues in Parliament. When the House of Lords rejected Lloyd George's 'People's Budget' in 1909 Snowden became convinced of the need to remove its veto over financial matters. When he returned to Blackburn in the autumn of that year, he nailed his colours to the Liberal mast: 'It is important that the electors should realise the fact that upon the issue of the coming election depends the future of social reform in this country'.[12] Indeed, in both of the 1910 General Elections, Snowden was unambiguous about his close relationship with the Liberal candidates. He admitted the need to play down the Labour programme and supported the Labour Party's willingness to give 'a helping hand to anybody who is trying to remove the obstruction' of the House of Lord's veto on financial matters.[13] He also supported the Labour Party's 'good commonsense position' in advising its supporters to vote for those candidates who opposed the veto of the House of Lords in those two member constituencies where there was no second Labour candidate.[14]

Table 5.3 Analysis of the Blackburn Poll, January 1910

		Barclay (Lib)	Bowles (Con.)	Cecil (Con.)	Snowden (Lab.)
Barclay	409	409	—	—	—
Bowles	56	—	56	—	—
Cecil	71	—	—	71	—
Snowden	415	—	—	—	415
Barclay–Bowles	163	163	163	—	—
Barclay–Cecil	253	253	—	253	—
Barclay–Snowden	11,239	11,239	—	—	11,239
Bowles–Cecil	8,807	—	8,807	8,807	—
Bowles–Snowden	86	—	86	—	86
Cecil–Snowden	176	—	—	176	176
Totals	21,765	12,064	9,112	9,307	11,916
Turnout 96.0 per cent					

Table 5.4 Analysis of the Blackburn Poll, December 1910

		Carpenter (Con.)	Norman (Lib.)	Riley (Con.)	Snowden (Lab.)
Carpenter	54	54	—	—	—
Norman	327	—	327	—	—
Riley	46	—	—	46	—
Snowden	449	—	—	—	449
Carpenter–Norman	307	307	307	—	—
Carpenter–Riley	9,262	9,262	—	9,262	—
Carpenter–Snowden	191	191	—	—	191
Norman–Riley	95	—	95	95	—
Norman–Snowden	10,025	—	10,025	—	10,025
Riley–Snowden	97	—	—	97	97
Totals	20,853	9,814	10,754	9,500	10,762
Turnout 92.4 per cent					

In effect, Snowden was endorsing the Lib–Lab alliance. Inexorably, despite some ritualistic pronouncements of the political independence of the Labour Party, Snowden had come to accept the need for the progressive alliance in both local and national politics. On 5 January 1910 Mrs Snowden appealed for votes for Barclay, the Blackburn Liberal candidate: on 7 January Snowden said he agreed with his wife. During the last week of the January 1910 campaign both Liberal and Labour organizations advised against plumping, suggesting that voters divide their two votes between the progressive candidates.

The resulting Lib–Lab alliance was evident in the voting patterns which emerged in both the January and December 1910 General Elections. The overwhelming majority of Liberal and Labour voters divided their votes between the progressive candidates and the Conservative–Labour vote practically disappeared. Snowden had no option but to follow the dictates of Blackburn politics – a strategy which accorded with some of his own ideological inclinations.

This move towards Liberalism was also facilitated by Snowden's exposure to a strong trade union movement. The locally powerful Weavers' Association and its leader David Shackleton were associated closely with the Liberals in East Lancashire. Even after the Association had voted in favour of joining the Labour Representation Committee in 1902 by the overwhelming majority of 85,154 votes to 19,886, it was obvious that a relationship with the Liberal Party was going to be maintained. This was most evident in the events surrounding the Clitheroe by-election of 1902, where Snowden was made fully aware of the link between Lancashire trade unionism and Lancashire Liberalism. At one stage, it appeared that Snowden would be the 'Labour and Socialist' candidate but the local Liberals offered not to contest the seat if David Shackleton, who had been chosen by local trade unionists, was nominated by the local LRC instead of Snowden. In a climate of wheeling and dealing, Ramsay MacDonald asked Snowden to withdraw, which he did, and Shackleton was returned unopposed as Labour's third MP. This arrangement helped to pave the way for the secret negotiations which led to the infamous Lib–Lab pact of 1903, whereby electoral clashes between Liberal and Labour candidates were to be avoided in some constituencies. Indeed, Blackburn was chosen to be part of this deal.

Snowden was never sponsored by any trade union. In the 1900 General Election he stood as an ILP candidate with SDF support. In 1906, and again in the January 1910 General Election, he was officially supported by the ILP in arrangement with the Labour Party. His campaigns were financed by selling threepenny stamps to workmen and he received only £200 per year from the ILP once he was in Parliament. The financial constraints he faced as an MP were considerable and, as he stressed in 1911, a visit to his constituency could easily swallow up his £4 per week income.

> I visited my constituency from twelve to twenty times a year and I cannot go down without incurring railway expenses for each different visit amounting to a sum of about £4, and to use a homely expression, an expenditure of £4 makes a very big hole in a weekly allowance of something like £4.[15]

The Blackburn trade unions did not help Snowden with his financial expenses, nor did he seek their support. His journalistic writings would, in any case, have contributed significantly towards his relative financial independence. He was never very happy about the rising importance of trade unionism within the Labour Party, nor the consequent tendency to make a narrow trade-union policy the distinctive appeal of the party. Nevertheless, he knew when to play the trade-union card. In the 1900 General Election campaign he had said very little about trade unionism. But between 1900 and 1906, the Taff Vale case, which imposed financial liabilities upon trade unions taking strike action, the shift of the cotton unions from the Liberal Party to the LRC/Labour Party, and Snowden's own dealings with Shackleton over the Clitheroe by-election, had emphasized to him the importance of winning trade-union support. Accordingly, in the 1906 General Election Snowden openly courted trade unionism, directing much of his criticism at Sir Harry Hornby's opposition to the Trades Disputes Bill, a Liberal attempt to compensate for recent judicial encroachments on trade union activities.

Snowden accused Sir Harry of voting 'to destroy trade unionism',[16] but there was never any great conviction behind his statements on an issue which was always of tactical rather than ideological importance to him.

Blackburn politics had certainly moved Snowden towards the Liberal Party, but what type of Radical was he? He certainly displayed an interest in the 'new' Liberal ideas which were proposed by Lloyd George and others. This brand of Liberalism, though it maintained that free trade was the best system of creating wealth, accepted that the distribution of that wealth was far from perfect. It therefore supported measures to provide old-age pensions, to deal with the Poor Law and to offer national insurance provision against unemployment and illness. Such measures, of course, cost money. As a result Lloyd George introduced his 'People's Budget', with its taxes on the rich and landed, to pay for his schemes and provoked the House of Lords to block his measures with its veto. It was Snowden's opposition to the use of this veto which finally forced him to accept the need to work openly with the Liberal Party in 1909 and 1910. It was even claimed that Lloyd George's Budget had been based upon the proposals advocated by Snowden. Whether or not this was true, Snowden was clearly struggling with the question of modernizing economic and social relationships within the parameters of a free trade system – an issue which associated him with Lloyd George. Nevertheless, Snowden's display of 'new' Liberal thought was shallow for, at root, he was a faithful adherent to the old Liberal shibboleths of 'Peace, Retrenchment and Reform'. In the final analysis, he believed that all budgets had to be balanced and that free trade must be maintained. If this meant delaying social reform then it was the price which had to be paid for a sound financial policy. It was this policy which would throw him into opposition against the expansionist policies advocated by the Liberal 'Yellow Books' during the 1920s. In 1910, as before and after, Snowden was an old progressive Liberal Radical at heart, not an advocate of the 'new' Liberalism, even if the events of 1909 and 1910 had temporarily fused the two strands.

The demand for the parliamentary franchise for women was an issue where a consistent Liberal Radical would back enfranchisement. In the changing atmosphere of Blackburn politics Snowden veered towards his Radical roots.

It appears that he had shown little interest in women's suffrage until 1900. From then onwards two factors dictated his support of the suffrage movement. The first was the obvious point that a substantial proportion of the members of the local branch of the Weavers' Association were women who were becoming increasingly conscious of their lack of a parliamentary vote. The second was Snowden's marriage to Ethel Annakin in March 1905.

From early 1900 until 1906 the suffragettes – women who fought not merely for the vote but for a wide range of women's rights – ran a successful campaign amongst the female Lancashire textile workers. The campaign, led by the North of England Society for Women's Suffrage (which was connected with the National Union of Women's Suffrage Societies) concentrated on the need to make women aware that their working conditions would only improve once they had the vote. The Society argued that, whilst women were disenfranchised, Parliament would take no interest in their problems.

The campaign was started in Blackburn on 1 May 1900 when the North of England Suffrage Society launched a petition in favour of women's suffrage to be signed exclusively by women working in the Lancashire cotton mills. The choice of Blackburn was apposite, for the town had more women working in the cotton mills than any other Lancashire town. The movement spread throughout Lancashire and, in the spring of 1901, it presented a petition, with 29,000 signatures, to Parliament. In its wake, there followed another such petition to be signed by all the female workers in the textile industries of Lancashire, Yorkshire and Cheshire and much vigorous campaigning to get the trade unions and the LRC/Labour Party to accept the justice of the cause. Indeed, David Shackleton was quickly reminded that a considerable part of his salary as MP for Clitheroe was paid out of the pockets of women weavers who were denied parliamentary suffrage.

Snowden could not remain aloof from these events. The women's suffrage campaign had begun in Blackburn and remained a vital issue amongst the cotton operatives. Mindful of the importance of the issue, he did make passing reference to women's suffrage at the Blackburn parliamentary election in 1900, and at the Wakefield by-election in 1902. Yet, though he referred to 'the shame of injured manhood and womanhood' in his speeches, he directed little effort to promoting the cause of women's suffrage. In common with many Radical Liberals, he suspected that the enfranchisement of women would be to the political advantage of the Conservative Party, although he recognized that the issue was a natural extension of Radical Liberal principles and necessary in order to extend electoral democracy.

Active involvement in the women's suffrage campaign came slowly for Snowden. It was not until April 1904, and through an article in the *Labour Leader* entitled 'The ILP and Women's Franchise', that he first outlined his views. At this stage he was quite clearly out of tune with the views being expressed by the Lancashire suffragists: he opposed any parliamentary bill to enfranchise women on the same property qualification as men, since such an arrangement would have given some propertied women the vote whilst some working-class men and women remained disenfranchised. The ILP had recently supported the principle of adult suffrage and Snowden could not see how it could promote an 'Adult Suffrage Bill and a Women's Representation Bill at the same time',[17] He added:

> It is, I think, much to the credit of the I.L.P. that they have not too prominently advertised the position as exceptional and requiring special treatment. The Socialists recognise a great principle – 'the principle of the unity of the human family'. Every industrial evil which afflicts women afflicts men to a lesser or greater degree. The evils we want to remove are not confined to one sex.
>
> ... Labour Members of Parliament would, I am sure, to a man, support every proposal for Women's Suffrage, but it would, I am equally sure, be effort diverted from the much more useful work of the I.L.P. to concentrate its forces upon a measure which would require enormous effort to carry to a successful issue, and when realised would not be worth the effort.

In effect, he was accepting the 'adultist' position favoured by the ILP and the LRC. However, towards the end of 1904 he had changed his mind and had come round to the view that any measure that would extend the property franchise to women, no matter how limited, was desirable.

Why did Snowden change his mind? Obviously the pressure of the local suffragist activities, working through the Weavers' Association, must have been a factor. Shackleton had come under pressure in Clitheroe and Snowden, though he was not a trade union candidate, undoubtedly came under some suffragist pressure and he admitted the strength of 'feeling among the Lancashire factory women' for the partial measure of which he disapproved.[18] Nevertheless, Snowden maintained, and Jill Liddington and Jill Norris have confirmed in *One Hand Tied Behind Us* (1978), that he was largely pushed towards accepting the need for a women's suffrage bill by his courtship and eventual marriage to Ethel Annakin. She was deeply interested in women's suffrage and stimulated Philip's involvement.

Ethel was born into a middle-class family in 1880. In her teens she trained to be a teacher at Edge Hill College, Liverpool, at which time she was much influenced by the Rev. Dr C. F. Aked of Pembroke Chapel who inspired her to enter the slums of Liverpool and lecture on the evils of drink. She subsequently joined the Fabian Society and was in regular correspondence with the ILP.

It seems that she first met Philip in 1903 at a time when she was a school teacher in Leeds. She made her debut as a socialist lecturer at the Keighley Labour Institute in September 1903 and, shortly afterwards, took a post at Walverden School, Nelson, a mere nine miles from Cowling. Little is known of the personal relationship between Ethel and Philip, but it is widely believed that it was she who proposed marriage and that Philip, flattered by her interest, accepted despite his mother's objections. They were in fact married on 13 March 1905 at the Otley registry office, Wharfedale, in the presence of a small group of friends including Fred Jowett, who became the first Labour MP for Bradford in 1906. Philip informed his mother of the wedding by telegram, after the event.

Their honeymoon was unusual to say the least, for they conducted a lecture tour around the district for the next three days. But they were presented with gifts at Blackburn and Ilkley, and a dance was held in their honour, attended by Keir Hardie and Dr Stanton Coit, the American-born leader of the Ethical Movement who stood for Wakefield in the 1906 General Election. George Bernard Shaw was also present and displayed his wit when Philip was dancing: 'No he isn't dancing. That's the Ethical Movement'.[19]

Ethel soon became a formative influence on Philip's career. She was always concerned to further his political reputation but had little tact and soon became widely disliked within the Labour movement. Nevertheless, Philip was besotted by her, defended her against critics even when it meant threatening his own political career, and was greatly affected by her dedication to women's suffrage.

On several occasions, Ethel toured the country on behalf of the National Union of Women's Suffrage Societies. She also wrote a pamphlet and two books on the need to rectify the economic and political plight of women: *Women and the State* (1907), *The Woman Socialist* (1907) and the *Feminist Movement* (1913). She accepted the need to obtain the property franchise for women and saw the enfranchisement of women as an essential step towards raising their social and economic standing.

Responding to the wishes of the Lancashire female textile workers and of his wife, Philip spoke in favour of the Women's Enfranchisement Bill in the acrimonious debate which took place at the LRC's Liverpool Conference in January 1905. He dismissed the demand for complete adult suffrage by reference to political reality: 'no sensible man can fail to realise that there is no likelihood in the imminent future of any House of Commons taking the important step of granting adult suffrage'.[20] But his words went unheeded and the conference rejected a motion to support a partial women's suffrage bill by the overwhelming majority of 483 to 270. Despite the counter-evidence there was a widespread belief that the Bill was designed 'to enfranchise well-to-do women whilst leaving working women voteless'.[21]

Once in Parliament, Snowden campaigned vigorously for women's suffrage. He supported the Women's Enfranchisement Bill of 1907 and formed a suffrage committee with the Hon. Geoffrey Howard, a Liberal MP whose family owned Castle Howard near York. This committee, of which both were joint secretaries, sponsored women's suffrage bills and, in 1910, was recouched as an all-party body known as the Conciliation Committee. It put forward the Conciliation Bill in 1910, 1911 and 1912 and Snowden outlined its policy in a short pamphlet entitled *In Defence of the Conciliation Bill*. He maintained that the Conciliation Bill – which would give the vote to every woman possessed of the household suffrage under the 1884 Representation of the People Act (provided that, if married, she was not registered in the same Parliamentary Borough or County Division as her husband) – commanded most parliamentary support and had the greatest chance of winning parliamentary approval. Such a measure, he argued, would enfranchise about one million women and out of every ten 'eight will belong to the working-class'.[22]

Yet the Conciliation Bill was defeated in 1910, 1911 and 1912 and the issue of women's suffrage was clouded by the rising level of militancy which emanated from Mrs Pankhurst's Women's Social and Political Union. Its members began to disturb meetings, raided the House of Commons and, when arrested, went on hunger strikes. Though they primarily harassed Liberal ministers, they also turned their attention towards Snowden, on the grounds of his reluctance to subordinate all questions to the demand for women's suffrage and to vote against the government regardless of the issue. Nevertheless, Snowden remained a fervent advocate of the cause and succeeded in forcing the 1913 Labour Party Conference to oppose any further franchise bills which did not include women.

If Blackburn politics helped to direct Snowden towards a re-alignment with the Liberal Party then Labour politics also helped to determine the same end. It is evident that Snowden became increasingly frustrated with the Labour Party and the ILP as they moved in political directions of which he disapproved.

Snowden had risen quickly within the ILP. Having joined the NAC in 1898 he was chairman between 1903 and 1906. As one of the 'Big Four', he exerted considerable influence within both the ILP and the Labour Party. But there were challenges in both parties which concerned him greatly. In particular, the political successes of the ILP/LRC in the 1906 General Election, which saw the return of 30 Labour MPs, led to the rapid growth of ILP membership and the emergence of a new type of recruit. These often lacked deference to the older members and looked to a new generation of socialists, such as Victor Grayson, for direction and inspiration.

It was Grayson's involvement in the Colne Valley by-election of 1907 which symbolized this challenge. Colne Valley was one of the seats which MacDonald had given to the Liberals in the Gladstone–MacDonald pact of 1903. The decision of the Colne Valley Labour League to select Grayson as its candidate for a parliamentary by-election in 1907 was thus controversial and led to some protracted discussions between the League, the ILP and the Labour Party, Snowden was in fact drawn into the Colne Valley negotiations to help settle the matter and reported that the local party was determined to contest with Grayson. He was also the only Labour MP to campaign for Grayson.

Yet Grayson proved to be a most contentious and, for Snowden, ungrateful figure. He did not stand as an ILP or LRC/Labour candidate but as a Socialist. Once in Parliament he refused to join the Parliamentary Labour Party, would not identify with the ILP group and offered himself as the only Socialist MP. He was also critical of the compromises which the ILP/LRC had made – the accommodation which had been made with the trade union movement when the Labour Alliance was formed in 1900 and its flexibility towards the Liberal Party in parliamentary elections. Grayson clearly felt the need for a more aggressive electoral policy in dealing with the Liberals and a need to revise the relationship with the trade unions. Snowden could accept the latter but not the former.

Grayson's arrival in Parliament thus presented the political Labour movement with the need to re-examine its position. What direction was it to follow? How was it to deal with him? Above all, how should it react to his blatant disregard of parliamentary conventions? In general, the Labour movement ostracized him, even though the ILP Conference of 1908 agreed to pay him a parliamentary salary of £200 per annum. The Labour group of MPs were critical of his behaviour and abhorred his lack of party loyalty. Snowden, was one of his sternest critics, recalling that Grayson was responsible for 'one of the most deplorable exhibitions I have ever seen in my Parliamentary experience' when he attended the Commons one day in October 1908 in order to suggest that the problem of unemployment should be discussed, defying the Speaker in the process. He added that Grayson's action 'was a clear piece of hypocritical acting. . . . The man who had been in Parliament for more than a year and had never once raised the question of the unemployed now became a hero of the unthinking mob'.[23]

Other issues added to this growing antipathy between Grayson and the Labour leaders, and hostilities deepened when Grayson joined the staff of *New Age* towards the end of 1908. For three months he worked as joint editor of the paper with A. R. Orage, but left to join the staff of the *Clarion* in February 1909. From these platforms he mounted his campaign against the Labour leadership.

The climax of this conflict came at the ILP Annual Conference at Edinburgh in April 1909. The NAC of the ILP had sought to censure Grayson for his actions inside and outside Parliament but the conference decided to refer the main passage of criticism back to the NAC for reconsideration. This one revolt by the conference was on a substantively trivial point, but to the NAC it was a symbolic threat to its control of the party. As a result Hardie, MacDonald, Glasier and Snowden resigned from the NAC. Hardie explained the dislike of the 'Old Gang' at being referred to as 'limpets clinging to the rock of office' and accused Grayson of being used by others 'who were even more unscrupulous than he was'.[24] The conference quickly changed its mind and passed the original resolution condemning Grayson by a vote of 249 to 110 and asked the 'Big Four' to withdraw their resignations. They refused and remained outside the NAC, despite a countrywide campaign to get them to rejoin the NAC.

For Snowden, the decision to leave the NAC came at a point in his life when the ILP was becoming less important to his career. His political reputation was already established and the substantial income he gained from journalism gave him a measure of independence. But his departure from the NAC of the ILP did not mean that he transferred his loyalty unreservedly to the Labour Party. In fact he became alarmed at its increasing domination by the trade union movement.

Like Grayson, Snowden had never been very happy at the Labour Representation Committee's compromise with the trade union movement in 1900 – despite the fact that, in Blackburn, he represented a constituency dominated by the cotton unions. For him, trade unionism was no more than a temporary method of maintaining the wage rates of a few and 'he never considered the trade union basis of the Labour Party as ideal'.[25] He wanted the LRC/Labour Party to aim at raising the living standards of all the working class rather than binding itself to the sectional demands of the trade unions.

He was even more suspicious of militant strike activity which led to national disputes in mining and railways between 1910 and 1912. He felt that it was unnecessary and, in his book *The Living Wage* (1912), suggested that parliamentary action should be used to force the state to set up an Arbitration Board with powers to fix minimum wage rates. In addition he was critical and dismissive of those syndicalists who advocated the use of the General Strike to bring about the collapse of capitalist society: 'The advocates of the General Strike have . . . assumed a working-class unity for which there is no support either in experience or in probability'.[26] By 1914, he was emerging as a very rigid progressive who discounted all but parliamentary methods of bringing about change.

Between 1900 and 1910, Blackburn politics had exerted a crucial influence upon Snowden's political career. Although he was already imbued with Liberal Radicalism, it had directed him back towards the Liberal Party as an organization, re-establishing in different terms, a connection which he had broken in the mid-1890s. By 1910 Snowden, as much as any Liberal, was elected by Liberal votes and was committed to progressive ideas – even if the fusion of Liberal ideas over the House of Lords' veto debate hid the fact that his primary interest lay in the 'old' rather than the 'new' Liberalism. At this stage of his career a progressive alliance seemed highly attractive to him. Not only did it guarantee his seat at Blackburn but it was more acceptable to him than the political directions in which the ILP and the Labour Party were travelling. He could not conceive of the development of a trade union-dominated Labour Party, fighting on the narrow base of trade union and working-class policies, as offering any real challenge to the Liberal Party. Despite this distinct trait of Labour policy, he also concluded that the Labour Party had failed to face up to the Liberal Party or to distinguish itself sufficiently from the policies of the 1906–14 Liberal Governments. It is thus paradoxical, given the new synthesis of progressive politics which Snowden had helped to establish in Blackburn, that he should, at the Bradford ILP Conference of 1914, accuse MacDonald of having negotiated with the Liberals. MacDonald had negotiated with the Liberals and Snowden, in his Blackburn constituency, had been a willing recipient of the benefits of that arrangement. Indeed, by 1914, he was very aware of the fragility of the Labour Party's presence in Parliament, noting that the 'present labour representation in parliament is there mainly by the goodwill of the Liberals'.[27] It was only the First World War which revived his old ILP idealism.

Notes

1 P. F. Clarke, *Lancashire and the New Liberalism* (Cambridge University Press, London, 1971), p. 224. Similar quote in *Blackburn Times*, 6 January 1906.
2 SDF, *Annual Conference Report, 1894*, pp. 21–2.
3 J. Hill, 'Social Democracy and the Labour Movement in Lancashire', *North West Labour History Society*, 9, 1982/83, p. 48. Also, J. Hill, 'Working Class Politics in Lancashire 1885–1906: A Regional Study in the Origins of the Labour Party', Keele, PhD, 1969.
4 *Blackburn Times*, 29 September 1900.
5 *Blackburn Weekly Standard and Express*, 15 September 1900.
6 *Blackburn Weekly Telegraph*, 29 September 1900.
7 *Lancashire Daily Post*, 25 September 1900.
8 *Lancashire Daily Post*, *Northern Daily Telegraph*, 3 October 1900.
9 Loc. cit., 22 March 1902.
10 Herbert Gladstone's diary, 12 November 1902. Quoted in P. F. Clarke, 'British Politics and Blackburn Politics 1900–1910', *Historical Journal*, vol. XII (1969), p. 309.
11 *Northern Daily Telegraph*, 15 January 1906. Quoted in D. Howell, *British Workers and the Independent Labour Party, 1888–1906* (Manchester University Press, Manchester, 1983).
12 *Northern Daily Telegraph*, 20 November 1909.
13 *Blackburn Times*, 15 January 1910.
14 Ibid.
15 Hansard, XXXIX, 1622–4 (14 August 1911). Quoted in Clarke, *Lancashire and the New Liberalism*, pp. 200–1.
16 *Blackburn Times*, 23 December 1905.
17 *Labour Leader*, 16 April 1904.

18 Ibid.
19 'Ephesian' (C. E. Bechofer Roberts), *Philip Snowden: An Impartial Portrait* (London, 1929), pp. 71–2.
20 Labour Representative Committee, Annual Conference, *Report*, 1905. Also quoted in J. Liddington and J. Norris, *One Hand Tied Behind Us* (Virago, London, 1978), p. 186.
21 Snowden, *An Autobiography*, op. cit., p. 281.
22 P. Snowden, *In Defence of the Conciliation Bill* (The Woman's Press, London, 1912), p. 2.
23 Snowden, *An Autobiography*, op. cit., p. 166.
24 *Labour Leader*, 16 April 1909.
25 Snowden, *An Autobiography*, op. cit., p. 281.
26 Philip Snowden, *Socialism and Syndicalism* (Collins, London, 1912), p. 238.
27 *Labour Leader*, 26 June 1913.

6 Snowden and the First World War 1914–18

The First World War was crucial to British history for it brought about significant changes in the role of the state, the power of trade unions and the political position of women. It also helped to change the alignment of the Liberal and Labour parties, encouraging Labour to seize political initiative from the Liberals. But whilst the War facilitated a major transformation in the position of the Labour Party, speeding up the growth it had achieved before 1914, it also created tensions within the Party which were almost as intense and divisive as those which convulsed the Liberal Party in 1916. Snowden was at the heart of this political storm within Labour ranks, leading an anti-war ILP against a Labour Party which, in supporting the war effort and joining the Coalition Government, was the 'most craven and supine working class party in the belligerent countries'.[1] The War helped to revive Snowden's flagging interest in the ILP and shot him leftwards within the wider Labour movement, creating barriers which were to delay his return to the Labour Party during the immediate post-war years. Yet throughout the War, Snowden became one of the darlings of the Left and projected himself as an honourable and consistent advocate of international socialism. The image was well deserved, although it owed more to his Radical Liberalism than to his Socialism.

The outbreak of war in 1914 came with startling suddenness. As late as 1 August 1914 Continental Socialist leaders were still not convinced that war was even a likely possibility. As George Haupt suggests, they were the captives of their own myths about their ability to prevent war and unaware of the depths of national chauvinism.[2] They were caught out by the events, pushed on the defensive and literally became disorientated spectators to be submerged by the gathering wave of nationalism. All their efforts to agree upon a policy to prevent war, from the Stuttgart Conference of 1907 to the Basle Conference of 1912, were to no avail. In the heat of conflict, the vague and pious commitments to oppose military tendencies and to promote *rapprochement* between Britain, France and Germany were swept away and many Socialists quickly forgot their socialist promises and joined or supported their own wartime governments in the prosecution of the war.[3]

This trait was evident in the case of the British Labour Party. On 3 August 1914, Ramsay MacDonald spoke for the Labour Party in the House of Commons stressing that Labour was as patriotic as any other political party but that it had been given no reason why Britain should remain other than neutral in the looming conflict.[4] When Britain declared war on Germany on 4 August it appeared that the Labour Party would remain faithful to the position which MacDonald had put forward. Indeed on 5 August the NEC of the Labour Party passed a resolution, by 8 votes to 4, condemning the war as a product of 'Foreign Ministers pursuing diplomatic policies for the purpose of maintaining the balance of power'.[5] But the situation changed quickly when, on the same day, the Parliamentary Labour Party decided to support the Government's request for war credits of £100 million. MacDonald promptly resigned the Chairmanship of the PLP: 'I saw it was no use remaining as the Party was divided and nothing but futility could result,' he wrote in his diary.[6] 'The Chairmanship was impossible. The men were not working, were not pulling together, there was enough jealousy to spoil good feeling. The Party was no party in reality. I was sad, but glad to get out of harness.'

MacDonald gave up the leadership of what he perceived to be a divided party and subsequently continued his opposition to its pro-war stance by writing passionate articles in *Labour Leader*, the organ of the ILP. He joined common cause with that section of the ILP which was opposed to the War but took the debate further and joined with a handful of anti-war Radicals on the left wing of the Liberal Party – most notably Philip Morrell, Norman Angell, Charles Trevelyan, E. D. Morel and Arthur Ponsonby.[7] On 10 August they decided to form a 'committee to voice our views'.[8] On the 17 November this committee officially became the Union of Democratic Control. From the start it advocated the adoption of four 'Cardinal points'. At the end of the War no province was to be transferred from one country to another without the consent of the population. No treaty or agreement was to be entered into by the British Government without the consent of Parliament. British foreign policy was to aim, not at maintaining a balance of power, but at setting up an international council with machinery for securing peace. Finally, as part of the peace settlement, Britain was to propose a drastic disarmament agreement between the powers and to nationalize the armaments industries.[9] In essence, the UDC offered the beguiling vision of democratic forces, rather than politicians working secretly, running foreign affairs. Philip Snowden was to share many of their attitudes towards foreign affairs, although this was perhaps not surprising given that they all shared a common background in Liberal Radical thought.

MacDonald, the UDC, the ILP and various other interest groups formed a small bloc of opposition to the War – amplifying the gap which existed in Labour, as well as Liberal, ranks. Nevertheless, it should not be assumed that these anti-war forces were of like mind, just as it should not be expected that the whole of the ILP was committed to peace. The fact is that ambiguities and contradictions riddled the ranks of the alleged opponents of the war and the term pacifist was applied too readily and too easily.

In the first place, a large proportion of the ILP membership did not oppose the war effort. When the *Bradford Daily Telegraph* attacked the ILP's opposition to the war effort and their reluctance to 'raise even a single finger to help the country to prosecute the war successfully', Fred Jowett, MP and Chairman of the ILP, replied that 'In proportion to its membership the ILP had more adherents serving in the army and navy by far than either of the other two political parties'.[10] Censuses of the Bradford ILP membership support this statement. One taken in February 1916 indicated that of 461 young men in the local party, out of a membership of 1,473, 113 were in the trenches, four had been killed, one was missing, nine had been wounded, three were prisoners of war, 118 were training in England, six were in the Navy and 207 attested under the Derby Scheme as necessary home workers.[11] A similar survey in 1918 found that of the 492 members liable for military service, 351 were serving in the forces whilst 48 were conscientious objectors or were on national work.[12] There is little to suggest that the members of the Bradford ILP were any more patriotic than those of many other ILP branches. Indeed they had the reputation of being pacifists.

Of those ILP members who opposed the War only a few, such as Clifford Allen, J. Bruce Glasier, Arthur Salter, Willie Leach and Fenner Brockway were pacifists: Brockway and Allen were later to be incarcerated in Dartmoor and Wormwood Scrubs because of their absolutist pacifist beliefs. This small group would have agreed with the sentiments expressed by Willie Leach, in an editorial about the views of the *Bradford Pioneer*.

> We hate all war, especially the present one. This is a pacifist or peace journal conducted, among other purposes, with the object of stating as well as we can, the ILP position on the hideous tragedy now being enacted in Europe.... Human life is the most sacred thing we know, and its preservation, its development, its best welfare, must therefore be our religion on this earth.[13]

Yet contrary to the impression often given such sentiments were not shared by the majority of even the anti-war members of the ILP. The majority of the anti-war section of the Party appear to have followed the lead of Fred Jowett, the Party Chairman, who was never an outright pacifist, but accepted the need for National Defence. Jowett attempted to articulate a view of what caused the War and how wars could be eradicated in the future. He maintained in his Chairman's speech to the 1915 ILP Conference at Norwich that 'Now is the time to speak and ensure that never again shall the witches' cauldron of secret diplomacy brew the war broth of Hell for mankind'.[14] He later expanded upon this view stating that

> I believe that the war would never have arisen if the government had carried out an open and honest foreign policy and disclosed to the people who had most to lose the relations between themselves and foreign governments with whom they were acting in collusion.[15]

His constant theme throughout the War was, like that of the UDC, that secret treaties had caused it. 'His fad', as the *Standard* said of Jowett, 'is democratic control of foreign affairs'.[16] It was a 'fad' shared by many others in the Party, including Snowden.

Although Jowett believed that the War was caused by secret treaties he also believed in the need for a British victory over 'Prussianism' and that there could be no settlement of the War without the 'restoration of Belgium to complete sovereignty'.[17] Indeed, the issue of 'Little Belgium' was a convenient bridge over which many Labour and Liberal politicians, not least of them David Lloyd George, travelled from an anti-war stance towards patriotism. Jowett, and his supporters, certainly declared that a nation had a right to defend itself and frequently paid homage to those who had given their lives in the War. In many respects the views of Jowett closely resembled those of James Keir Hardie, expressed in his famous article 'We must see the War through, but denounce Secret Diplomacy'.[18] Although Jowett's views, like those of Hardie, often appeared ambiguous and at odds with the ILP's declared opposition to the War, he was categorical in his wish to see the War speedily concluded in favour of the allies. On his attitude towards the anti-war resolution passed by the 1916 ILP Conference, of which he was Chairman, he reminded one critic that

> The ILP resolution to which you refer only expressed the view that Socialist Parties as organised bodies should support no war. It did not attempt to lay down such a policy for individuals. If it did I should be opposed to it in principle.[19]

Such a distinction between the actions of individuals within a party and the policy of the party was confusing to many critics of the ILP and permitted those with Jowett's sympathies both to support and oppose the war in different guises – though Snowden did suggest that this was no different from individuals opposing a war which the state had entered into without prior consultation.[20]

It is evident that the outbreak of war divided the Labour movement. On the one hand the Labour Party, and the trade union movement, supported Asquith's Government and entered into a Coalition in May 1915. They reflected the dominant sympathies of the trade union movement, even in 1917 when the ILP led a powerful peace campaign. Nevertheless, there was a small, but vociferous, section of the Labour movement which objected to this meek acceptance of capitalist conflict, although it expressed many shades of opinion. It was this section, the rump of the ILP, which Snowden helped to organize into a pressure group against the War. In this atmosphere Snowden was in his element, offering his messianic message of peace against a Labour Party whose trade union supporters did well out of the conflict. War seemed to act as a political catalyst for him, reviving his Radical Liberal sentiments and convincing him of the foolishness of war for the Socialist cause.

Yet prior to 1914 Snowden had revealed only fitful interest in the issue of war. In common with many other Labour leaders, he had expressed his opposition to British involvement in the South African War. 'It was a mean war: the power of a mighty Empire used to crush the independence of a small farmer state.'[21] He had expressed concern at the rising expenditure on armaments and acted as a principal speaker in the ILP's campaign against 'militarism' in 1913 and 1914. Indeed in March 1914, he spoke in the most lofty manner of the power of international socialism.

> It is not in the courts of kings nor in the chambers of diplomacy that the war problem is going to be solved. The workers of all lands are increasingly recognising that militarism and capitalism are the common enemies of the workers of all lands. Thirteen millions of men in Europe are enrolled under the red flag of Socialism, and in that fact you have a stronger safeguard of peace than in all your battleships and all your armed camps.[22]

Nevertheless, all these actions were incidental, not central, to his political activities and were conditioned largely by the fear that rising expenditure or armaments was economically ruinous and that the consequent military might endanger international trade which he believed was vital to the continued prosperity of nations.

Like many ILP members, Snowden held an optimistic view about the victory of Liberal values for he felt that socialism could only come through the growth, not the collapse, of capitalism. The First World War shook Snowden's faith in that view for it threatened the rosy picture of unbroken progress on which he had been raised. From 1915 he was thus concerned to promote peace negotiations in an attempt to prevent the economic collapse of the nation and to reduce the hiatus in the democratic march towards socialism. This became all the more urgent when the Bolshevik Revolution of October 1917 raised the prospect that socialism could be more quickly won by force.

When war broke out in August 1914 the Snowdens were touring Canada en route to the United States and New Zealand. Frustrated with the state of British Labour politics, and drawn back to his nonconformist roots, Philip had accepted an invitation to join in the National Prohibition Campaign to be held in New Zealand during late 1914. The Snowdens had left Britain on 10 July 1914 and Philip did not return until February 1915. During this period, though Ethel clearly expressed her opposition to Britain's involvement in the conflict, Philip declared his intention not to comment until his return: 'political life has convinced me that in politics it is not the distant observer who can understand the game'.[23] He later recalled that he had cabled Arthur Henderson, the Secretary and later Chairman of the Labour Party, enquiring whether or not he should cut short his lecture tour. Henderson advised him to continue with the tour:

> I could not at the time understand this, but I learnt after why he was not anxious for me to come back. There was a split in the party on the question of war, and Mr. Henderson rightly assumed that I should be on the side of the minority who were opposed to Britain's participation in it.[24]

In fact Philip returned by himself in February 1915, Ethel not returning from the lecture tour until December.[25] His first action was to visit his Blackburn constituency to pronounce upon the War. He spoke for more than an hour to 2,000 people in the Prince's Theatre, declaring that he had 'never been prouder of the I.L.P.'.[26] He complained that foreign policy was in the hands of the sons of peers and that they were able to conduct their activities without Parliamentary control. He complained of the armaments ring, attacking the activities of the firms of Krupps and Vickers. But he remained equivocal about the prosecution of the War, leaving the matter of volunteering for the army to individual conscience. Yet, unlike some leading members of the ILP, he did not participate in the Recruiting Campaign, informing the Mayor of Blackburn that 'I refuse to ask any young man to sacrifice his life for me.' He added that:

> I am not going to ask any young man to do something for me which I am not able to do myself. The consequences are so serious that I believe the decisions should be left entirely to individual conscience. If a man thinks it is wrong to go, he ought not to be persecuted. If a man thinks he ought to go, then he ought to go and I honour that man.

Despite his concern for individual conscience, or perhaps because of it, he quickly gravitated towards a pacifist position, although he never claimed himself to be an absolute pacifist. Indeed, in pre-war years he had been convinced of the absolute necessity 'for the defence of our shore'[27] and later reflected that he had 'never taken up the attitude of the extreme pacifists who object to war in all possible circumstances'.[28] This contrasted sharply with MacDonald's opposition, which was principally based on the belief that Britain should have remained neutral because she was not directly threatened, or that of some other ILP leaders, such as Jowett, who criticized the secret treaties that had led to war but supported the conflict until Belgium was restored to complete sovereignty. Snowden's view accepted MacDonald's implicit assumption that a nation might have to defend itself but qualified this by arguing that the economic and human cost of the war was prohibitive.

Snowden attached himself to the relatively small group of ILP stalwarts who, through a variety of attitudes, opposed the War. He and they were soon isolated from the mainstream of trade union and Labour Party opinion and he amplified these differences by his personal attacks on some of the trade union patriots, who dominated the trade union movement and the Labour Party during the War. He particularly made a broad sweep against the 'tyranny of the massed vote of the great industrial organisations in the Labour Party', which he considered was responsible for the apparent continuation of the patriotic and right-wing attitudes within the Labour Party throughout wartime.[29] But he reserved his most vitriolic attack for Will Thorne, who had been a champion of militant action and left-wing causes before the War and was now leading the large General Workers' Union and MP for West Ham. In the War he acquired the uniform of a lieutenant-colonel in the West Ham Volunteers, and a fur coat as a gift from F. E. Smith, later Lord Birkenhead. These adornments, and his support for the War and for conscription made him a target for opposition in his own union and from Snowden who referred to his 'unlettered ignorance and unfitness for Parliament'.[30] Yet such attacks served to isolate the ILP and, in Thorne's case, backfired for having broken down on the platform of his union's Biennial Conference the whole audience 'rose *en masse* and cheered and sang until I recovered myself'.[31]

In 1915, after a self-imposed exile of six years, Snowden allowed himself to be re-elected to the NAC of the ILP, and threw doubt on the suggestion that his silence at the Conference revealed his dissent by stressing that 'his silence was a sign of agreement'.[32] He also became one of the *Labour Leader*'s most regular contributors, writing lengthy articles for most editions throughout 1915 and 1916. He was quickly absorbed into propaganda work and suggested the extent of his involvement in a letter to J. Bruce Glasier, editor of the *Labour Leader*, in October 1915.

You have given me little time for the article you want. When is the latest that will do? I always write my things on the latest date. I am full up every moment of the time during the coming week, and next week-end I am away from Friday to Monday with ILP meetings. If you get it by the post on Thursday October 19th would this be in time? As far as I can see I shall have the afternoon of the 18th free.[33]

Almost a year later, in September 1916, he became the regular writer for the 'Review of the Week' column which was switched from the second page to the front page. He continued to write for that column until March 1919.

One senses that Snowden was rising to the political challenge of war, relishing the opportunities it provided and hurrying towards the chairmanship of the ILP. Indeed, the way was now open for his assumption of control: Keir Hardie died in September 1915, Bruce Glasier was ill and not inclined to lead, and the varied interests of Ramsay MacDonald took him away from the centre-stage of ILP politics. Snowden was the only one of the 'Big Four' with the time, opportunity and desire to take charge of the ILP's peace campaign. He was returned to the NAC in 1915, top of the poll in 1916 and became Chairman of the ILP in 1917, replacing Jowett who had completed his three-year term of office. Snowden remained Chairman until April 1920.

Snowden was now leading a party which was officially opposed to the War and which, in the words of one historian, 'created . . . an excellent, almost religious atmosphere of dedication and solidarity of persecution'.[34] Consequently, there was a 'more intimate comradeship in the party than in his pre-war days'.[35] It offered an atmosphere which Snowden knew well from his Keighley days. His oratory and writings began to show the flourishes of his early days in the ILP, offering a vision to his audiences that they

would see beautiful rays of sunshine throwing their radiance far beyond the black clouds they saw from below. What they had to hope for, fight for, and work for was a universal peace amongst nations without distinction of creed, or colour or race.[36]

He quickly won the label of being left wing, a revolutionary no less, hiding from police raids on his meetings and provoking unrest.[37] The mythology which surrounded his activities, encouraged by the press, built up an aura of respect around him from the Left which was only gradually dissipated in the post-war years.

At this stage, Snowden had clearly rediscovered his appetite for Labour politics, though not to the exclusion of all other interests. Indeed, in 1915, he accepted Lloyd George's offer of a seat on the Central Control Board (Liquor Traffic), motivated more by his dislike of drink than by the desire that this body might prevent the consumption of alcohol impairing the war effort. He had previously been a member of the Samuel Commission which had recommended that the state should purchase breweries, tied houses and licensed premises at a cost of £250 millions. David Lloyd George had rejected its recommendations but had set up a Control Board which did assume wide enough powers to purchase breweries and licensed premises in Carlisle, which housed many of the munitions workers who worked at Gretna.[37]

Nevertheless, Snowden's abiding political passion throughout the War was his demand for peace. From the outset he felt that the cost of the war would be calamitous for Britain.[38] The wartime government borrowed heavily and were increasing the National Debt by £2 millions per day, a situation which he felt would delay the implementation of essential social welfare measures in the postwar years. Consequently he generally voted against all measures designed to increase wartime expenditure by borrowing, although there were occasions when the need for party unity prevented this. Responding to the criticisms of C. H. Norman, a prominent member of the No-Conscription Fellowship who was incarcerated in Dartmoor as a pacifist, Snowden summarized his position.

> In respect to other matters you say the operation to War Credits has not taken the vote of dividing the House. In that you are wrong. The last Vote of Credit was divided upon on the 3rd reading of the Bill. This is a matter which is constantly being considered by our small group in the House of Commons and really you should allow us to judge as to what is the best thing to do. Personally I have always been in favour of voting against the Credits, but when you are a member of a small Party beset on all sides by a strong opposition, it is very necessary to hold together and act as a united group.[39]

Snowden believed that if the War had to be paid for then it should come from the unearned income of the rich and the war profiteers who would not be rendered to a 'condition of starvation' by the imposition of a tax of 15s. in the £.[40] When military conscription was introduced in January 1916, he took the opportunity to emphasize the point further: 'We should extend the conscription of life to the conscription of wealth.'[41] He then outlined his capital levy scheme for financing the War out of the taxation of the rich, advocating the introduction of a graded system of taxation which would exempt holdings under £91,000 but impose a rising scale of taxation from one to ten per cent on capital values up to £1 million.

Snowden's scheme was typical of several others which were being floated at that time for the Labour Party, and the Labour movement, in its widest sense, was discussing a variety of ways of conscripting wealth.[42] It drew some support but the emergence of an alternative 'Conscription of Wealth' plan, which gained Labour Party backing, plus the hostility of trade unionists to Snowden's pessimistic economic assessments of the War left it without support. It should be remembered that to many trade unionists Snowden appeared to be out of touch with reality. The War had increased the membership of their unions, raised wages, ensured the continuity of work and enhanced the status of their leaders. Despite the wartime restrictions imposed upon normal trade union activities, the movement had never been so powerful and effective.

Although most trade unionists were not seduced by Snowden's economic concerns they were in agreement on at least two points he espoused – opposition to the Munitions Bill and opposition to military conscription. The first of these issues had arisen in the summer of 1915 when the Government introduced a bill which restricted the freedom of Labour to move from munitions factory to munitions factory without holding a certificate from his first employer and restricted the right to strike or maintain trade union practices, especially in those factories concerned with war production which were taken into the direct control of the state. Speaking against the Bill in the House of Commons, Snowden emphasized that whilst he had supported state measures to control strikes 'he had never advocated compulsory State arbitration, under such conditions as proposed by the Bill. I have never advocated compulsory arbitration except upon a basis of Trade union rights and Trade union safeguards.'[43] In fact, he put up a determined defence of trade union rights, although he reiterated his opposition to all strikes which were, in any case, 'unthinkable at a time like this'. His position was that he personally did not believe in trade unionism or their resort to strike but that his commitment to civil and individual liberties meant that he would defend their rights. For his efforts many trade unions, including the London Building Industry Federation and the Furnishing Trades' Association, passed measures of support for Snowden's action at the same time as they condemned the failure of the Labour Party to oppose them in Parliament.[44]

The second issue was the introduction of military, and indeed industrial, conscription in January 1916. The Derby Scheme, a type of voluntary conscription in which the idea was that all men of military age should indicate their willingness to serve when called up, was apparently failing to attract sufficient volunteers. As a result, the government introduced a Military Service Bill in January 1916, which, when passed by Parliament, permitted the conscription of single men of military age and paved the way for further such bills to extend conscription to married men. The trade union movement, through the Labour Party's conference at Bristol in January 1916, overwhelmingly confirmed its opposition to conscription by 1,716,000 votes to 360,000 –

though it confirmed its commitment to the war effort and refused to support agitation against the Military Service Bill.[45] Nevertheless the parliamentary representatives of the Labour Party, led by Arthur Henderson, supported the Bill in Parliament in contravention of the conference decision. It was left to Snowden and a small band of largely Liberal Radical MPs to oppose the measure. He made a waspish speech in Parliament in which he described the Bill as 'a strong weapon for enforcing the chains of slavery on democracy',[46] and concluded that

> I oppose the measure for the reasons I have stated, because the case is not made out, neither on the ground of military necessity nor on the ground of the redemption of the Prime Minister's pledge, and I oppose it also because I believe it will undermine those foundations upon which alone the greatness of the country depends.

To him, there was no need for compulsion, the Prime Minister had deceived the country into believing that there would be no conscription in the wake of the Munitions Bill and the whole package simply offended his concern for civil rights and individual liberties. *The Times* regarded Snowden's speech as the 'ablest onslaught upon the Bill that had been made in the House'.[47] But all was to no avail. Henderson charged Snowden with inconsistency – on the grounds that he wanted compulsion on every issue other than conscription – and the Bill was carried by the overwhelming vote of 431 to 39.

Snowden and the ILP took the matter to the Labour Party Conference at the end of January 1916 where he charged Henderson and the PLP with becoming 'blind tools of the Government'.[48] But torn between Snowden's powerful oratory and loyalty to their trade union leaders, the Conference produced a typically contradictory resolution attacking all forms of permanent militarism but justifying the present system as a result of the war.

The most important consequences of these debates for Snowden were that they strengthened his connection with the Liberal Radicals and isolated him from the Parliamentary Labour Party which, under Henderson, felt free to continue its collaboration with the Coalition Government and to ignore those aspects of Labour Party Conference policy of which it disapproved. As a defender of trade union rights, which both the Munitions Bill and the Military Service Bill attacked, Snowden won admiration, although never sufficient to wean the rank and file away from their leaders. Consequently, he directed much of this effort into working with the UDC, which he had associated with since his return from New Zealand, and with the No-Conscription Fellowship which had been formed in 1915. Through the latter body he began to associate with other Liberal Radicals such as H. B. Lees Smith and Arthur Ponsonby.

From January 1916 thousands of young men poured through the tribunals, which were set up to examine those who claimed exemption from military service, and had their objections to conscription overruled and were handed over to the military authorities. Snowden raised the issue of their treatment and, in connection with this work received over 30,000 letters in 1917.[49] He also attended the second conference of the No-Conscripiton Fellowship as a platform speaker, offering a passionate defence of individual liberty which the 2,000-strong audience applauded by waving white handkerchiefs.[50]

It was in Parliament, however, that he was most effective. On two occasions, in March and April 1916, Snowden raised the issue of the unfair treatment of conscientious objectors. His main complaint was that the local Tribunals and the War Office were grossly violating the provisions of the Act. The military officers were threatening those who claimed exemptions; Tribunals were failing to listen to appeals against conscription, failing to administer the Act properly and clearly rejecting the cases of men who were obviously medically unfit for military service. He gave many examples of the way in which the Act was being flouted. In one case, the chairman of the Middlesex Appeal Tribunal agreed that a claimant was a conscientious objector and the claimant's counsel asked for an absolute exemption which the Act provides for.

> Then the military representative intervened, and suggested that the case should stand over pending the decision of the Central Tribunal in a similar case. The chairman said:
>
> The appeal is dismissed.
>
> Counsel: With great respect I press the desirability of postponing the case until the point is decided by the Central Tribunal.
> Chairman: Next case.
> Counsel: I apply for leave to appeal as provided by the Regulations.
> Chairman: Refused.
> Counsel: On what grounds.
> Chairman: Next case.[51]

The main thrust of Snowden's argument was that claimants for exemption from military service were not receiving fair and impartial treatment.

The matter was taken further when he, and the Radical MPs, managed to embarrass Asquith, the Prime Minister, with the revelation that 34 conscientious objectors who had been sent to France had then been smuggled out of France, sentenced to death and then had had their sentence commuted to ten years' penal servitude. This provoked Asquith to state that no executions would be carried out. And on 25 May 1916 there was another triumph for the anti-conscription movement with the issue of Army Order X, which laid down that after being court-martialled conscientious objectors should be handed back to the civilian authorities for incarceration in one of His Majesty's prisons. In June the Government also decided to set up the Pelham Committee, which was responsible for finding alternative national work for men who were prepared to take it. Eventually about 4,000 of the 16,000 conscientious objectors accepted national work under the Pelham/Home Office Scheme.

Notwithstanding the changes which Snowden and the anti-war MPs forced upon the Government, the campaign against conscription was lost in Parliament. Faced with this situation, Snowden returned to and revived his attempt to force the Government to consider the need for a negotiated peace, and it was for the Peace Movement that he was best remembered in the War.

As early as April 1915 Snowden had declared that the Allies should 'make known the terms upon which they would be willing to bring the war to an end' and that there were already signs that the German Social Democratic Party were contemplating the need for a negotiated settlement, without annexation.[52] From then onwards he stressed three main themes, which he shared with the UDC. In the first place, the Allied and Central powers should decide their terms for a negotiated peace settlement. Secondly, that this should be achieved without annexation of territory by force of arms, unless those people involved agreed to the changes. Thirdly, that foreign policy should be decided by the people of Britain, not by a small number of statesmen who carried on secret negotiations oblivious of the wishes of Parliament and the people: the peace would be a people's peace. Universal free trade was deemed essential for future peace for it would remove the possibility of economic grievance and conflict.[53]

From the beginning of the War, Snowden had demanded that the Allied nations must make known the 'terms upon which they would be willing to bring the war to an end'.[54] He was encouraged in this view by the fact that the German Social Democratic Party, convinced that Germany was involved in a defensive war, was pushing for a negotiated peace based upon no annexations.[55] Indeed, in June 1915, Eduard Bernstein, Hugo Haase and Karl Kautsky, of the German SDP, put forward proposals for peace.[56] The momentum for peace was gathering and was pushed further forward by the decision, in December 1915, of the German Social Democratic Party to put a question to the Imperial Chancellor asking whether he would be prepared to make a settlement as to the conditions under which he would enter into peace negotiations.[57] His answer was that he would be prepared to consider any proposals put forward by Britain. Snowden asked Asquith a similar question the same week and elicited the vague reply that any terms would first be discussed by the Allied Governments.[58]

Snowden took the matter further when he made the first speech in

Parliament in favour of a negotiated settlement on 23 February 1916. It was subsequently published by the Blackburn Labour Party as a *Plea for Peace*. His main charge was that peace could be negotiated by Britain without the loss of honour for the outstanding lesson of the War was that 'militarism stands discredited. It is now proved to be a futile method of serving aggressive designs.' It only required the Prime Minister to go one step further to promote peace.

> He can give encouragement to offers of peace and he can translate into more definite and precise language his Guildhall speech. There are many channels open to the Government through which negotiations may be opened up, and we have the right to demand that the Government shall state in much more definite and precise language the terms upon which they would be willing to consider peace.[60]

There is little to suggest that Snowden's campaign punctured the desire of the British people or the Government for military victory, despite the high military cost of the Battle of the Somme, being waged in 1916. The moment was not propitious for a peace campaign. But Snowden's efforts were rescued from oblivion by the fact that President Wilson, of the United States, spoke on 27 May 1916 in favour of a negotiated peace settlement. The Axis or Central Powers welcomed the message but the Allies replied that their war aims were well known, that they were entitled to reparations and that details could only be discussed at the moment of negotiation.[61]

Between December 1916 and March 1918 there were nine opportunities for a negotiated peace settlement to have been developed, but all were rejected by the Allied powers. The first effort was made in December 1916 by the German Chancellor who announced that he had despatched to the ambassadors of the Neutral Powers and to the Pope, a Note intimating his 'desire to enter now into peace negotiations'.[62] The Allies replied on 30 December suggesting that the offer was a sham but were forced to consider the matter further because of the renewed efforts at peace made by Wilson in mid-December 1916. On the 10 January 1917 they rejected the President's suggestion that the belligerents should begin preliminary soundings with a view to arranging for peace. In rejecting Wilson's Note, however, the Allied powers indicated that they would pursue the War until the Allied provinces were returned to them and until Italians, Slavs, Rumanians and others were freed from foreign domination.[63] This added a new dimension to the issue of peace, for many of those who had supported the War and volunteered in the first instance had done so to rescue Belgium from the Germans.

There were other appeals for negotiated peace. The Pope issued his appeal for a negotiated settlement on 1 August 1917 and Lord Lansdowne had a similar appeal published in the *Daily Telegraph* in November 1917.[64] Other efforts occurred until February 1918 when Allied Governments issued a declaration closing the door against further appeals for peace negotiations. They declared that 'The only immediate task before the Allies was the prosecution with the utmost vigour and in the closest and most effective co-operation of the military efforts of the Allies'.[65]

Snowden was deeply involved, at all points in this debate, attempting to press the Allied powers to respond in a positive manner to the efforts to open peace negotiations. Indeed, he added to his demands the theme of 'no annexations'. He had already been influenced in this direction by the Union of Democratic Control, which had this demand as one of its cardinal principles, and the attitude of the German Social Democratic Party on this matter appears to have influenced him further. The issue became even more important once the Allied powers widened their war aims in January 1917. Very quickly Snowden's attitude became almost identical to that of the UDC: 'No annexation means no transfer of any territory against the will of the people concerned'.[66] It was in line with the peace demands of the Allies, and Snowden asked, in a sarcastic manner, whether or not the Allied enthusiasm for nationalism extended to Egypt and India.[67] Unlike the Allies, he fully believed that the people should be involved in determining foreign policy.

To begin with, Snowden fought for these principles through the ILP's Peace Campaign, speaking in Parliament and campaigning throughout the country. He was helped in this by his wife, Ethel, who had left the ILP because of the failures to develop the women's suffrage, but who returned due to the War. Contrary to Snowden's comments in his *An Autobiography*, Ethel began the Women's Peace Crusade in August or September 1917 and not in support of Lord Lansdowne's letter of the 29 November 1917.[67] Indeed, she had outlined her crusade in the *UDC*, in September 1917. She stressed that the idea had sprung from a variety of movements in a variety of areas throughout the summer of 1917. In Glasgow the Women's International League took the initiative; in Manchester the women of the ILP were the first to move in this direction; in Leicester it was the Women's Labour League who began the Crusade. Their theme was the demand for a negotiated peace. They held demonstrations which attracted 10,000 at Glasgow on 8 July, 20,000 at Nelson on 21 August and 4,000 at Leicester on 12 August.

Unlike the Christian Peace Crusade, the Women's Peace Crusade was not composed of pacifists alone. Its commitment was not to pacifism but to the belief that '*this* war should be ended *now*, by negotiations'.[68] In many respects the real stimulus for Ethel's activities and those of the Women's Peace Crusade was the Russian revolution, not Lord Lansdowne. Ethel asked

> Why do not the Allies explicitly accept the Russian formula, 'No annexations and indemnities, and the right of the peoples to determine their own Government?' Why do not the Allies make as clear as sunlight to the German people that they have no designs on their territory, nor on their trade hereafter?[69]

All three threads of Snowden's peace campaign – allied terms, no annexation and the involvement of the people – in fact came together and were made more relevant by the Russian Revolution of February and March 1917. The revolution had been precipitated by the action of the Tsar in issuing a Ukase dissolving the Duma and the Council of Empire, although this had been provoked by the chaotic internal state of Russia. The General Strike of the workers at Petrograd on 9 March, following the defection of the troops, forced the Tsar's Government to resign. The Duma resolved not to disperse but formed itself into a Council of Deputies which eventually worked with the soldiers and the people to form a Provisional Revolutionary Government. It was the actions of this Government which inspired Snowden and the Peace Movement with the hope that the War could be brought to an end in line with the type of policies which they had advocated.

The new Provisional Government in Russia adopted a two-part peace policy: to press for a general peace without annexations and at the same time to defend the homeland and the revolution against the German invader. It was popularly known as Revolutionary Defence and appeared to provide the way for Russia to disengage from the War. The success of this situation partly depended upon the military situation but also on the participation of the Allied socialists in a proposed conference at Stockholm. Though Alexander Kerensky, who had become Minister of War under the Provisional Government, did harbour some interest in continuing the War the majority of the Mensheviks and their allies wished to extricate Russia from the conflict and, in his April theses, Lenin made it plain that in any case others would act to try to end the slaughter.

In an attempt to get the House of Commons to endorse the declarations of the 'democratic Government of Russia', Snowden waxed lyrical on the way in which the Revolution fulfilled all the objectives of his Peace Campaign.

> No event in our generation has so thrilled the world as the Russian Revolution. It has given us new hope in democracy and revived our faith in Internationalism. It has given up a hope that the war aims which have been declared by the statesmen of the various countries – the maintenance of civilisation and the triumph of democracy – are going to be realised in the only way in which these ideals and our own can be realised, that is by the people of different countries.[70]

To him, it was the people, not statesmen, who were going to force the end of the War and the Russian Revolution proved that this was possible.

In this context, Snowden and the ILP joined with other socialists to form the Workmen's and Soldiers' Council at the Leeds Convention of June 1917. The Leeds Conference, in fact arose from two main political tributaries. It emerged partly from the desire of the quasi-Marxist British Socialist Party (BSP) to pursue international peace, following the overthrow of the nationalistic and patriotic Henry Mayers Hyndman in 1916, and it was also clearly relevant to the ILP's demands for peace. The peace designs of these organizations had been temporarily conflated by the events in Russia. The United Socialist Council of the ILP and the BSP, a body formed as a result of the deliberations which had taken place between both parties on the eve of War, called the Leeds Conference. Snowden was chairman of that body and played a major part in the activities at Leeds.

The details of the Leeds Conference are well known. It passed four resolutions: hailing the Russian Revolution; advocating moves towards establishing a general peace based upon the rights of nations to decide their own affairs; demanding the creation of a charter of liberties by the British Government; and demanding the formation of a Council of Workmen's and Soldiers' delegates in every town, urban and rural district. Snowden was responsible for putting forward the second resolution and drafting the resolution which was sent to the Petrograd Soviet, informing it of the Conference, endorsing Russia's foreign policy and pledging efforts to obtain a democratic peace.[71]

The Leeds Conference was generally distanced from organized labour, and it never captured the public imagination, but Snowden did have hopes that the Stockholm Conference of Socialists would lead to peace. As early as April 1917 Arthur Henderson had received a letter from Camille Huysmans, the Belgian socialist, inviting the Labour Party to a special meeting of European socialists at Stockholm. Henderson, aware that the French socialists were opposed to a conference which might be attended by German and Austrian socialists, persuaded the Labour Party NEC on the 9 May to pass a resolution that the Labour Party should not be represented at the conference. Instead he suggested that a British delegation should go to Russia with the intention of inviting the Russian Council of Workmen's and Soldiers' Delegates to send representatives to a London Conference to be held at the end of June 1917. The London Conference was never a realistic possibility but Henderson, with the reluctant approval of the British Cabinet, did go to Russia at the end of May, returning at the end of July. He went convinced of the need to reject the Stockholm Conference but came back a converted man. He persuaded the Labour Party NEC to call a special conference on 10 August, at which the resolution to go to Stockholm was passed by a three to one majority. But it also decided that the Labour Party representatives would not be supplemented by representatives from any other affiliated or unaffiliated socialist body in Britain. This meant that the ILP would have been prevented from sending a delegation and was strongly opposed by Snowden. Accordingly, the Conference was adjourned to discuss the matter further. Snowden was pressured to drop his objections, and the reconvened meeting on 21 August narrowly confirmed its earlier decision. In the event, the British Government intervened and announced that it would not issue passports for the British delegates who were to attend the peace conference and, indeed, the Stockholm Conference was never held.

Snowden's hopes for peace had been partly frustrated by the attitude of the Labour Party, from which he was being increasingly estranged. This isolation was further compounded at the beginning of 1918 by the introduction of the Party's new constitution. Although this contained the socialist commitment to establish the common ownership of the means of production, it also included changes which ended the federated structure of the Labour Party NEC, giving trade unions much greater control of the NEC and removing the ILP's right to direct representation.

These constitutional changes were strongly opposed by Snowden. There were many obvious objections, not least being the feeling that the Labour Party was not to be trusted, having proved to have been 'more capitalist than the employers, and more militant than the Government' during the War.[72] But his main objection was that the changes did not guarantee that individuals would have a say in the Party but rather confirmed 'The tyranny of the massed vote of the great industrial organisations. . . '.[73] What he perceived was the need for a party of individual members who, theoretically at least, would be able to contribute fully to the development of policy in the Party for 'Men with political ideals and political enthusiasm will not be content to be crushed by the heavy weight of huge numbers who have brought into the Labour Party the ideas and methods of Trade Unionism, which are admirably suited to industrial purposes but quite unsuitable for political aims'.[74] For this reason Snowden campaigned strongly for the view that the ILP should build up its membership and continue to act as the socialist conscience of the 'so-called' Labour Party. He disagreed with those, such as Jowett, who expressed the view that the ILP should cease its independent existence now that the Labour Party had acquired a socialist clause – Clause Four.

By 1918, however, it must have become clear to Snowden that many of the visions which he cherished were not going to occur. The new Labour Party Constitution was now in force and had strengthened the hand of the trade union leaders just as surely as it had reduced the influence of the ILP. The Peace Movement was also failing. Though Snowden explained that the decision to form Workmen's and Soldiers' Councils throughout the country had been considered unnecessary by the organizing committee of the Leeds Conference several attempts had been made to form such bodies which had alienated many trade unions who felt that these bodies were being formed to compete with them.[75] The fact is that they got nowhere and the Peace Movement had begun to falter by the end of 1918. The entry of the USA into the War had devalued the coinage of President Wilson's appeal for a negotiated peace and the Allies were now adamant in their refusal to negotiate with the Central powers. It was a very isolated Snowden and a disillusioned Peace group in the House of Commons who debated the issue of peace in the House of Commons on 13 February 1918. A. J. Balfour, the Foreign Secretary, heaped the obloquy of the House upon Snowden and his supporters, though it did not prevent Snowden offering a meticulous analysis of the contradictions of Government policy and reiterating the view that 'There is no enthusiasm for the war. There is an almost universal desire for peace.'[76] By that time Snowden must have realized that whilst the Red Flag floated over the Tsar's Palace it was unlikely to float over Westminster.[77] The Peace Movement was running out of steam.

He was also becoming worried by the developments within the ILP. Although he was on the left of the Labour Party he was firmly committed to democratic change and far to the right of the BSP and many other quasi-Marxist groups. This became clear with the occurrence of the Bolshevik Revolution in November 1917. The events in Russia, the introduction of a proletarian dictatorship and the rigidity of the Marxist ideology applied by Lenin, offended Snowden's softer, more liberal, British experience of change. Snowden was distressed to hear ILP pacifists supporting Lenin and the Bolshevik Revolution and matters came to a head at the ILP Conference held at Leicester in March 1918. He was largely responsible for the toned-down message of support sent to the Russian Bolsheviks which merely noted the stand made for the social and economic freedom by the workers of Russia. In reality, the developments in Russia had undermined Snowden's conception of democratic change.

The First World War had revived Snowden's political life and thrust him to the forefront of ILP politics. But it had also sharply defined his political position. He was hostile to the Labour Party, being particularly opposed to its support for the wartime coalition governments and the generally patriotic fervour of its leaders. Yet he was also suspicious of the revolutionary intent of the Bolsheviks, fearing that their violent tactics might offer a viable alternative to his democratic path to socialism. He remained firmly embedded in the old Liberal Radical and ILP traditions of his youth and retained an almost emotional attachment to the issues of civil rights, individual liberty and progress. Yet, by the end of the war, this stance had left him relatively isolated in the whole compass of the Labour movement and at the head of an ILP whose support and influence was threatened. In the immediate post-war years, he lost even this limited base as the ILP came under the influence of new political forces.

Notes

1 *Labour Leader*, 4 January 1915.
2 G. Haupt, *Socialism and the Great War: The Collapse of the Second International* (London, OUP, 1972), Chapter 10, pp. 195–215.
3 Ibid., pp. 103–4.
4 D. Marquand, *Ramsay MacDonald* (Jonathan Cape, London, 1977), p. 167.
5 Labour Party, NEC Minutes, 5 August 1914.
6 J. R. MacDonald, Diary, 23 September 1914, quoted in Marquand, op. cit., p. 169.
7 Marquand, op. cit., p. 171.
8 Ibid., pp. 183–4.
9 Ibid., p. 183.
10 *Bradford Pioneer*, 21 May 1915.
11 Ibid., 25 February 1916.
12 Ibid., 1 March 1918.
13 Ibid., 22 October 1915.
14 Ibid., 9 April 1915.
15 Ibid., 2 June 1916.
16 F. Brockway, *Socialism over Sixty Years: The Life of Jowett of Bradford 1864–1944* (George Allen & Unwin, London, 1946), p. 152.
17 *Bradford Pioneer*, 2 June 1916.
18 Republished from *Merthyr Pioneer*, in *Bradford Pioneer*, 21 April 1916.
19 *Bradford Pioneer*, 2 June 1916.
20 *Labour Leader*, 15 April 1915, 1 July 1915.
21 Snowden, *An Autobiography*, p. 417.
22 *Hansard: Parliamentary Debates*, vol. LIX, col. 2148, 18 March 1914.
23 *Christian Commonwealth*, 26 August 1914.
24 Snowden, *An Autobiography*, p. 332.
25 *Labour Leader*, 18 February, 16 December 1915.
26 Ibid., 18 February 1915.
27 *Hansard: Parliamentary Debates*, vol. LIX, col. 2148, 18 March 1914.
28 Snowden, *An Autobiography*, p. 362.
29 *Labour Leader*, 28 October 1917.
30 Cross, *Philip Snowden*, p. 154.
31 Ibid.
32 *Labour Leader*, 15 April 1915.
33 Glasier Collection, Liverpool University Library, 1915/78. Letter from Snowden to Glasier dates 9 October 1915.
34 Marquand, op. cit., p. 184.
35 *Labour Leader*, 12 April 1917.
36 Ibid., 4 November 1915.
37 Snowden, *An Autobiography*, Chapter xxvi, pp. 377–86.

38 P. Snowden, *How to Pay for the War – Tax the Unearned Income of the Rich* (1916).
39 ILP Archive, Francis Johnson Collection, 1917/192.
40 *Labour Leader*, 20 May 1915.
41 Snowden, *How to Pay for the War; Labour Leader*, 20 May 1915.
42 J. M. Winter, *Socialism and the Challenge of War 1912–18* (Routledge & Kegan Paul, London, 1974), pp. 207–23.
43 *Labour Leader*, 1 July 1915.
44 Ibid., 8 July 1915.
45 *Labour Leader*, 3 February 1916.
46 Ibid., 20 January 1916.
47 Ibid.
48 Ibid., 3 February 1916.
49 Snowden, *An Autobiography*, p. 406.
50 A. Marwick, *Clifford Allen: The Open Conspirator* (Oliver & Boyd, London, 1964), p. 31.
51 P. Snowden, *British Prussianism: The Scandal of the Tribunals: Full Reports of two Speeches delivered in the House of Commons by Philip Snowden, M.P., March 22 and April 6, 1916* (National Labour Press, Ltd, 1916), pp. 17–18.
52 *Labour Leader*, 15 April, 1 July, 1915.
53 Ibid., 10 August 1916.
54 Ibid., 15 April 1915.
55 Ibid.
56 Ibid., 1 July 1915.
57 Snowden, *An Autobiography*, p. 430.
58 Ibid.
59 P. Snowden, *A Plea for Peace* (ILP, Blackburn, 1916), p. 8.
60 Ibid., p. 12.
61 Snowden, *An Autobiography*, pp. 436–7.
62 Ibid., pp. 437–45.
63 Ibid., p. 438.
64 *Daily Telegraph*, 29 November 1917.
65 Snowden, *An Autobiography*, p. 441.
66 *U.D.C.*, July 1917, article of F. Seymour Cocks on the Leeds Conference.
67 *Labour Leader*, 7 June 1917.
68 *U.D.C.*, September 1917.
69 Ibid.
70 *Labour Leader*, 24 May 1917.
71 Ibid., 7 June 1917.
72 Ibid., 12 July 1917.
73 Ibid., 25 October 1917.
74 Ibid.
75 Snowden, *An Autobiography*, p. 456.
76 *War or Peace?: Report of a Speech delivered in the House of Commons on Wednesday, February 13, 1918 by Philip Snowden* (National Labour Press, London, 1918), p. 10.
77 *Labour Leader*, 12 April 1917.

7 From the ILP to the Labour Party 1918–22

The direction of Snowden's political career changed rapidly in the immediate post-war years. At the outset he was firmly committed to rebuilding the ILP after its disastrous election performance in the 1918 General Election. By 1922 he was firmly located in the Labour Party. Why did he change political camps? In the absence of any evidence that Snowden's political attitude had evolved in any way it appears that his decision to change political horses was largely pragmatic and opportunistic. The Labour Party was rapidly becoming the second party in British politics and the expanding ILP membership was proving to be less in tune with Snowden than it had been in the War.

At the outset of this period, Snowden's faith in the ILP seemed complete. Though he had some misgivings about the support which some members of the ILP gave to the Russian Bolsheviks, he was fired by the spirit of unity which had emerged in the wake of the dreadful electoral drubbing the Party had received in the 1918 General Election.

Snowden's own campaign in Blackburn had served to harden his commitment to the Party. The sole focus of his political opponents' campaign had been his wartime record in directing the ILP's peace campaign. To this was added some vitriolic press attacks, the most notable of which came from Joseph Burgess, a founder member of the ILP and a prominent journalist, who wrote a series of articles attacking him throughout November and December 1918. According to Burgess, 'There are some politicians who are termagents. Mr. Snowden belongs to this type.'[1] He accused him of being a traitor to the British worker, of 'trafficking with the enemy',[2] of unfairly criticizing Lloyd George, and of betraying the old ILP which had been forged by Keir Hardie. He concluded that 'since he [Keir Hardie] died, and largely due to the inspiration of Mr. Snowden, the ILP has degenerated into a revolutionary Bolshevik Party, imitating Lenin's confiscating policy'.[3]

Burgess was clearly wide of the mark but his views reflected the sentiments felt by many of the Blackburn electorate who also found newspaper reports on Snowden's 30 election addresses shrouded in invective. In fact Snowden conducted quite an active campaign, raising familiar issues such as temperance and the nationalization of industry and land, alongside the wartime concerns about the need to abolish conscription and to restrict the 'vaulting ambition of Lloyd George'.[4] But this was a 'khaki' election and the calumny and hostility which surrounded Snowden's wartime activities dominated the outcome. Blackburn was still a two-member division and the two coalitionist candidates were returned with about twice the vote which Snowden received.

Table 7.1 Blackburn Poll, 1918

Sir Henry Norman	(Liberal–Coalition)	32,078 (elected)
Lt-Col Philip Dean	(Unionist–Coalition)	30,158 (elected)
Philip Snowden	(ILP/Labour Party)	15,275

Snowden was not rueful about his defeat when he gave his presidential address at the ILP's Easter Conference in 1919.

> The full force of opposition was, of course, brought to bear upon the I.L.P. candidates who had been members of the late Parliament. They had all lost their seats, but they kept their self-respect, and maintained the honour of their cause unsullied. They polled votes which, in the circumstances were remarkable, and which justify the claims they had made in Parliament – that they represented a body of opinion in the country far greater than their proportionate numbers in the House of Commons.[5]

Released from his parliamentary duties, he now set about the task of rebuilding the ILP. His letters to Bruce Glasier are rich in ideas and enthusiasm for the task. He saw the necessity of reorganizing the NAC of the ILP and was adamant that it should proclaim its political independence. It needed to bring in new blood.

> The NAC needs this contact with fresher minds. Benson has plans for remodelling the NAC. I think this is much needed. We should have a body with Executive powers which can meet more frequently. Unless this is done the Labour Party will submerge us.[6]

He was soon occupied in a round of coffee-table conferences, at which a variety of ideas were discussed.

> We had a most wonderful time at Jordans – the most useful conference I think I have ever attended.... The need for an energetic forward movement by pamphlets and books was reached and schemes were suggested for meeting the need. I want to see the Labour Press with its great resources turned into a munition factory for our Socialist propaganda. I am quite willing to give a good deal of my time to this work. We want

> leaflets and we want pamphlets and, we projected last week, a series of Socialist books to sell at 1s.[7]

In another letter, he wrote that

> For the last fortnight my mind, day and night, has been full of the *Leader*. I have scores of brilliant ideas for making it the biggest, brightest, best, most useful, most popular paper in the world. I feel so keenly about this that I would like to take on the editorship with Mrs. Glasier as partner. I could live to make it a success as I have never lived for a purpose before.[8]

As a result of these meetings he was drawn into writing a variety of pamphlets and books at this time, the most notable being *Twenty Objections to Socialism* and *Labour and the New World* (1921).

Such enthusiasm belied the fact that the ILP was beginning to move in directions which would drive Snowden out of effective participation in the Party by 1921. The balance of power within the Party was beginning to move away from its traditional areas of dominance, such as the West Riding and Lancashire, towards the expanding region of Scotland, where the war had strengthened support for the Scottish ILP. Snowden soon found his position threatened by John Wheatley and Jimmy Maxton, men of a very different style and temperament from himself, who were inclined to lead the Party towards regaining the working-class vote. His concept of an ILP drawing support from all classes was under threat.

He also became frustrated at the ILP's difficulties in establishing links with international socialists. In 1920, J. Bruce Glasier had sent a letter to Snowden, the contents of which he conveyed to the 1920 Easter Conference. He argued that the ILP ought not to be divided over the issue of joining the Second and Third Internationals:

> I had hoped that long ere now we should have been successful in bringing about a reassembly of the full International in which every nation and section, valid in its Socialist constitution, whether majority or minority, would have due representation. . .[9]

At the time, the ILP had been divided between those who wished to join the Second International, now composed of reformist socialist parties, and the Third International, or Comintern, which was dominated by Moscow and contained the revolutionary socialist parties. Snowden had feared that the revolutionary element within the Party would force the ILP to join the Comintern but on the second day of the conference 'every speaker who rose was against the Bolsheviks. . . . It was unfortunate that so many of the delegates had come to the Conference pledged, or I am sure the vote for Moscow would have been much smaller than it was'.[10] In the end, Glasier's influence seems to have prevailed and the ILP eventually joined the Vienna Union, or the 2½ International, which was committed to bringing the revolutionary and reformist socialist organizations together. The Vienna Union was ignored by most major parties and quickly collapsed. But, in the rising debate over the internationals it is clear that Snowden had become frustrated at the level of revolutionary influence within the ILP. The outcome of the 1920 Conference was greeted by Snowden with 'relief rather than satisfaction. I had feared that things might go worse.'[11]

Such developments and tensions served to undermine Snowden's faith in the ILP. He admitted in 1920 that 'The new N.A.C. seems strange to me. . .'.[12] But what eventually drove him out of the mainstream of ILP politics was the party's treatment of his wife. She had visited Russia on a fact-finding mission in 1920 and returned with an extremely critical account of her experiences. She wrote a description of what happened in her book *Through Bolshevik Russia* criticizing, amongst other things, the persecution of the Menshevik and Social Revolutionary parties. Because of this, and the opposition of some members of the ILP who were still besotted with the Bolshevik Revolution, she was not re-elected as the ILP candidate to the National Executive Committee of the Labour Party in 1922. But even before this event, she had been strongly criticized and Philip took this as a personal insult for, as he once informed the ILP Conference, 'My wife and I are in a very full sense two souls with a single thought, two hearts that beat as one.'[13] His period of office as Chairman of the ILP came to an end in 1920; he accepted the post of Treasurer but then gave up the post in 1921.

Snowden, on his formal resignation as Chairman of the Party, appeared to harbour hopes that he would continue to work within the ILP and reflected upon the sentimental attachment which he enjoyed with the Party for almost a quarter of a century.

> I do not think that I could have lived through the terrible times of the last five years . . . if I had not known that I was sustained by the good wishes and prayers of my comrades in the I.L.P. There have been times when the temptation of retirement has been strong, but I have resisted that temptation when I have remembered the thousands of men and women in the country who were looking with hope on what assistance I and a few friends might be able to give to the movement. It would have felt like desertion in a great crisis, like desertion in the face of the enemy.
>
> I never could leave the I.L.P. .... It has meant too much to me for nearly 30 years. It has had my interests, my efforts, and my thoughts. If I left the I.L.P. I could never be the same man again. It was that which induced me to accede to the request that I should accept the office which has been rendered vacant by the retirement of Mr. T. D. Benson.[14]

This was clearly more than a few kind words from a founding father of the Party to his offspring. There was real feeling and empathy behind these statements. But Snowden was looking back, and the ILP which he knew was fast disappearing.

The ILP was developing new attitudes, influenced by the Bolsheviks and the guild socialists. Guild socialism, in particular, began to capture the mind of the Party and was evident in its 1922 Constitution.This Guild idea rejected capitalism, and the wage system for treating human beings as mere commodities but also rejected the idea of many socialists that the state would take control of every aspect of life. Guild socialists believed that political and industrial democracy cannot be identical. Politicians must not be made responsible for running industry.

> Accordingly in a free Socialist community industry, as well as politics, must be governed from within and from below. For the State-controlled industry we must substitute the independent and democratic Guild working in participation with the State.[15]

These guilds would be based upon the existing trade unions, but instead of simply being bargaining agencies within the framework of capitalist industry they would control industry, representing the community as producers. The political state would represent the community as consumers. The balance of power in this dual society would be defined by the formula that, while the political state would own the means of production the guilds would control them.

These were ideas which attracted some of the new leading spirits of the ILP, most notably Clifford Allen. In January 1919 he attended a disucssion conference of the NAC of the ILP at which the main topic was Guild socialism:

> Cole magnificent, MacDonald vague and a little 'debatey'. Snowden by far the worst. He seemed to have very little grip on the industrial side of things.[16]

Allen's personal visit to Snowden did little to revise his opinion of Snowden.

> To Philip Snowden's for supper, where had 4 hours delightful talk. He is frightfully imbued with the old idea of the divine right of Democracy and majorities, and only very hardly coming to see the new developments in the Socialist Movement. These older leaders of the ILP are terribly reactionary but they are able and sincere.[17]

By 1919 Snowden and Allen were politically poles apart. Snowden continued to preach the old Liberal Radical and ILP gospel on which he had been raised and would not adapt his ideas to the new political atmosphere which had emerged within the ILP.

Yet why did he place his faith in the Labour Party, an organization which he had severely criticized during the First World War? One clue is offered in a letter which he wrote when he resigned from the ILP on 28 December 1927.

> I have not taken this decision hurriedly. For several years the conviction has been growing upon me that the I.L.P. as a separate body has served its purpose, and that its continued existence is neither necessary nor useful.
>
> ... The old I.L.P., by creating the Labour Party, has made a far greater and more powerful instrument for establishing the Socialist State than it could ever hope to be, and it might well be content now to merge itself in larger life.[18]

But can this explanation be taken seriously? There were signs that Snowden had been moving away from the ILP before the War, and it is arguable that he would have already left had it not been for the War. Yet in 1919 and 1920 he was still staunchly defending the continuation of a separate ILP. But if he was quixotic about the future of the ILP why should he leave it to mark out his career in the Labour Party? He had been similarly critical of the Labour Party before 1914, feeling that it had not sufficiently separated itself from the Liberal Party. He remained critical of it during the War and disliked and distrusted many of its trade union activists. Nevertheless, his attitude towards the Labour Party appears to have been changing throughout 1919 and 1920.

Immediately after the December 1918 General Election, Snowden reflected that whilst the Labour Party had increased its parliamentary representatives from 59 to about 150 it had not succeeded as it should and he was doubtful about its prospects.

> But if the Labour Party in Parliament is going to be a fighting force, if it is going to fight for great political principles, and for a democratic industrial policy, the great majority of its members will have to be reborn. There are amongst them some of the most reactionary of the Trade Union leaders.... No Parliamentary group ever had such a magnificent opportunity as the Labour Party is now provided with by the circumstances of political situation. If they fail to take full advantage of that opportunity they may destroy the political Labour movement in this country. They will drive the Trade Unionists from political action, in despair of its futility illustrated by the Parliamentary Labour Party, and they will give an irresistible impetus to the most extreme form of industrial action. A straight fighting policy in the House of Commons by the Labour Party will quickly make a vulnerable breach in the armour of the Coalition.[19]

In this rather disingenuous piece, Snowden reflects all his fears for Labour. It would be dominated by the trade union leaders whose right-wing policies might force their members to industrial rather than political action. It might miss the opportunity with which it was now presented, now that it had effectively replaced the Liberal Party as the effective opposition to the Coalition Government.

If we are to accept Snowden's 1927 statement as an accurate, rather than contrived, explanation of his move to Labour then his conversion of thinking had to occur between January 1919 and his departure from the NAC of the ILP in 1922. If that is the case then what was attracting him to the Labour Party? Perhaps it was the fact that the Labour Party appeared less likely to be influenced by Bolshevik sympathizers than the ILP. More likely, it was the fact that the Labour Party was now appearing to represent a genuine alternative to the Liberal Party.

The Liberal Party had lost some political ground to the Labour Party before 1914. But the War had speeded up the transference of the progressive vote in two ways. In the first place the Liberal Party had split in 1916 between the Asquith and Lloyd George factions, thus creating a lacuna for the Labour Party to fill. Secondly, the new Franchise Act of 1918 providing adult male suffrage and female suffrage for women over the age of 30, had increased the electorate from about seven millions to 20 millions. Many Labour supporters were therefore able to vote for the first time.

The Labour Party was also making significant improvements to its organization and propaganda. The number of its constituency and divisional parties had increased from 215 in January 1918 to 498 in 1921 and 527 in 1922. Many branches had formed women's sections and there was a fair degree of activity connected with individual membership campaigns and propaganda activities. New agents were being appointed and the Party appeared to be on the verge of a political breakthrough.

Indeed, there is evidence to suggest that Snowden was beginning to change his attitude towards the Labour Party shortly after his pessimistic forecasts of January 1919. In February 1919 he was forced to admit that

> The Labour Party have begun very well. If they will maintain this fighting policy they will earn and they will deserve the support, not only of the Labour Movement but the men and women of every class who want to see the House of Commons leading the country along the road of ordered progress and reform.[20]

He later modified his views to suggest that it was performing better on industrial matters than on questions of civil liberty and international relations.[21] But he was heartened by the stand of British trade unions and the British Labour Party against the Allied interventions in Russia towards the end of 1919.[22]

Liberal disarray, Labour growth and frustration with the activities of the ILP seem to have combined to persuade Snowden to switch his primary political allegiance from the ILP to the Labour Party despite his distrust of both MacDonald and the trade union movement. The switch was evident by 1922, and was facilitated by his return to Parliament.

Notes

1 *Blackburn Times*, 9 November 1918.
2 Ibid., 7 December 1918.
3 Ibid., 30 November 1918.
4 Ibid., 7 December 1918.
5 P. Snowden, *Peace and Retrospect* (ILP, London, 1919), p. 4.
6 Glasier Papers, 1/1919/99. Letter from Snowden to J. R. Glasier, 26 January 1919.
7 Ibid., 1/1919/100. Letter dated 28 January 1919.
8 Ibid., 1/1919/101. Letter dated 2 February 1919.
9 Ibid., 1/1920/95. Letter dated 2 April 1920.
10 Ibid., 1/1920/97. Letter dated 2 April 1920.
11 Ibid.
12 Ibid.
13 *Labour Leader*, 8 April 1920.
14 Ibid.
15 A. Marwick, *Clifford Allen: The Open Conspirator* (Oliver & Boyd, London, 1964), p. 47.
16 Ibid., p. 52.
17 Ibid., p. 53.
18 Snowden, *An Autobiography*, p. 645.
19 *Labour Leader*, 2 January 1919.
20 Ibid., 20 February 1919.
21 Ibid., 24 April 1919.

8 Snowden and the Colne Valley Constituency 1922–31

Snowden was at the top of Labour Party politics for nine years between his return to Parliament in 1922 and the end of the second Labour Government in August 1931. Yet it was only the close relationship which he enjoyed with his Yorkshire Pennine constituency of Colne Valley which allowed him to pursue, without hindrance, his role as a Labour grandee. This chapter, the first of three which will examine Snowden's career in a thematic manner, will attempt to assess the nature of his relationship with his local party.

Snowden's links with Colne Valley can be traced back to the 1890s. He had lectured in the constituency on many occasions and was part of an ILP deputation which had advised that the National Administrative Council of the ILP should endorse Victor Grayson's candidature in the 1907 parliamentary by-election. Snowden's ethical approach was, indeed, consonant with the political mood of a constituency in which trade unionism was weak and the dissenting and nonconformist tradition was strong. His missionary style of lecturing was akin to that of Victor Grayson, dominated by an almost religious emphasis in the need for brotherhood. He was thus an obvious choice for the Labour candidature when the position fell vacant in 1921. He was selected as Labour candidate in October 1921 and returned as Labour MP for Colne Valley in the 1922 General Election, representing the constituency until 1931.

According to Snowden, his move from Blackburn to Colne Valley was the result of pressure from his ILP colleagues who 'were anxious to make a certainty of my return to Parliament at the next Election, and they did not share my optimism about my prospects at Blackburn. They pressed me hard to accept this opening in Colne Valley.'[1] And accept it he did. After being released from his candidature in Blackburn he went to Slaithwaite, a community near Huddersfield which was just within Colne Valley, where he won the candidature of the division at a Colne Valley Divisional Labour Party meeting by an overwhelming majority:

'practically all the delegates voted for Mr. Snowden. No votes being received for Mr. Shaw.'[2]

Once selected, Snowden set about winning the seat with a determined lecturing campaign, addressing nine meetings between 7 and 25 November 1921. He provided money from his own pocket, out of the reported £1,500 to £2,000 he was earning from his journalistic work. He employed a woman organizer for one month to help form a Women's Section of the Colne Valley Divisional Labour Party (CVDLP) and was active in inviting national speakers to the constituency.

Such action was necessary because of the scattered nature of this large constituency. There were 38 small towns and villages in the division, which involved all election candidates in considerable travelling. Indeed, during an election campaign candidates would probably be expected to give three or four speeches per day. Snowden's campaigning quickly yielded results and, following a campaign in which he highlighted Labour Party policy and the high level of unemployment in the textile trade which dominated the area, he was returned as MP for Colne Valley in the autumn of 1922.

Table 8.1 Colne Valley Constituency, General Election, 1922

Philip Snowden	(Labour)	12,614 (elected)
J. Brooke	(Conservative)	11,332
J. W. Mallalieu	(Liberal)	8,042

Once returned to Parliament, Snowden appears to have retained a respectful, though distant, relationship with his constituency. Like Ramsay MacDonald at Aberavon and Seaham Harbour, he could not always visit his constituency on a weekly basis and was often absent from the annual meetings of the CVDLP: J. H. Hudson, Labour MP for Huddersfield, often attended in his place. In July 1924 'he was too busy with the work of his office of Chancellor of the Exchequer to attend'[3] and in 1926 he was absent 'owing to the industrial crisis'.[4] Yet these absences do not appear to have blighted support for him, his majority continuing to rise at successive general elections.

Local satisfaction with Snowden was partly sustained by the kudos which the constituency gained from his political importance and his triumphs. In February 1923 it was recorded that 'Mr. Snowden's work in the House of Commons, since the Election, had undoubtedly extended his reputation both in the constituency and throughout the country'.[5] When he became the first Labour Government's Chancellor of the Exchequer 'Colne Valley was honoured' and it was felt that the chancellorship was a 'position which we believe he is filling with credit to himself and the constituency he represents'.[6] His local reputation was further enhanced by the fact that he was one of the two Labour representatives on the Court of Inquiry which was formed in order to resolve the issues raised by the wool textile dispute of July and August 1925. This strike and lock-out was the first regional dispute to occur in the Yorkshire woollen and worsted industry. It was contemporaneous with the coal crisis of June and July 1925, which later led to the Coal Lock-out and the General Strike nine months later, and so has become obscured in the history of industrial relations by these more dramatic events. Yet the dispute was more important. The weak woollen textile unions took on the employers and prevented them reducing wage rates against a background of five years of wage cuts. It was hailed as a great victory for the unions and Snowden, as a member of the Court of Inquiry which resolved the dispute by recommending that there be no wage reductions, participated in that victory against the perceived employers' and government's assault on wages. Naturally this decision was well received in the woollen and worsted textile community of Colne Valley.

Such successes meant that Snowden was usually toasted with uncritical acclaim in his constituency. Even his essentially deflationary budget of 1930 did not receive the criticism which might have been anticipated.

> In the budget our member Mr. Snowden, by replacing the large amount of extra taxation required on the shoulders of the rich income-tax payers, did something to reverse the disastrous policy of his predecessor, Mr. Churchill. The Government's record, when the difficulties with which it had to contend are taken into consideration, is a very creditable one.[7]

Snowden's position was further bolstered by the fact that the West Riding of Yorkshire was one of Labour's heartland during the 1920s. The once Liberal-dominated textile district was overwhelmingly Labour controlled in that period and Snowden reflected, in 1928, on the political landscape of the area north of Sheffield. 'You can start at Sheffield, and drive through Penistone, Colne Valley, Huddersfield, Elland, Dewsbury, Halifax, Bradford, Shipley and Keighley, and you are never out of a Labour constituency.'[8]

Yet Colne Valley was hardly the usual type of Labour stronghold. It suffered from a weakness of trade-union organization, had no obvious urban centre and, with the exception of Grayson's period as MP between 1907 and 1910, had been a centre for Liberalism. Not surprisingly, Snowden was anxious to improve the organization of the CVDLP. In July 1924 J. H. Hudson MP, standing in for Snowden, expressed the Labour Party's concern that Snowden, as a national Labour figure, should be freed from having to deal with the organizational work of his constituency, that individual membership should be increased and that the '£200 in hand be spent on organisational work.'[9] The CVDLP appears to have made efforts to respond and, in 1924 and 1925, it held meetings to bring about the 'better development of the Educational side of our Movement'.[10]

Snowden's distance from his constituents, combined with his national reputation, helped to produce a deferential attitude amongst his Labour supporters. His departure from the Labour Government to the National Government in 1931 obviously shocked them. Yet there was relatively little of the personal rancour which surrounded the departure of Ramsay MacDonald and J. H. Thomas. This may be partly explained by the fact that Snowden had decided not to contest another parliamentary election. He had informed Ramsay MacDonald on 11 June 1931 that 'he had fought his last fight'.[11] As a result, unlike MacDonald, he did not stand against his old colleagues when a general election was held at the end of 1931. Snowden was candid about the whole episode. In a letter to Mr Heywood, Chairman of the CVDLP, on 30 August 1931 he admitted that his decision to join the National Government had been the 'most painful experience of his life' and, having outlined the reasons for his action, hoped that 'you will be able to secure a candidate who will keep the seat for Labour'.[12] This letter was, of course, written when future relationships were still obscure. At this time, the CVDLP was prepared to be generous and merely recorded its desire to place on record 'our appreciation of the very valuable services he has rendered to the constituency during the nine years he has been its representative in the House of Commons'.[13] Only J. H. Hudson, a close personal friend, MP for Huddersfield until defeated in the 1931 General Election, and editor of the *Huddersfield Citizen*, the local Labour paper, revealed bitterness rather than sorrow: 'It is no use denying the facts. The treachery of Snowden and MacDonald had a profound effect upon many of our people.'[14]

Whatever the merits or demerits of Snowden's relationship with the Colne Valley constituency, it did give him the parliamentary platform he so desired. His reputation also made it a safe Labour seat from which he could project himself into national politics.

Notes

1 Snowden, *An Autobiography*, p. 553.
2 Colne Valley Divisional Labour Party, Minutes, 8 October 1921.
3 Ibid., 26 July 1924.
4 Ibid., 1 May 1926.
5 Ibid., 28 February 1923.
6 Ibid., 29 February 1924.
7 Ibid., 22 February 1930.
8 *Huddersfield Citizen*, 24 August 1928.

9 Colne Valley Divisional Labour Party, Minutes, 26 July 1924.
10 Ibid.
11 James Ramsay Macdonald papers, Public Record Office, 30/69, item 1753, the MacDonald Diaries, 11 June 1931.
12 Snowden, *An Autobiography*, pp. 960–1.
13 Colne Valley Divisional Labour Party, Minutes, 29 August 1931.
14 *Huddersfield Citizen*, December 1931.

9 Shadow Chancellor and Chancellor of the Exchequer 1922–29

During the 1920s, unemployment was absolutely vital to the electoral dynamics of the Labour Party; where it was high, Labour usually polled well. And to many contemporaries, it was the Labour Party, rather than the Conservative and Liberal parties, which was effectively the party of the unemployed. It was therefore crucial that the Labour Party should offer constructive solutions to unemployment – a problem which affected about 10 per cent of the workforce, the 'intractable million', throughout the 1920s. Yet it is equally clear that the Labour Party, confident in the belief that unemployment was a product of a capitalist society and would disappear once socialism was achieved, felt little compulsion to offer solutions. Snowden did little to disturb such equanimity. On his first speech as Shadow Chancellor he simply announced that 'we shall always have the problems of unemployment with us under a system of competitive capitalism'.[1]

He was impeccably orthodox in economic matters, a believer in the need to return to pre-1914 normality. This meant returning Britain to the gold standard and re-establishing the high pre-war parity of $4.86 to the £, and he accepted that such a policy necessitated deflationary policies. As part of this package he had a pressing desire to see balanced budgets replace the deficit budgets which had occurred during and immediately after the war. He also accepted the need to pay off the National Debt which had risen from £650 million in 1914 to £6,000 million by 1919. In common with most other chancellors of the exchequer, he committed himself to paying off the National Debt at £50 million per annum through a Sinking Fund. The logic behind this was pure *laissez-faire* capitalism: the payment of the debt in the context of balanced budgets would force interest rates down and stimulate industrial activity. Underpinning all these policies was an intensely deep commitment, almost a fetish, to the need for free trade combined with an absolute horror of tariff protection.

The Labour Party, and especially Snowden, faced the problem of unemployment with a range of *laissez faire* responses which would have done justice to the purest of capitalist parties. It is hardly surprising then that when J. M. Keynes, Oswald Mosley and the ILP offered more interventionist and expansionist policies in the mid- and late 1920s, Snowden should dismiss them out of hand, and that the Labour Party should follow his lead.

Snowden's faithful adherence to economic orthodoxy was noted by many contemporaries. When he became Chancellor of the Exchequer in the Labour Government of 1924, Churchill reflected that 'The Treasury mind and the Snowden mind embraced each other with the fervour of two long-separated kindred lizards'.[2] Bob Boothby's comment was even more apposite:

> To every outworn shibboleth of nineteenth-century economics he clung with fanatic tenacity. Economy, Free Trade, Gold – these were the key-notes of his political philosophy and deflation the path he trod with almost ghoulish enthusiasm.[3]

Recent writers have shared these opinions, noting his 'visionless orthodoxy'.[4]

But why did Snowden advocate this economically orthodox policy rather than develop a more iconoclastic policy within the parameters of capitalism? There appear to be two major answers to this question. In the first place, the Treasury view obviously appealed to many aspects of his Liberal Radical upbringing. Secondly, most of the socialist and Labour Party perspectives on unemployment appeared to accept that it was inevitable under capitalism, that it could only be alleviated by socialism, and that it was only the coming of socialism which would solve the whole problem of poverty, of which unemployment was just one part. They thus dismissed the ideas of economists such as Keynes as mere 'reformist tinkering', and offered little by way of policies which would help the unemployed, even in an expected transition period between capitalism and socialism.

At the root of Snowden's acceptance of the 'Treasury view' was his grounding in Gladstonian Liberalism. He was raised in an atmosphere which regarded borrowing as an evil and free trade as an essential ingredient of prosperity. He was imbued with a strong belief in stable international relations, which was considered to be the basis of a thriving free trade world economy. As already noted, he was thus dismayed at the outbreak of the First World War, for it had broken the progress of capitalism which he saw leading to socialism. He was eager to regain the normality of the pre-war years. To Snowden, then, balanced budgets, the gold standard and free trade paved the way to socialism and had to be rightly applied. The fact that it was possible that the policies of sound finance might be anathema to socialism does not appear to have crossed Snowden's mind but two recent writers have suggested that Snowden, MacDonald and Thomas 'had sought to combine a misty-eyed, emotional commitment to socialism with an unquestioning acceptance of orthodox principles of finance and administration which, for all practical purposes, made progress to socialism impossible'.[5] This judgement appears fair in the light of the failures of the first two Labour administrations.

Yet, in the 1920s, there was no substantial body of socialist opinion on how to deal with unemployment. Like most putative socialists, Snowden believed that unemployment was a manifestation of the working-class poverty which was bound to exist within a capitalist framework. The only solution to poverty was socialism. Like many other members of the Labour Party, he rejected the more expansionary policies of Lloyd George, Keynes and other Liberals which he saw as palliatives, not solutions. Snowden had few socialist resources to draw from when it came to dealing with unemployment in a capitalist society. John Hobson, a Liberal economist, had suggested that the tendency for capital to oversave in slumps might be rectified by taxation which would permit governments to restore the normal saving–spending ratios and help economic recovery. But it was left to Beatrice Webb, through the medium of the Minority Report of the Royal Commission on the Poor Law of 1909, to outline an argument which was rapidly becoming accepted as Labour Party policy. In this report, she suggested that, once unemployment rose above 4 per cent, government departments ought to speed up their programmes in a 'counter-cycle' move to prevent the trade cycle moving into deep slump. This action could not then be regarded as a public works policy because work proposals would have started before unemployment became acute. These proposals could be financed by borrowing, at low interest rates, the large amount of capital – the 'idle balances' – not being invested in industry during a depression. There would also be normal taxation and budget surpluses during periods of relative prosperity. These ideas had emerged in the Labour Party's Unemployed Bill which was presented to Parliament on four occasions between 1907 and 1911. However, this Bill also added another component to the 'socialist' ideas from which Snowden could draw. It suggested that every man had a right to work but that, since capitalist society could not guarantee that right, the first duty of a Labour Government would be to provide humanely for the unemployed.

Snowden accepted the general outline of this policy, but the economic conditions of the 1920s and his own economic philosophy restricted its application. Unemployment averaged 10 per cent in the 1920s and was thus judged to be too high to take 'counter-cycle' action. In addition, government departments tended to concentrate upon public works schemes – for which Snowden had little enthusiasm.

Secondly, his Gladstonian convictions on balanced budgets conditioned his hostility to the idea of borrowing 'idle balances' during a depression. Snowden was always reluctant to use the budget as an instrument for creating jobs, for fear that it might stimulate inflation and ultimately bring about the financial collapse of the nation.

Loyalty to Gladstonian economics always meant that Snowden was unlikely to fully accept even the most limited of Labour Party responses to unemployment. His constant line of argument was that a prosperous capitalist economy was necessary to finance socialist policies and that there was a strict road to such prospects. Thus his first priority was to encourage economic prosperity by adopting 'balanced budgets' and 'sound finance'. He clarified this approach in 1920, when he wrote a book entitled *Labour and the National Finance*, arguing that all industries would have to be self-financing under a Labour administration and that they could not expect to rely upon Government subsidies.

In truth, there was little to distinguish Snowden's economic philosophy, and that of the Labour Party, from that adopted by other political parties. Indeed, there were only three symbols of any distinctiveness. The first was Snowden's advocacy of the Capital Levy – an idea which had first emerged in 1915. His plan was to regain the interest and profits, which were accumulating in the pockets of businessmen, financiers and industrialists due to the rapid extension of war credits at high interest rates by introducing a capital levy on fortunes over £1,000. He believed that this would yield £3,000 million and thus help to reduce the National Debt. He maintained that this could reduce normal taxation rates by £200 million per year and that all but the richest sections of society would be better off. But, even before Snowden became Chancellor of the Exchequer in 1924, the scheme seemed less attractive than anticipated. The scheme practically disappeared from Labour's pre-election statements in 1923, as Snowden suggested, because it was not electorally attractive.[6]

The second distinctive feature was that Snowden presented the Labour Party as the caring party which was prepared to provide better unemployment benefits and improve the conditions for obtaining such benefits. But even this was a long way from the vision of the Budget 'as a means not only of raising revenue to meet unavoidable expenditure but as an instrument of reducing inequalities in distribution' which Snowden had written of in his *Socialist Budget* (1907).

Thirdly, Snowden and the Labour Party were committed to nationalization or public ownership of some kind – though Snowden was less enamoured of the idea than many other Labour leaders. However, the Labour manifesto of 1923 failed to mention nationalization as a consequence of MacDonald and Snowden's decision to produce neutral policies which would not damage Labour's chances in the general election.

In substance, then, there was little to distinguish Labour's economic strategy from those of the other political parties and Labour's financial proposals in the 1920s were clearly dominated by Snowden's acceptance of the 'Treasury view'. His response to every economic situation was predictable. He objected to anything which might generate inflation, opposed borrowing, maintained that socialism would be paid for out of taxation – and would have to wait if it could not be paid for in this manner – and was strongly committed to the belief that all public works projects had to be self-financing. Underlying all of these policies, during the inter-war years, was the need to reduce the National Debt.

His economic and financial strategy reflected this blinkered vision. As Shadow Chancellor in 1923, he criticized the Conservative Budget, 'The Big Business Budget', for cutting the rates of super-tax when the 'first thing is to reduce the debt in a thorough manner'.[7] When he introduced 'The Housewife's Budget', on 29 April 1924, the first budget ever presented by a British Labour Government, he offered some minor reductions in indirect taxation on sugar and tea and announced the removal of the McKenna Duties on motor cars, motorcycles and various other items. Yet his main concern was to demonstrate his financial soundness and economic orthodoxy by stressing that a reduction of the National Debt was an essential precursor of industrial growth and real tax cuts.

> Meanwhile it is clear that we must take every opportunity and devote as much of our resources as possible to the redemption of Debt (Cheers). Some people seem to think that Debt reduction is something which confers no public advantage. I know a reduction of 1s. in Income Tax is much more spectacular than paying off £50,000,000 of Debt. In the first case the relief is obvious, in the second it is indirect, but none the less real, and in fact more widespread and penetrating in its benefits. Improvement in national credit in its turn regulates the rates at which money can be borrowed for industrial purposes. Moreover, in view of the great conversion schemes which we shall carry out in a not far distant future, the maintenance and improvement of British trade is a matter of vital importance.[8]

The last sentence was a reference to the need to return to the gold standard in 1925.

What is disturbing, though not entirely surprising, is that the Budget was well received on all sides of the House of Commons. It drew general approval from the Liberals and the Conservatives and at the same time seems to have confirmed Snowden's socialist respectability to some Labour MPs. Thomas Johnstone, a Labour MP, reflected upon its impact.

> Time was, and that was not too long ago, when Mr. Philip Snowden's opposition – unbending and relentless – to all phases of the Bolshevik

> experiment in Russia . . . created around him an atmosphere of 'moderation' as was thought in some quarters to betoken a drift towards repudiation of the principles he had spent his life in propagating. But events have again confounded the prophets.[9]

Johnstone's comment is in fact very curious given that the budget was hardly evidence of Snowden's distance from moderation. It indicates how little of a redistributive nature was required to appease most Labour MPs and to attract the loyalty of the party.

Snowden's position as Chancellor of the Exchequer was short-lived, brought to an end by the defeat of the first Labour Government in October 1924. From then until May 1929, he acted as Shadow Chancellor, but found relatively little to quarrel with in Winston Churchill's budget speeches. Most criticism was cosmetic for he fundamentally agreed with the policies which Churchill pursued – though, interestingly, Treasury officials had found him more 'malleable'.[10] He applauded Churchill's decision to return to the gold standard in 1925, approved of his policy of balancing the budget and welcomed his commitment to reducing the National Debt. He was silent on the general strategy of wage reductions which the government pursued throughout 1925 and 1926 up to and including the events which led to the General Strike of May 1926. When he did level criticism it was usually on the grounds that Churchill had steered away from the straight and narrow of economic orthodoxy.

Snowden once stated that 'you cannot have a tax reduction on sound economic lines so long as the National Debt exists'[11] and was critical of Churchill's 1925 Budget, 'The Rich Man's Budget', on precisely those grounds. His objection was that Churchill had given part of the £26 million budget surplus to relieve the supertax payers. The correct policy would have been to reduce the National Debt.

In 1927 the focus of Snowden's annual budget attack upon Churchill was that 'Winston's conjuring trick' had deceived people into thinking that he had balanced the budget and created a surplus. He was even more pernickity about the 1928 Budget, arguing that the budget surplus was more due to good luck than to good management: 'Had not a number of millionaires taken pity on his former misfortunes and died to give him an unexpected surplus in Death Duties, he would have had another big deficit.'[12]

In the final analysis, all that Snowden did was criticize the Baldwin Government for reducing taxation for the supertax payers. He added to this some general comments about the failure of the Baldwin Government to tackle unemployment. Yet it is difficult to see how his own declared economic policies would have been much different, or would have produced markedly better results. If there was a difference in strategy it lay in the fact that Snowden wished to redistribute income and wealth from the rich to the poor by taxation although, given his orthodoxy, the opportunities to do this were extremely limited.

The limited economic perspective of Snowden's financial policies became increasingly evident as the 1929 General Election approached. *Labour and the Nation*, the first shot in the election programme of the Party was a vague and rambling document as far as economic and financial policies were concerned. Consequently, the main focus of attention for the Labour Party was Snowden's conference speech where he made it clear that he did not intend to use the budget as an instrument for creating jobs in any future Labour government:

> I have seen and I know something of the danger of the control of credit and the means of starting an inflation policy, and it might be highly dangerous in the hands of a Government that wanted to use this means in order to serve some purpose or to gain popular support. We know there is going to be a General Election in nine months' time. What would be the greatest cry for this election? In those nine months to have reduced the unemployed from 1¼ millions to a quarter of a million, and an unprincipled Government in the absolute control of currency and credit could do that, but they would do it at a terrible price which the country would have to pay sooner or later.... That is a power I am not prepared to put without reserve and control into the hands of any political government.[13]

There was practically no criticism of Snowden's speech, and even the ILP, which had developed its alternative policies, raised little objection.

Snowden's domination of the economic and financial policies of the Labour Party went almost unchallenged during the 1920s. As already noted, it was suggested that even relatively minor reductions in indirect taxation were sufficient to confirm Snowden's socialist credentials within Labour ranks. But why was this the case? Several explanations have already emerged. The Liberal Radical background of many of the Labour leaders impaired their ability to make significant changes in economic policy. As socialists they were reluctant to consider palliatives to deal with unemployment when the arrival of the Socialist State would remove capitalism – the cause of poverty and unemployment. It is also obvious that few Labour leaders had mastered the details of financial matters in the way that Snowden had done. But Robert Skidelsky made the most telling point when he wrote that

> The intellectual bankruptcy of Labour's leaders were evident to all who cared to see. They expected to build the temple of socialism on the foundations of a 'correct' financial policy, and were quite unaware that those foundation were being busily undermined by the best capitalist economists.[14]

The fact is that there were few socialist thinkers developing alternative economic and financial policies to those which were identified with the Treasury. The only significant signs of a challenge to these views, and to Snowden's orthodoxy, came from the ILP, from which Snowden had formally detached himself in 1927.

One of the reasons for Snowden's departure from the ILP in the early 1920s was the fact that new groups of people with different ideas to those he defended were beginning to win support with the Party. The leading spirit, and driving force, behind these developments was Clifford Allen. He brought a number of middle-class economists and financial experts into the Party, including J. A. Hobson, E. F. Wise, H. N. Brailsford and Oswald Mosley.

It was Mosley who, with John Strachey and Allen Young, produced one of the major challenges to Snowden's orthodoxy with the publication of *Revolution by Reason* in 1925. Mosley had been greatly influenced by Keynes and presented own proposals for the credit expansion of the economy to the ILP conference in 1925.[15] The Mosley plan was one designed to nationalize the banking system and, through it, to offer consumer credit to the unemployed and producer credits to manufacturers with the purpose of stimulating demand in the economy. This policy was never formally accepted by the ILP but Mosley, with his collaborators, developed his plan further in *Revolution by Reason*. From the start it was quite clearly Keynesian in type, suggesting that the key to any solution to unemployment was to expand credit and then to redistribute income and wealth - whilst many of those, such as Hobson, who explained Britain's economic problems in terms of underconsumption, placed more emphasis upon the redistribution of income and wealth in order to stimulate demand.

Mosley believed that such credit expansion could follow either a capitalist or a socialist pathway. The former would lead to inflation, according to his analysis, whilst the latter could provide a coordinating intelligence, in the form of an Economic Council, which would balance demand and production. To stimulate mass consumption, the wages paid by individual firms would be fixed at general levels and firms would be forced to accept overdrafts from the nationalized banks, thus forcing private industry into the hands of the Economic Council. Producer credits would also be given to manufacturers in socially useful industries to raise output and lower prices. Any resistance by industry would be met with 'summary socialization'. In addition Mosley was prepared to abandon the gold standard and allow the pound to find its own level. Thus, *Revolution by Reason* united aspects of the expansion of policies of the new monetary theorists with the possibility of imposing a web of socialist controls.

Although Mosley's plan was impressive, and surfaced in the economic debates of the second Labour Government, it is clear that he missed the mark. The ILP was not in the mood to discuss reformist ideas and was beginning to produce its own internal policy papers. In 1923 Clifford Allen had established a number of expert inquiry commissions.[16] The most important was that on the living wage, chaired by J. A. Hobson. It produced an interim report, *Socialism in Our Time*, which was debated at the 1926 ILP Conference, and its final report, *The Living Wage* was published towards the end of the year.

The Living Wage accepted some of the ideas advocated by Mosley and his colleagues, but the primary strategy was different. It maintained that unemployment and poverty would be cured by redistributing wealth and income. This was clearly shaped by Hobson's under-consumptionist ideas rather than the credit expansion ideas of Keynes. This redistribution would be brought about by more steeply progressive taxation and a system of family allowances to provide additional income for families with children. Further purchasing power would be injected by imposing statutory wage minimums throughout industry which would be paid for by printing money. Though this was obviously inflationary, it was felt that the added purchasing power of the workers would soon absorb surplus industrial capital and lead to a rise in production. These actions were to be supported by a variety of socialist controls – including the explicit commitment in the final version to nationalize the Bank of England and those industries which failed to introduce a minimum wage level.

Many of these suggestions were anathema to Snowden. The abandonment of the gold standard and the adoption of inflationary policies to stimulate industry and cure unemployment were alien to his whole economic approach. But the increasing political isolation of the ILP from the rest of the Labour Party in the mid- and late 1920s, its decline into factionalism, the hostility of the trade unions, and MacDonald's antipathy to its ideas, ensured that there was little possibility that its proposals would ever rival those of Snowden. The 1927 Labour Party conference debated *The Living Wage* and referred it to the NEC where MacDonald condemned it, with his trade union backers, and assigned it to political oblivion.

By 1929 Snowden was in complete control of the financial and economic policies of the Labour Party and even Mosley, a close friend of MacDonald during the late 1920s, made little headway against Snowden's almost febrile obsession with orthodoxy. This meant that the Labour Government of 1929–31 would face the world recession with ineffective policies but would only be judged by the 'humanity' of its treatment of the unemployed. Yet it is interesting to note that Snowden's domination of Labour's economic and financial strategy went far beyond his political strength within the Party between 1922 and 1929.

Notes

1 Cross, *Philip Snowden*, p. 185.
2 R. Skidelsky, *Politicians and the Slump: The Labour Government of 1929–1931* (Macmillan, London, 1967), p. 69.
3 Ibid.
4 Ibid., p. 38.
5 A. Booth and M. Pack, *Employment, Capital and Economic Policy* (Basil Blackwell, Oxford, 1985), p. 136.
6 Snowden, *An Autobiography*, p. 595.
7 Archives of the Labour Party, *The Big Business Budget* by P. Snowden, 1924/94, p. 5.
8 Archives of the Labour Party, *The Housewife's Budget* by P. Snowden, p. 5.
9 *Leeds (Weekly) Citizen*, 2 May 1924.
10 T. Jones, *Whitehall Diary*, vol. I (Oxford University Press, Oxford and London, 1969), edited by K. Middlemass, entry 17 May 1925.
11 Archives of the Labour Party, *The Big Business Budget* by P. Snowden, 1923/64, p. 5.
12 *Huddersfield Citizen*, 20 April 1928.
13 Quoted in Booth and Pack, op. cit., p. 28.
14 Skidelsky, op. cit., p. 47.
15 Booth and Pack, op. cit., p. 29.
16 Marwick, *Clifford Allen*, pp. 84–5.

10 Snowden and Labour Politics in the 1920s

Snowden's political career in the 1920s was dominated by three themes of longstanding relevance to him – his antipathy towards MacDonald, his desire that the Labour Party should appeal to all classes and his contemplation of an alliance between the progressive forces of Liberalism and Labour. If he sought to build up his own personal support around these issues and problems there is little evidence that he was able to do so. MacDonald had a tight hold on the support of the non-trade union members of the PLP, the trade unions put resources behind him after the defeat of the General Strike of 1926. Lacking an obvious power base, Snowden was forced to cooperate with MacDonald, a man who shared many of his views and aspirations but for whom he harboured a personal 'spiteful' animosity.

Snowden was never a serious candidate for the leadership of the Parliamentary Labour Party and the whole issue of the Labour leadership was quickly settled in 1922. The 1922 General Election had seen the return to Parliament of a greatly increased number of Labour members, including Snowden and MacDonald. The first task of this group was to elect a 'Chairman and Leader'. The previous chairman had been J. R. Clynes, widely supported by the trade union-sponsored MPs, but his position was now challenged by MacDonald. Snowden may still have harboured some interest in the leadership but, lacking ILP and trade union support, his ambitions were totally unrealistic. In the end the contest was between MacDonald and Clynes. MacDonald canvassed support from the younger members of the Party and Clynes gathered the trade union support. In an open vote, MacDonald obtained 61 votes to Clynes's 56. Snowden voted for Clynes, explaining, many years later, that he did not feel that MacDonald would give the Party a 'vigorous lead' and that his pre-war activities highlighted his 'passion for intrigue and compromise'.[1] These comments may well have been written with the events of 1931 in mind but it is only fair to recall that Snowden had come into conflict with MacDonald on this very matter in the ILP Conference of 1914.

Notwithstanding his open opposition to MacDonald, he was invited to be Labour's Shadow Chancellor and, when the need arose, Chancellor. Snowden and MacDonald worked closely together to present the Labour Party as 'the coming party'. Both feared the consequence of Labour being forced to form a government without a clear majority and advised against such a course of action. Yet they enthusiastically grasped the opportunity when it arose. Indeed, Snowden reflected the almost contagious enthusiasm of the Labour Party when it was offered office: 'It had come at last! Few of us who had toiled through the years to achieve this object had expected to see it realised in our lifetime.'[2]

Faced with rising unemployment, Baldwin had decided to go to the country on the issue of protection in December 1923. Though the Conservatives were returned as the largest political party in the House of Commons they could always be outvoted by the combined vote of the Liberal and Labour parties who advocated free trade. Baldwin thus relinquished office in favour of the Labour Party, the larger opposition party.

The new Labour administration was formed in early January 1924 and lasted for ten months. During this period Snowden focused on financial matters, the only major exception being his concern for foreign affairs. There were two matters which threw him into conflict with MacDonald. One was the inter-Allied Conference and the reparations issue. The other was the Geneva Protocol.

The first of these sources of conflict arose from the fact that Germany, as Snowden had always feared, was unable to pay the reparations demanded by the Allies at the end of the First World War. Partly in consequence the French had occupied the Ruhr in 1923 and the Dawes Committee produced its plan for German recovery. The Dawes Plan recognized that Germany could not meet her obligations unless her currency was stabilized and her budget balanced. This could not be done unless Germany's economic unity was restored and, though the French occupation was outside the brief of the Dawes Committee, it was suggested that foreign troops ought not to impede Germany's economic activities. It then arranged a complicated procedure whereby Germany's reparations would rise from £50 million to £125 million over five years, though no reparations could be paid at all in the first year without a foreign loan of £40 million.[3]

The whole document was controversial for it implicitly condemned the French occupation of the Ruhr and skated over the danger of the Germans defaulting on payments by declaring that sanctions would only be applied in the case of 'flagrant failure' by the Germans to carry out their obligations. In addition, there was the problem of obtaining security and guarantees for the £40 million foreign loan.

MacDonald hoped that the fine detail of the issues would be settled at the inter-Allied London conference of July and August 1924. Three committees were formed: one to deal with the role of the Reparation

Committee which would declare upon German default and the security to be given to the subscribers of the loan; a second to settle the plan for the restoration of German economic unity; and a third to deal with technical matters about how reparation payments could be best put to use.

Snowden was appointed to be chairman of the first of these committees, the one which would deal with many of the explosive issues which would arise at the conference. From the start he made it clear that he was not going to be rushed or brow-beaten by the French. He argued that it was up to the committee to decide upon matters and that the security to subscribers to the foreign loan to Germany was inadequate. This angered the French who felt that the financial and reparation concessions which had been on offer under the Dawes Plan and in subsequent discussions would be ruined by Snowden's perverse behaviour. Matters got worse as Snowden constantly took the German side in demanding the precise terms on which Germany would be deemed to have been in 'flagrant failure' of her obligations, and in determining the timescale for the French evacuation of the Ruhr. In a complicated set of negotiations Snowden managed to deeply offend the French delegation and MacDonald wrote to him that 'Your remarks yesterday have played havoc & the whole French delegation has been mischief-making the livelong day'.[4] MacDonald later wrote in his diary that 'Snowden absurdly mischievous. Raised every imaginable petty fogging point, the underlying one being that we could trust the French in nothing. Gave him all the rope he took ... in the end everyone was against him.'[5] At one point, Snowden threatened resignation.[6]

In the end, despite Snowden's opposition, the inter-Allied London conference produced four agreements. The first, and the most important, being the decision of Germany and the Reparation Commission to carry out those parts of the Dawes report which applied exclusively to Germany.

Snowden also found himself opposing MacDonald over the Geneva Protocol. This arose from negotiations between Britain and France, following MacDonald's emotional speech to the League of Nations Assembly on 4 September 1924. He had asked that Germany should be admitted to the League and that a system of arbitration should be set up to deal with grievances between nations. The resulting Anglo-French negotiations, the Geneva Protocol, provided for an elaborate system of arbitration backed by force. Those states which refused to go to arbitration when required to do so by the League council would be regarded as aggressors, and a variety of sanctions could be taken against them. The supplement to this was to be a disarmament conference in June 1925. Yet, though MacDonald's initiative and Protocol appeared to offer a way of avoiding future conflict, it worried Snowden since it appeared to commit Britain to a system of collective security, the like of which had led to Britain's involvement in the First World War.

These clashes of opinion between Snowden and MacDonald soon intensified. They were fuelled by the feeling of Snowden, and several other ministers, that MacDonald was becoming distant in his policy making – a frustration which led MacDonald to hold informal early morning meetings with some of his ministers from April 1924. The Snowdon–MacDonald relations also worsened as a result of the Russian loan.

One of the cardinal points of MacDonald's foreign policy was the effort he made to come to terms with Soviet Russia. One of the first acts of the Labour Government was to establish diplomatic relations with Russia. Snowden accepted that this was desirable, and had always been opposed to attempt to isolate Russia from the rest of the world. But what he could not accept was that Britain should provide a guaranteed loan of about £30 million to Soviet Russia, on the basis that they spent £20 million or so on British goods. His main objection was that the Russians had seized British property during the Bolshevik Revolution and that she had offered no compensation to the British bondholders.

Arthur Ponsonby was given the responsibility of negotiating with the Soviet delegation and preparing a formula which would meet the requirements of both the Soviet delegation and Parliament. These were tricky and protracted discussions and it is clear that efforts were made to defuse Snowden's opposition which might threaten Cabinet accord and Parliamentary approval. After some particularly difficult negotiations with the Russians, which broke down and forced Ponsonby to come up with an alternative set of proposals, he recorded in his diary:

> I examined all of them, took Chapman's in my pocket, tore over to Downing Street, by a miracle met Snowden in the lobby, got him in a waiting room with a Treasury expert. A moment of hesitation, but he accepted.[7]

The Labour Government was defeated in October 1924 and this precipitated a general election which brought about an increase in its vote but saw a decrease in the number of Labour MPs returned. Snowden regarded this general election, caused by events surrounding the infamous Campbell case and fought within the context of the Zinoviev letter scare, as unnecessary and blamed MacDonald for Labour's defeat. He wrote to Fred Jowett, referring to the 'great opportunities we have wantonly thrown away by the most incompetent leadership which ever brought Government to ruin'.[8] This was a view which he also expressed to Manny Shinwell.

During 1925 Snowden's name was mentioned, along with those of

Henderson and Clynes, as a possible leader of the Labour Party. Ernest Bevin, and many other trade union leaders, were beginning to doubt the wisdom of continuing with MacDonald as leader and the search seemed to be on for an alternative leader of stature. But nothing came of this suggested palace revolution, although the soundings were indicative of the mood of frustration which was developing towards MacDonald. Throughout the mid- and late 1920s, there was a feeling abroad in the Parliamentary Labour Party that MacDonald was drifting away from his colleagues. In a letter to MacDonald in 1927, Snowden reflected upon this mood. He maintained that 'Now that the Protocol has been buried at Geneva I do not see any reason why we cannot all agree upon an agreed policy for securing its fundamental aims of arbitration and disarmament.' But there were problems, and he continued

> you must excuse me for writing quite plainly. I am expressing the feeling of all my colleagues who have talked with me on the subject. We are feeling that somehow – it is difficult to explain – we cannot get inside you. You seem to be protected by some impenetrable barrier. I called it aloofness in my last letter. It was not so in the old days of the N.A.C.[9]

At this stage, Snowden was certainly considering the possibility of an organizational alliance with the Liberal Party. But why, given his own established political position within the Labour Party, should he have considered such an arrangement?

One factor must have been his frustration with MacDonald. The split over the Geneva Protocol had been deep and MacDonald had remained distant from his political colleagues. But there were others. Snowden's affinity with Liberal Radical ideas meant that he was never entirely unsympathetic to the formation of a viable centre party in British politics. His earlier objections to the Liberal Party had often been on the grounds that its organization, rather than its ideas, were opposed to Labour. In 1922 he had written a Labour Party pamphlet entitled *What is the Labour Party? A Reply to Liberal Misrepresentation* in which he argued that:

> The attitude of the Liberal Party to the Labour Party is changeable like a chameleon. At one time we are told that Liberalism and Labour are two wings of the Progressive forces. Pathetic appeals are made to Labour to unite with the Liberals, for really, we are assured, the two parties are agreed upon nine points in every ten. At other times the Liberals change their tactics and attack the Labour Party more bitterly than they ever attacked the Tories. The Labour Party is represented as a revolutionary organisation bent upon overthrowing all our cherished institutions.[10]

Yet even these essentially tactical criticisms appeared less relevant when the first Labour Government was formed in 1924 and remained in power owing to the support given to it by the Liberal Party. When that understanding was endangered by Asquith's attack upon John Wheatley, a Clydeside MP and Minister of Housing in the first Labour Government, and one of the 'wild' men of the Labour Party Ethel Snowden, always less guarded than her husband, wrote to Lloyd George:

> You know my sympathy for the idea of a Union of all Radical forces for common ends. You know how greatly I have antagonised friends in my own party by this advocacy for the last two years, and in the circumstances and after events which might reasonably have turned me the other way.... You cannot suspect me of sympathy with the wild men of the Party. You know I disapprove of the mischievous policy of Wheatley. But because of Asquith's attack ... I have declined several invitations from Liberals and have warned my husband to behave with cautiousness.[11]

Ethel's letter implies that Philip was also critical of Wheatley and on good terms with Lloyd George. It is tempting to suggest, in the light of Philip's earlier comments about the closeness of thinking of him and his wife, that he shared his wife's idea of a union of Radical forces.

The experience of the 1924 Labour Government may well have persuaded Snowden that such a combination was a distinct possibility. Certainly there were rumours that Snowden was involved in the development of a Lib–Lab alliance, so much so that, in 1926, Snowden was considering the necessity of denying that he had ever been involved in the discussion of a political and Parliamentary alliance with the Liberals. He wrote to David Lloyd George that

> It has come to my knowledge that a very definite statement is being made that on the 7th May there was a meeting at my house at which you met certain of my colleagues and discussed with them the question of a political and Parliamentary alliance, and that the terms and conditions of such an alliance were agreed upon.
>
> I desire to say most emphatically that neither on the 7th May nor any other date did such a meeting take place, and that the question of a political alliance, or of your joining the Labour Party, has never, within my knowledge, been considered or discussed with you.
>
> In justice to myself and colleagues, and in justice to you, I make this unequivocal denial of the report to which I have referred.[12]

Yet the fact that he forewarned Lloyd George of his impending statement, which he was never forced to make, raises some doubts about the frankness of his denial. And all the most vigorous displays of innocence would not have hidden the fact that he had obviously discussed the possibility of a Radical Alliance with Lloyd George in some informal manner, and possibily through Ethel. Their initial contacts may have been of a cursory nature, based upon a blossoming friendship. Yet by the late 1920s they had given the matter some thought. Indeed on 3 October 1928, Snowden sent a letter to Lloyd George suggesting that neither of them were obstacles to such an alliance but that 'Neither of the two parties is ripe for it', but that 'the Labour Party generally would be' opposed.[13] His firm belief in the need for an alliance was demonstrated by his comment that 'It is very sad that two parties who should go together a long way along the road to progress should be forced to fight each other for the benefit of the reactionaries and revolutionaries.'[14]

Snowden may well have harboured some aspirations about the formation of a Lib–Lab or radical alliance but there was, in fact, no possibility of such an arrangement. He may well have been on good terms with Lloyd George – the Liberals did support the 1924 Labour Government, and he was at odds with MacDonald and the trade union movement – but this did not necessarily constitute the basis of a Radical alliance. Indeed, the value of the relationship with Lloyd George is questionable. On economic and financial matters it was the Asquith section of the Liberal Party which supported Snowden's economic orthodoxy, not the Lloyd George section which was developing its own brand of reformist and interventionist capitalist policies. His friendship with Lloyd George masked the divergent economic policies which they were pursuing. Within the Labour Party, it is not clear who Snowden would have expected to take over to such an alliance. As already suggested, Mosley and the ILP were attacking the economic orthodoxy of the Labour Party in 1925 and 1926. In 1927, Snowden finally severed his connections with the Party. As for the trade union section of the Labour Party, they were generally loyal to the Labour leadership and unlikely to entertain a Radical alliance. And, after their defeat in the General Strike of 1926, they were more determined than ever to exert their influence within the Labour Party. Furthermore, although they were generally supportive of Snowden's economic orthodoxy, if unhappy about its impact, they were hardly likely to respond to the political ambitions of a man who was well known for his antipathy towards trade unionism.

The complexity of British progressive politics and the amorphous and secretive nature of discussions meant that Snowden would never be able to form the centre Radical alliance which he saw as a viable alternative to the political dominance of the Conservative Party. In the end, Snowden came to recognize the impossibility of his political dream.

Ironically, given Snowden's attitude towards trade unions, his political reputation in the Labour Party was enhanced by the political repercussions of the General Strike. During the nine-day General Strike period, Snowden, to use Winston Churchill's phrase, remained 'as mum as a mouse'.[15] Later, his well-known hostility to strike activity and syndicalism emerged: 'If the Trade Unionists had fully realised the forces that would be ranged against them they would never have embarked upon the strike.'[16] Nevertheless, it was left to Snowden to make the staunchest defence of the trade union movement at this time.

Baldwin's Conservative Government had strongly criticized the TUC over its action and, in 1927, introduced legislation – the Trades Dispute and Trade Union Act – aimed at preventing sympathetic strike action and at undermining the financial connection between the trade unions and the Labour Party through the demand that the political fund of trade unions should be subject to the more restrictive 'contracting-in' clause than the more favourable 'contracting-out' clause. In May 1927, when the measure came before the House of Commons, Snowden gave a ninety-minute speech which Lloyd George considered to be the best of his career. He began by asserting that a General Strike could not succeed for industrial purposes and that it was only meaningful, and likely to succeed, when the government was totally out of tune with the workers of the country. He added that fifty Acts of Parliament would not stop a General Strike if the workers were determined to have it. As for the first clause of the Bill

> which is supposed to give effect to the Government's intention to make what they call a strike against the community illegal is so ridiculously worded that nobody understands it. No lawyer in the House of Commons will venture an opinion as to what it means.[17]

He was effectively criticizing the government for its destructive extremism in similar terms to those he used in connection with the workers' commitment to the General Strike. He challenged the government to think through the consequences of its action and wondered whether or not it could put five million men before the courts and into prison, by applying the legislation. His attack was to no avail, but evoked a positive response from Lloyd George and some Liberal MPs and was considered to be a most powerful condemnation of such trade union regulation.

One gets the feeling that Snowden was testing all possibilities in the interregnum between the first two Labour governments, though nothing appeared to challenge the Labour Party as the chief rival to the Conservative Party. Adrift from the ILP and the trade union movement, realizing the impossibility of the Radical Alliance, Snowden found himself once again collaborating most closely with MacDonald. In May 1929, following Labour's victory in the General Election, albeit as the largest rather than majority part, he became Chancellor of the Exchequer in the second Labour Government.

Notes

1 Snowden, *An Autobiography*, p. 573.
2 Ibid., p. 604.
3 Marquand, op. cit., pp. 334–9.
4 Ibid., p. 349.
5 MacDonald Diary, 15 August 1924, quoted in Marquand, op. cit., p. 349.
6 Marquand, op. cit., p. 349.
7 Ponsonby Diary, 13 August 1924, quoted in Marquand, op. cit., p. 362.
8 Cross, op. cit., p. 212.
9 PRO, 30/69 item 1753, MacDonald Diaries, 1910–1937.
10 Archives of the British Labour Party, Pamphlets, 1922/51.
11 Lloyd George Papers, House of Lords Library, G 18/18/12.
12 Cross, op. cit., p. 228.
13 Lloyd George Papers, G 18/7/16 dated 3 October 1928.
14 Ibid., also Cross, op. cit., p. 229.
15 Cross, op. cit., p. 221.
16 Snowden, *An Autobiography*, op. cit., p. 730.
17 *Huddersfield Citizen*, May 1927.

11 The Hague Conference, 1929

In a round of acrimonious discussions, Snowden was one of the few Cabinet ministers to be given office without dissent – such was his hold over the financial and economic policies of the Labour Party. It was also decided that he would lead the House of Commons when MacDonald was away, in effect making him deputy Prime Minister. He was at the pinnacle of his career. As Chancellor of the Exchequer, he quickly set about making small improvements in unemployment benefits and approving a relatively minor programme of public works through local authorities. But his most immediate concern was to deal with the complex problem of German reparations which was to be the topic of discussion at The Hague Conference in August 1929.

Snowden had always been an opponent of German reparations from the moment they became incorporated in the Treaty of Versailles (1919) at the end of the First World War. He felt that reparations in cash would cause the depreciation of German currency and that payment in kind would simply help to create worldwide unemployment. In addition, he had frequently noted the difficulties which were involved in operating the reparations system and feared that the bitterness it engendered would ultimately provoke another world war.

These fears were well founded for the German currency did collapse in the immediate post-war years and the German nation was never able to meet her obligations under the Treaty of Versailles. In 1921 it was agreed that Germany owed £6,700 million and that she would pay off £330 million per year. This proved too burdensome and in 1924 the Dawes Committee reduced the figure to £50 million, rising to £125 million in five years. In the first year £40 million would come from a foreign loan and, to ease the burden, Germany would be allowed to pay some of her reparations debts in kind. It was blatantly obvious to all that there was little prospect of Germany paying off the debt burden imposed after Versailles.

During the 1920s British Governments of all political colours began to recognize this fact. In 1922 the British Government offered to cancel all claims against Germany and all Allied debts if the United States and other creditor nations would do the same for Britain. This offer was not favourably received and, instead, the British Government despatched the Balfour Note, whereby she agreed to ask no more from the Germans and the Allies than she was asked to pay to the USA. Acting on the Balfour Note, Britain effectively reduced the German and Allied debt from £3,000 million (£2,000 million owed by France and Italy) to £1,000 million, which was the equivalent of Britain's debt to the United States. Yet between 1922 and 1927 not even this arrangement had worked. German and Allied debts to Britain had not been paid in full whilst Britain had honoured her debt commitments to the United States. Between 1923 and 1928, Britain was out of pocket to the tune of £29.1 million. If interest of 5 per cent were added to this deficit then it would rise to about £116 million.

In 1929 the Baldwin Government had been instrumental in setting up the Young Committee to settle the reparations issue once and for all. It decided that German reparations should be reduced – to £100 million per year for 36 years and £70 million per year for another 22 years – France was also to evacuate the Rhineland and, in order to soften the relations with France and Italy, Britain provisionally accepted the need to reduce her share of the net total German reparations.

At this stage the second Labour Government came to power and Snowden decided to oppose the Young Plan at The Hague Conference in August 1929. He did not see why Britain should have to make further financial sacrifices for the benefit of Italy and France. However, this flew in the face of MacDonald's more cautious approach. He had written to Snowden on 2 August 1929 advising him of the gist of his talk with Sir Josiah Stamp, one of the two British representatives on the Young Committee.

> As to the letter [Reparations Conference] he said he thought we could get some concessions on Reparations in kind, but that we had little hope of an increase in the percentage of money payments. He says that Balfour Note will hang like a millstone around his neck. He gave me a somewhat more assuring survey than Brand but said that things were still exceedingly delicate and advised 'no shocks'....[1]

Snowden ignored the advice and went out to The Hague on 4 August 1929 determined to demonstrate that British generosity had reached its limits and that there would be no further sacrifice of British interests. The result was that The Hague Conference did not prove to be the formality that everyone expected. Snowden demanded that Britain should be given back the extra £2,400,000 which the Baldwin Government had provisionally agreed to forgo and that Britain should receive all her payments in cash, rather than kind. Snowden put the matter bluntly.

> You will forgive me if I appear to speak with great firmness in regard to the distribution of annuities. The House of Commons will never agree to further sacrifice of British interest in this matter. There are no divisions between the Parties on this question. We are agreed upon this. We are prepared to wipe the slate clean of all international debts and all Reparations. That was promised in the Balfour Note. It was the declaration of our Party when we came to power. But, so long as debts are payable, Great Britain and every Government in Great Britain would insist upon her being fairly treated in this matter.[2]

Snowden's internationalism was clearly qualified by his national concerns. These threatened the harmony of interest, the concert of Europe, which had been built up in the 1920s. His approach was a clear alteration in the direction of British foreign policy, much to the chagrin of the Foreign Secretary, Arthur Henderson, who became a mere spectator at The Hague. MacDonald later recalled that 'At The Hague Henderson & Snowden laid in a vast store of ill-will for each other & thus Pluto has been working ever since.'[3] But MacDonald was also unhappy at Snowden's intransigence. On 27 August 1929, after more than three weeks of negotiations, MacDonald noted that

> I wrote & had sent this morning early a long message to the Chancellor asking to stop being negative & to negotiate on the understanding that if he get a substantial offer he would concede it; also giving him to understand that I wanted to settle.[4]

In fact three weeks of negotiations came to an end the next day when it was agreed that the British share of the reduction of reparations would be £400,000, instead of the £2,400,000 indicated by the Baldwin Government, and that German reparation goods paid in kind could not be sold in the foreign markets. MacDonald concluded that 'Snowden will have a great show & the results deserve it'[5] and he sent him a telegram congratulating him upon his 'splendidly successful fight for fair play for our country'.[6]

When Snowden returned to Britain, he was toasted as the 'Iron Chancellor' and treated as the personification of John Bull. A *Punch* cartoon summed up the situation neatly. With a clear reference to the fact that Snowden had won back 83 per cent of the concessions which Britain would have made under the Young Plan, the cartoon had John Bull talking to Philip Snowden. John Bull remarks to Philip, 'Well played'. Snowden replies 'I wanted a hundred', to which John Bull adds 'Well eighty-three's pretty useful. Anyhow it is a lot more than they meant you to get'.[7] James H. Hudson, MP for Huddersfield, one of Snowden's closest friends and editor of the *Huddersfield Citizen*, had accompanied Snowden to The Hague. He wrote effusively of Snowden:

> He has brought back with him a settlement which has filled the hearts of his countrymen with thankfulness.... His name has today become a household word among the nations of the world, and few statesmen in Europe are recognised as his peers.[8]

Another political sketch noted that he 'presents his case remorselessly ... as though it was a proposition in Euclid' and added that the Europeans were unused to the frontal-attack style of argument, typical of Lancashire and Yorkshiremen, adopted by Snowden.[9]

These reactions are interesting for what they reveal of both the Labour movement and Snowden. It was to be expected that the Yorkshire Labour heartland, which at this stage lacked the critical edge as far as Snowden was concerned, should be euphoric at his success. What is less expected is the extent to which a sense of Labour nationalism should underpin Snowden's success, with the clear implication that he had served the national interests by forcing concessions from European nations who had not been playing fair with Britain.

More to the point, Snowden also appears to have abandoned some of his previously declared internationalism for establishment nationalism. He obviously enjoyed the adulation and honours, including the Freedom of the City of London, the Freedom of the City of Leeds and an honorary doctorate at Victorial University of Manchester. All were fitting tributes from the national Establishment. The 'traitor' of the First World War was now a patriot enjoying widespread popularity. But all this outpouring of national pride revealed a lack of perception about the results of The Hague Conference. Personal vanity and national pride were satisfied but the whole conference amounted to very little. At a potential risk to international harmony, Snowden had spent more than three weeks in making some trivial financial savings. Such pettifogging activities were soon to be overwhelmed by the mammoth economic problems which Britain faced under Snowden's economic stewardship between 1929 and 1931.

Notes

1 Public Record Office, 30/69, item 1753, the MacDonald Diaries, 27 August 1929.
2 'Ephesian' in C. E. Bechofer Roberts, *Philip Snowden: An Impartial Portrait* (London, 1930), p. 226.
3 PRO, 30/69/1753, MacDonald's Diaries, 20 November 1930.
4 Ibid., 30/6/672, a letter from MacDonald to Snowden dated 2 August 1929.
5 Ibid., 30/69/1753, MacDonald Diaries, 28 August 1929.
6 Ibid., 30/69/254, telegram dated 28 August 1929.
7 Philip Snowden, *An Autobiography* (1934), p. 822.
8 *Huddersfield Citizen*, 6 September 1929.
9 *Leeds Weekly Citizen*, 6 September 1929.

12 The Economic Crisis and the Second Labour Government 1929–31

Snowden's stubborn adherence to economic orthodoxy contributed enormously to the financial difficulties faced by the second Labour Government. There were economic choices being suggested to Snowden and the Labour Cabinet. Britain could have come off the gold standard, devalued the pound and adopted protectionist policies, similar to those introduced by the National Governments in 1931 and 1932. The prices of British exports would have been reduced by devaluation and British competitiveness in the home market would have been increased. Alternatively, there was the possibility of expanding out of slump by pump-priming British industry with heightened demand through the introduction of a 'living wage' policy or by offering cheap credit to the working class. There was, perhaps, even a third major alternative: the nationalization of industry and the introduction of a broad set of collectivist policies – though they may not have got very far given the second Labour Government's minority position. But Snowden had objections to all these devices. His political upbringing in Cowling and Keighley had stamped him as a Liberal Radical, and his Blackburn experiences – despite some involvement with new Liberal ideas – had confirmed him to be a Liberal of the old progressive type. He did not develop his economic ideas beyond those he had come to accept in the confining, almost claustrophobic, atmosphere of Pennine village, or town, politics. His economic ideas lacked width or political sophistication but were important due to his position and their affinity with orthodox opinion. They compare, in impact, to the situation in modern British politics which allows the economics of a Grantham grocery shop to underestimate the constructive contribution which can be made by government intervention. The fact is that Snowden's political socialization and his own personal political history made it virtually impossible for him to act in any other way than he did. His was a self-help mentality which still held sway in the Labour Party during the 1920s.

Lacking vision, Snowden had no alternative strategy to offer. He thus met rising unemployment with a greater determination than ever to balance the budget by increasing taxation and reducing expenditure. This strategy helped to increase unemployment. Nevertheless, Snowden's policies went largely unchallenged within the Labour Party. He was masterful and convincing in Cabinet and had the support of the Treasury, which could operate to deny his Cabinet critics access to financial information. He was supported by the Prime Minister, and the majority of Labour Party members accepted his financial advice without question. It would have taken a well-organized revolt to shift him. As a result, devaluation was ruled out, expansionist policies were ignored and tariffs were firmly rejected. Indeed, it was not until his support for the gold standard, free trade and deflationary policies directly threatened Labour's pre-war commitment to treat the unemployed 'humanely', that his views were seriously challenged. Given Snowden's early political experiences and his zealous commitment to economic orthodoxy, the issues, the events and the outcome of the financial crisis of 1931 become intelligible, indeed almost predictable.

The Labour Party was returned to office in May 1929 in what Snowden referred to as 'one of the most strenuous contests I have known'.[1] It had won 287 seats to the Conservatives' 261 and the Liberals' 59. Although the Party had secured only 8,360,000 votes, compared with the 8,664,000 who voted Conservative, it had the most seats in Parliament and it became inevitable that it should form a second minority government, once again relying upon Liberal Party support to keep it in office. The decision to form this second government was in fact taken by MacDonald, in conjunction with Clynes, Snowden, Henderson and Thomas, at his house in Hampstead on 1 June.

There was the usual haggling over Cabinet posts, which was settled on 5 June according to MacDonald and 6 June in Snowden's autobiography.[2] Snowden assumed a detached interest in these proceedings for there was no doubt that he would be returned to the Treasury.

In the first instance, Snowden's interest was drawn to the issue of reparations. He had fought his Colne Valley election campaign on the basis of National Reconstruction and War Debts and it was the latter which immediately concerned him. He objected to the Dawes Plan, by which Britain gave up some of her claims to reparations to the benefit of France and Italy. As already suggested, Snowden did not see why British taxpayers should suffer for the benefit of France and Italy, a view which became readily apparent at The Hague.

On the broader issue of the economy and National Reconstruction, Snowden seems to have achieved rather less than he offered the Colne Valley electorate in 1929. His parliamentary election address had stated

> The Labour Party gives an unqualified pledge deal immediately and practically with Unemployment. We undertake to put in hand at once schemes which will find useful work and provide the country with valuable assets and stimulate all our great staple industries.[3]

It very quickly emerged that such statements were pious hopes and his pledges were never redeemed. Part of the problem was that his vision of a fully-employed society was impaired by his economic orthodoxy. But this was also true of the Labour Party as a whole.

The Labour Party's 1929 election manifesto, *Labour and the Nation*, referred to the first Labour Government's schemes of a comprehensive and far-reaching character which it had already begun to put into effect and 'which could be revived'.[4] It is difficult to understand what these vague comments meant, though they fitted well into the high-minded approach of the whole document, which saw the Labour Party as a party of all the classes, ranged against a small minority of property owners in its attempt to create a Socialist Commonwealth.[5] There was, however, a reference to the need for surtax, as a replacement for Snowden's capital levy, which, in the process of drafting, had been objected to by Snowden.[6]

On the more precise question of unemployment and economic policy, the programme had little to offer. There were brief references to the control of the Bank of England and to sound schemes for providing work which would be promoted by an employment and development board. Even more radical was the suggestion that industrial recovery would be assisted by a 'direct increase of purchasing power in the hands of the workers'.[7] But there was little to suggest how these schemes would be introduced, the order of their importance and how they would fit with Snowden's well-known hostility to printing money and fuelling inflation. The manifesto, unlike the Liberal Party's *We Can Conquer Unemployment*, offered more pious hope than a realistic and determined assessment of what could be done. It denounced the 'placid assumption that, in the twentieth century, the recurrence of involuntary idleness is still to be regarded, like tempests and earthquakes, as an act of God'.[8] Yet it was also quite clear that its authors had no concept of what to put in the place of the capitalist system. This left Snowden with a free hand to pursue his own policies for, as J. C. C. Davidson reflected,

> Snowden was immensely gifted when compared to his Socialist colleagues.... Some people said he was very narrow or, to put it differently, it was true to say that he knew, instinctively, that it was no good growing barley on deep clay soil. He knew that the Labour Party was useless when it was talking about finance.[9]

The King's Speech, outlining the intentions of the Labour Government, was little better, even though Snowden had personally changed some of the details about unemployment. According to Thomas Jones, Deputy Secretary to the Cabinet, there was serious discussion about the contents of the King's Speech.

> Then we reached Unemployment. Snowden was very caustic. 'I can see Ll.G. getting up and tearing all this to bits.' These Ministers, like their predecessors, are apparently haunted by the spectre of Ll.G., never absent from the Cabinet Room. The clock struck 5.0 p.m., and the P.M. had to go upstairs to receive Dawes, and Hugh Gibson. Snowden undertook to redraft the unemployment paragraphs, and to agree them with the P.M. to-night, and I shall have to circulate them hurriedly to the Cabinet by 11.0 to-morrow morning.[10]

Yet the final product was simply a vague undertaking 'to deal with the continuing evil of unemployment'.[11]

In the relatively good economic conditions of the summer of 1929, the vagueness of Labour's policy drew little attention. But with the Wall Street Crash of October and November 1929 there was an abrupt decline in world trade. Official unemployment figures in Britain rose quickly, reaching 1,537,000 in January 1930 and 2,753,000 – practically 25 per cent of the insured workforce – in June 1931. How was the Labour Party going to react to this worsening situation?

Snowden's domination of financial matters ensured that the options were limited. Tariffs and protective measures for specific industries were not to be entertained and Snowden informed his Cabinet colleagues, on 26 June 1929, that he would no longer support any more 'safeguarding of industries' measures – that is, protectionist arrangements applied to specific industries which had first appeared in the early 1920s and had been the basis of the Conservative Party's electoral campaign in 1929. The expansionary ideas of Lloyd George, which had formed the basis of the Liberal programme in 1929, were also dismissed. The vast public works programme advocated in *Britain's Industrial Future* (the Yellow Book, 1928) and the more detailed two-year programme of public investment – paid for by government borrowing and largely based upon road construction and house building – offered in *We Can Conquer Unemployment* (March 1929), were anathema to Snowden.

In the new Labour Government, J. H. Thomas was given the task of developing schemes to deal with unemployment through the Unemployment Committee, better known as the 'Thomas Committee', but soon found that this duty was beyond him due to departmental and Treasury opposition. Thomas quickly accepted that his Committee was ineffectual but Oswald Mosley, who was one of its members, decided to draw up his own radical solutions to unemployment, challenging the views of Snowden and the Treasury. The 'Mosley Memorandum' which circulated government circles between December 1929 and February 1930 attacked the very pillars of Snowden's orthodoxy. Mosley proposed that free trade should be set aside in favour of import controls in order to allow the home market to expand. Meanwhile there would be increased government expenditure to pay for public works, a scheme for early retirement and the raising of the school-leaving age. These ideas were presented directly to MacDonald in February 1930, and were quickly discussed in Cabinet.

Mosley's views were strongly opposed by Snowden. One Cabinet official noted, 'It was a case of Snowden v Mosley and plainly Mosley must go'.[12] In fact, Mosley resigned from the Labour Government in May 1930 but later presented his views to the 1930 Labour Party Conference at Llandudno in October. He made an impressive speech, only lost a resolution supporting his Memorandum by 1,046,000 to 1,251,000, and was also elected to the National Executive of the Labour Party.

Why was there so much support for Mosley? Did it represent a genuine desire within the Labour movement to overthrow Snowden's economic orthodoxy? Were Labour politicians beginning to doubt Snowden's economic strategy?

Although no trade union leader supported the Mosley Memorandum resolution at Llandudno it is obvious that the vote gave trade unionists, and local Labour parties, the opportunity to express their concern at the rapidly rising level of unemployment. But in the end the Labour movement remained almost slavishly loyal to the government and Snowden, and the TUC accepted that the minority position of the government prevented it from 'operating effective Socialist measures for the only solution of unemployment'.[13] There was almost a passive acquiescence in Snowden's strategy. Herbert Morrison and other ministers had to work very hard to win even minor concessions from Snowden for public works schemes. There was also some Cabinet discussion of tariffs, but the matter always got short shrift in Snowden's presence.

With the deteriorating financial situation, it is clear that Snowden was coming under increasing pressure from the City to take some action to cut the cost of unemployment throughout 1930 and 1931. His 1930 Budget was determinedly deflationary, though some party faithfuls in Colne Valley were prepared to see it as a redistributive package which placed the financial burden on the rich. He argued that the nation faced a budget deficit of more than £42 million, which by technical adjustments could be reduced to £26 million, and that the deficit should be made good by increasing Beer Duty by 3s. per standard barrel (equivalent to adding 1d. to the gallon) and by the increase of income tax at the standard rate from 4s. to 4s. 6d. [20 to 22½p.] in the pound. Given Snowden's determination to balance the budget there was little scope for increased expenditure to finance unemployment schemes and the rapidly rising levels of unemployment were raising the cost of unemployment benefits and building up a budget deficit. As a result Snowden came under increasing pressure from the opposition parties to curb the escalating cost of unemployment.

At this time unemployment provision essentially consisted of three types of benefit. First, there was insurance benefit paid out of an Unemployment Insurance Fund to anyone who had paid 30 contributions in the previous two years. Unfortunately, the Fund was going deeply into debt and the Labour Government was constantly faced with extending its borrowing powers throughout 1930. Secondly, there was the so-called 'transitional benefit', which was paid out by the Exchequer to those who were not entitled to unemployment benefit, but who made contributions to the Fund. Thirdly, there was public assistance which was paid to those who had depended on the Poor Law until the late 1920s. This cost was borne partly by the state and partly by the local authority, and paid through a Public Assistance Committee.

By 1930 the Labour Government was faced with an exhausted insurance fund, the mounting payment of 'transitional benefits' and the rapidly rising cost of Public Assistance Committee expenditure. The cost of 'transitional benefit' alone indicates the scale of the problem. The Treasury estimated costs at £10,500,000 for 1930, but the actual cost was £22 million. By January 1931 the Treasury was estimating an expenditure of £33 million for 1931 and as a result the Labour Government was faced with a serious budget deficit that year.

MacDonald had to act to avert an impending financial crisis and to indicate that his government was attempting to deal with the unemployment problem. In June 1930 he took over the special responsibility for unemployment from Thomas and awaited the report of an Economic Advisory Body which he had set up in February 1930. But, soon realizing that this body was unlikely to offer a clear programme, he then set up a committee of five economists under J. M. Keynes. This committee reported in October 1930, suggesting that unemployment benefits should be restricted, that public works schemes should be financed and that a general tariff should be introduced.

Snowden was clearly opposed to the tariff idea, had given way to Morrison on the need to finance some public works schemes and was firmly in favour of imposing restrictions upon unemployment benefits. Above all, he recognized that the cost of unemployment benefits would have to be cut if his 1931 Budget was to be balanced.

Throughout 1930 unemployment benefits were under financial scrutiny. They could be reduced in line with the fall in retail prices, or alternatively, entitlement to 'transitional benefit' could be limited –

especially in view of the alarming rate of increase that was occurring. Thirdly, the 'anomalies' of the system could be checked. It was argued that many married women, who did not intend to return to work, were drawing benefit. There were allegedly also numerous other loopholes widely referred to in the press.

In the summer of 1930 a committee of the Economic Advisory Council, chaired by G. D. H. Cole, reported in favour of a radical reform of the unemployment system. There were all-party discussions, which suggested some harsh changes, and MacDonald deferred the issue by setting up a Royal Commission, under Judge Holman Gregory, in December 1930 with the duty of examining the whole issue of unemployment and the financing of the Unemployment Insurance Fund.

To the TUC, this action was evidence that the government was attempting to legitimize future benefit cuts. Nevertheless, it gave its views to the Gregory Commission in May 1931, recommending that the rates of benefit should be increased, not reduced. But when the Commission reported on 4 June 1931, it had clearly rejected the TUC's advice. It maintained that the Unemployment Fund should be balanced by a 30 per cent reduction in benefits, that 'anomalies' should be eliminated, that unemployment benefit should be rigidly confined to 26 weeks per year, and that applicants for 'transitional benefit' should be means tested. In the end, all the Government did was to introduce a bill to deal with the 'anomalies', allowing the minister to vary the conditions, amount, and period of benefit for casual, seasonal, and short-time workers and for married women. Despite its views, the TUC acquiesced to this decision although Mosley and the ILP fought vigorously against the bill in one all-night sitting on 15 July 1931.

Notwithstanding the Labour Government's retreat from the Gregory Report, the reduction of unemployment benefits was now central to British politics. The events of early 1931 had made the issue even more relevant than it had been made in 1930. The financial crisis worsened and Snowden only survived parliamentary censure in February 1931 by accepting a Liberal amendment committing the Government to setting up an all-party committee of inquiry into the financial crisis. It was headed by Sir George May and would advise Snowden on how to reduce national expenditure in such a way as to ensure a balanced budget.

In the meantime, Snowden was faced with drawing up an interim budget. This proved to be a traumatic affair for the Labour Government, not least because Snowden fell ill three weeks after the February debate with an inflammation of the bladder. His condition required an operation after which he rested for seven weeks. His illness caused consternation in the House of Commons, where there was considerable concern when it was reported that his routine work would be undertaken by the Financial Secretary to the Treasury, who was not a member of the Cabinet. It was felt that the Cabinet needed to be kept well informed about the economic crisis. MacDonald was also worried, especially since the absence of Snowden allowed speculation about other economic policies – even protectionist proposals – to arise. On 8 March he noted:

> illness of Chancellor important, not only because he should be going on with his Budget but because he ought to be at Cabinet for decisions on quota & Ottawa policy. His absence put me in a fix because alternatives are 1. Delay further 2. Decide against him in his absence. Whenever the Cabinet has been united & someone was free to pursue a policy we have been a great success; but Cabinet hopelessly divided on home economic policy & we have been paralysed. Conf. with Sec. to Treasury on work of Budget.[14]

Events were not aided by press speculation that Snowden intended to resign. Indeed this was more than a rumour. In early 1931 he had indicated such an intention to the Webbs, and his political colleagues expected his resignation daily. MacDonald recorded that 'Thomas applies for the post if any gap to be filled'.[15] Resignation was certainly uppermost in Snowden's mind throughout the critical months of 1931 and later, on 11 June, he indicated to MacDonald that he had 'fought his last fight'.[16] Soon afterwards, on 14 June, he offered his resignation but it was rejected by MacDonald.

Despite his illness and impending resignation, he presented the Budget himself on 27 April 1931. It was clearly an interim measure, a 'stop-gap'.[17] In it, he reaffirmed the Government's decision to continue to pay money to the Sinking Fund and introduced measures to deal with the projected deficit of £37 million. The Budget was to be balanced, though the fine tuning was to be left until the May Committee reported.

Apart from the Budget crisis two other issues had attracted Snowden's attention in the first two years of the second Labour Government. The first was the ever-present threat of protectionism. The second was the difficulty which Snowden faced over his land tax scheme which had been outlined in his 1931 Budget.

It seemed to Snowden that he was fighting against protectionism on all fronts. The Government's attempt to reorganize the Coal Industry, even if it was not directly protectionist, threatened to interfere with the free operation of the market since it involved the closure of mines and the creation of coal quotas in the attempt to restrict output and force prices up. Attempts by the Ministry of Agriculture to establish similar measures for its industry seemed even more dangerous. In February

1930 the ministry had campaigned for marketing boards and quotas on imports. Despite the rejection of protection by the Cabinet, the Ministry of Agriculture produced a draft White Paper in April 1930 advising an import quota. Faced with this situation Snowden complained of the higher prices and lower wages which would result. In a letter to MacDonald, he warned:

> It seems to me that we are in grave danger of involving ourselves in a policy of raising prices to the consumer all round: first Coal, next Cereals and then Agricultural Produce generally. If our real object is to raise prices and so reduce wages we had better adopt wholeheartedly the inflation policy of McKenna or Keynes or the whole-hog protection policy of Baldwin. Personally I am in favour of a policy which will protect the consumer, maintain real wages and compel our industries to make themselves efficient by exposing them to the cold blast of reality.[18]

Thereafter the free trade v. tariff debate was waged in Cabinet.

The issue was keenly fought throughout 1930 because in February 1930 eleven countries, of which Britain was one, signed a convention at Geneva committing themselves not to increase tariffs until April 1931. The convention had to be ratified by November 1930 and Willie Graham and Philip Snowden were largely responsible for getting Cabinet approval – despite the fact that MacDonald and other Cabinet members wanted to wait and see if the other signatories of the convention were prepared to act in the spirit of the convention. On 29 August 1930, in the absence of MacDonald who had flown to Lossiemouth, Snowden was the acting prime minister at the Cabinet meeting. With Snowden making an impassioned plea for the ratification of the convention, declaring that 'the national honour of the country was at stake', the Cabinet voted by eight to two in favour of ratification.[19] On 4 September Snowden wrote to MacDonald reassuring him that 'I am sure we have done the right thing. We shall show good faith and still remain free if other countries do not play the game'.[20] He added that 'I think there are slight signs of an improvement in trade. Cotton mills and steel works are re-opening.'

MacDonald was evidently annoyed that his hands had been tied for at least eight months – until the truce was due to expire in April 1931, when protection would become possible. In the intervening period Snowden had a brush with R. B. Bennett, the Canadian prime minister, at the imperial conference in October and November, where Bennett had put forward the idea of imperial preference. As MacDonald noted, the 'Chancellor would have none of it. He was out for a debate on tariffs & to tear protectionism to tatters.'[21] Snowden's resolve did not prevent MacDonald privately reflecting upon a 'Revenue Tariff put on now to balance Budget'.[22]

Nevertheless, from April 1931 tariff protection once again became a possibility. The Geneva convention was at an end and a Cabinet committee, set up by MacDonald in December 1930, reported in favour of a wheat quota in March 1931.[23] It seems, however, that MacDonald decided to delay any decision about introducing revenue or protective tariffs until Snowden was well and for fear of forcing his resignation. Indeed to have forced Snowden's resignation over the issue of free trade and protectionism would have been to endanger the Liberal support upon which the Labour Government depended.

The important point to stress is that Snowden always got his way on free trade. It was this factor which was to dictate the events of the financial crisis of August 1931, when free trade was maintained despite the fact that two-thirds of the Cabinet generally favoured some form of protection as being preferable to a reduction in unemployment benefits.

Yet he did not always get his own way on other financial and political matters. The most obvious example of this was the difficulties he faced with the implementation of the Land Tax scheme which he outlined in the 1931 Budget.

It is crucial to understand the context in which this issue arose. From the start, the second Labour Government had been dependent upon the parliamentary support of the Liberals – without which it could have been defeated at any time. When the financial crisis began to worsen in June 1930, MacDonald extended an invitation to both the Liberals and the Conservatives to join with him in dealing with the issue of rising unemployment, it was only Lloyd George and the Liberals who replied in a positive manner.[24] In March 1931 the discussions between the Labour Government and the Liberal Party became a weekly affair – at a time when the Liberal Party had just declared its continued support for the Labour Government by a vote of 33 to 17 amongst its MPs.

It was at this juncture that the Liberal Party objected to aspects of Snowden's Land Tax Scheme. Snowden's 1931 Budget proposed provisions for the preliminary step of the valuation of land of the country and further measures for the imposition of a tax upon the valuations thus obtained. The land valuation had to be completed before the tax could be properly levied and it was therefore expected that Land Tax would not come into effect until 1933. The tax which was to be imposed was to be at the rate of 1d. (0.4p) in the pound on the capital land value. Yet he did not propose that the tax should be levied on agricultural land so long as it had no higher value than its value for agricultural purposes. Where agricultural land had a higher value than its agricultural value it would be subject to tax, but only on the excess of the value over its agricultural value.

Since the taxation of land values had long been an item in the Liberal programme, Snowden expected that he would gain the support of the

Liberal Party for this scheme. Indeed, when it was announced David Lloyd George gave it his unqualified support. But later he, and the Liberals, realized that this tax would be in addition to what landowners already paid in income tax [1s. 8d. in the £ on annual values, about 8p] under Schedule A. The Liberals therefore opposed the measure, their official spokesman stating that

> With regard to the tax I should like to say a few words. Frankly it is undoubtedly an extra tax and an additional burden upon land-owners. There is only one justification for the additional tax, and that is that it is based on the value of the site which has been created by enterprise other than the enterprise of the owner.[25]

David Lloyd George made it quite clear that this double taxation of land-owners was an issue which could 'precipitate a grave political crisis . . . and charged the Government with a lack of consultation upon the measure which was due to the unfortunate serious illness of the Chancellor of the Exchequer'.[26]

There were several Liberal amendments to this aspect of the Finance Bill, some of which were clearly impractical. At first the Labour Cabinet decided 'not to yield to Liberal Land Tax amendment [and] so run the risk of defeat'.[27] But such resolve soon evaporated with the realization tht Labour could lose marginal seats if there was a general election at that time and MacDonald asked Snowden to find a compromise arrangement. Snowden found this to be difficult and, indeed, offered his resignation on the 14 June, although it was quickly rejected by MacDonald. But on that day it appeared that Sir Stafford Cripps, Solicitor General, had found a compromise whereby the Government would continue with the single tax on the capital values of land, while graduating it on developed land according to the degree of development. At first, Snowden seemed amenable to this suggestion but at a meeting with MacDonald, Lloyd George and several others, Snowden voiced his disapproval. According to MacDonald, the meeting went as follows:

> Chancellor's first words to Ll.G.: 'Well, you have been thinking things over. What have you to say?' Shortly we agreed to the principle of the Cripps proposal, Chancellor getting increasingly at cross purposes & provocative. Joint Committee appointed by complete consent to fill in certain required figures. . . . Then followed discussion on how amendments agreed upon should be put on paper & moved. Ll.G. wished Liberals to initiate & when that objected to he lost his temper & walked out of the room. . . . No one took any notice. . . . Adjourned till afternoon & Joint Committee set to work. . . . Liberals came in as in the morning & proposed Cripps' proposal altered only as regards tax on fully developed sites. . . . Chancellor silent coldly & critically examined whispering with Graham and Cripps. Would say nothing. Meeting adjourned. We con-

> tinued. Chan. got report that he would get only £400,000 from 8,000,000 herediaments. Rejected & offered no alternative. Would not be bullied by Ll.G., surrender to Liberal &, &. We pointed out surrender by & not to Liberals. No effect. Liberal Party meeting waiting for our decision meanwhile adjourned. We adjourned for a meal & resumed at 8.15 pm. . . . We went on with Chancellor. Would listen to nothing. All consequences put before him, the rest of us being unanimous. Deadlock. Called members of Cabinet & 14 present. All unanimous though Graham took a seat on the fence & his uncertain mind wiggled like a compass. Chan. refused to cooperate with the decision in favour of agreeing to principle[sic] Liberal (originally in substance our own to which he had agreed in the morning) offer. When pressed, rose & said he would not cooperate. Asked for ten minutes to consider. We sat discussing for 50 minutes. . . . No message. 11 pm by then & went on the bench to announce decision on clause 19. I saw him in interval & put full issues and consequences before him. 'I do not care about the money. I shall not be humiliated by Liberals'. Mind has ossified on that irrelevancy. Just as I was moving him, Hudson promoted by the Treasury secretaries, who played a most subversive part playing on the Chan's obstinacy came in fussy state & said 'Revolt amongst M.P.s against surrender to Liberals'.[28]

At that point, Snowden, who later admitted that he could not understand why he was so angry with the Liberals,[29] let it be known that he would meet the Cabinet the next day to give his decision. In the meantime, MacDonald wrote to him, stressing that the Party was in no fit shape for an election contest. He argued that the taxation of land values was hardly 'the issue on which to divide the Labour Party' and appealed to him 'Do not destroy – as far as it can be destroyed – the work of our life-time by scattering our flock and leaving it torn, and disgusted with its leaders and itself.'[30]

MacDonald's appeal appears to have changed Snowden's mind for he announced to the Cabinet meeting on 16 June that, following a letter from the Prime Minister, he felt that 'he could no longer persist in his refusal to fall in with the views of his colleagues in regard to the Liberal amendment. After the meeting, MacDonald recorded that

> Cabinet met at 10 am. Chancellor opened with a statement that he had letter this morning from me which he could not resist and yielded. Thus the crisis ends. Still there was a postscript & it was touched with ridicule. When the Liberal amendment came up, it was ruled out of order.[31]

The whole eposide reveals Snowden's ability to get matters out of proportion. His indignation seems to have stemmed from the fact that the Liberals, who ought to have been aware of the implications of advocating a Land Tax in their programmes, were suddenly turning tail because of the political reaction which they foresaw. Snowden simply didn't see why he should accept amendments to a policy which had been a declared policy of the Liberal Party before he introduced the measure in the 1931 Budget. He disliked the inconsistency of the Liberal Party and was only swayed by MacDonald's appeal to keep the Labour Party together. In the end, however, he got his way for the Liberal amendment was ruled out of order and Snowden's original measure was accepted. It was only the Conservative opposition in the National Government which led to the abandonment of the Land Tax in 1934.

The Land Tax, if not the issue of free trade and protection, was only a side issue to the main event. The financial crisis was spreading rapidly throughout Europe and developments at home ensured that the issue of cuts in unemployment benefit would be central to public debate. The Gregory Commission had reported in favour of cuts in early June. At the end of July and May report was published. By including the £55 million paid to the Sinking Fund and £50 million borrowed by the Unemployment Insurance Fund, it estimated the budget deficit for 1931–2 as £120 million and suggested tax increases and savings to balance the budget. Of the £97 million to be saved, £67 million was to come from increases in unemployment insurance contributions, limiting benefit to 26 weeks in a year, reducing standard rates of benefit by 20 per cent and by introducing a means test for 'transitional benefit'. Whatever rhetoric was to be used, it is clear that the reduction of unemployment benefit would be the crucial issue in August 1931.

Snowden was to be a major influence upon the actions of the second Labour Government in the heady atmosphere of financial crisis. When the May Committee report was presented to the Cabinet on 30 July, he was a member of the Economy Committee which had been set up to consider it, along with MacDonald, Henderson, Thomas and Graham. Throughout August 1931, he laid down the parameters for discussion and decision making, although the focus of concern began to widen. Declining international confidence in the pound, despite the continuance of high interest rates in London, had led to an out-flow of money and gold from London. On 24 July Snowden was warned by officials that the 'gold exodus is unprecedented. . . . Unless we take such steps as are open to us to rectify the situation, there is a real danger of our being driven off the gold standard.'[32] At this stage, Snowden obviously feared that Britain could be forced off the gold standard and into protectionism. Snowden's priority now became the securing of an £80 million loan from New York and Paris to help the City bankers. In order to secure this loan he endorsed the Treasury view that the budget had to be balanced. But at the moment of most severe crisis he also had to deal with the Cabinet, the General Council of the TUC, the Labour Party and the opposition parties – all of whom had varying objectives and concerns.

The first meeting of the Economy Committee was arranged for 25

August. But the drain on gold continued and Snowden urged an early meeting. MacDonald arrived back in London on 11 August and, along with Snowden, met representatives of the major banks. They were afraid that the Government would have to borrow £80 million because of the run on the pound. The following day the Economy Committee of the Cabinet met and Snowden announced an expected budget deficit of £170 million for 1932–3, more than the £120 million projected by the May Committee. The Economy Committee gave its support for a package of cuts worth £78 million and new taxation of almost £100 million. Snowden had put several proposals to the committee relating to the unemployed: most notably a 20 per cent cut in benefit, an increase in contribution and the transfer of £20 million of the cost of transitional benefit to the local authorities. Nevertheless, the Committee rejected the cut in benefit, despite MacDonald's advocacy of the need for 'equality of sacrifice': 'yesterday I proposed the "1924 standards" as a basis for working out scheme of economy of value of money eg cuts in unemployment pay and reductions in fixed'.[33]

On the following day, 13 August, MacDonald and Snowden held their first meeting with an opposition leader, Sir Herbert Samuel, to inform him of the nature of the crisis and the intentions of the Government. Thereafter the Economy Committee met on a number of occasions. Its main problem was to agree measures which could be put to the full Cabinet on the 19 August. In its deliberations it had put forward some proposals to reduce 'transitional benefits' though it had rejected the idea of reducing the standard rate of benefit requested by the May Committee. The possibility of a revenue, rather than protective, tariff was also discussed. All members of the Committee, with the exception of Thomas, were against the principle of a revenue tariff, but all except Snowden preferred this to a cut in unemployment benefits, and there was, according to MacDonald, a 'vote of 4 in favour and the Chancellor against'.[34] After their discussions they submitted a list of economies to the full Cabinet, at 11 am on Wednesday 19 August, totalling £78,575,000. They were as follows:

Table 12.1 Economies recommended to Cabinet, 19 August 1931

	£
Unemployment Insurance	43,500,000
Teachers' Salaries	11,400,000
Service Pay	9,000,000
Police Pay	500,000
Roads	7,800,000
Other Economies	6,375,000
	78,575,000

The unemployment insurance item was divided into two parts. There were to be increases in contributions by employers and there was to be a reduction of the Treasury contribution to 'transitional benefits'. The standard rate of benefit was to remain unchanged.

The full Cabinet proved more obdurate than the Economy Committee expected, rejecting most of the proposals relating to the unemployed and reducing the economies to £56,250,000.[35] Essentially the difference was made up by the £20 million reduction in the Treasury contribution to 'transitional benefit', an item which was referred to a sub-committee for further discussion. There was also a discussion of a possible 10 per cent revenue tariff on manufactured goods, but this was dropped in deference to Snowden's opposition to protectionism – though the absence of official comment fuelled press speculation of a 'Cabinet All-day Tariff Battle'.[36]

MacDonald and Snowden met the opposition leaders in a 'three-party' conference on Thursday 20 August with the outline Cabinet proposals – indicating that £56 million of economies had been arranged and that another £20 million was under debate. Sir Samuel Hoare wrote later that 'Snowden was obviously speaking to a Cabinet brief, and made no effort to conceal his personal opinion that it did not go far enough.'[37] The opposition leaders were alarmed at the possibility of £100 million in new taxation which was outlined in addition to the economies and became insistent that the May Report cuts should be implemented. MacDonald and Snowden reported back to the Cabinet later the same day advising that there was a need for 'equality of sacrifice' and stressing that unemployment benefit was about 30 per cent up on its 1924 value 'at a time when Budgets were showing handsome surpluses'.[38] MacDonald noted at this meeting that 15 members of his Cabinet favoured a revenue tariff, that 11 wanted a 10 per cent reduction in benefits and that seven favoured a 5 per cent reduction.[39] It is quite clear that decisions about balancing the budget now lay between introducing a revenue tariff, which Snowden would reject, and reducing unemployment benefits.

There has been some recent discussion about Snowden's role in these events. One author has noted that the Treasury had informed Snowden on 18 August that the tax increases he had suggested were impracticable and would have to be reduced. This was at a time when he and MacDonald were arguing the need for cuts in unemployment benefits as part of a programme of 'equality of sacrifice' which would see the rich soaked with increases in direct taxation. It is argued that

> Snowden knew that [taxation demands would be less] from the 18 August. But he said nothing in all the meetings of the Cabinet from the 19 to 23 August. On this last day, in fact, he sat silently as MacDonald, in a last effort to save the Government, turned the principle of 'equality of sacrifice' on its head, arguing in perfectly good conscience that

> 'A scheme which inflicted reductions and burdens in almost every other direction, but made no appreciable cut in Unemployment Insurance benefit, would alienate much support and lose the Party their moral prestige which was one of their greatest assets! (Cab 23/67)
>
> MacDonald was not aware of these changes in the prospective budget. Neither was the Cabinet, and one cannot help wondering whether the eleven Ministers who finally agreed to cut benefit would have done so had they been told ... they had taken Snowden at his word, and trusted him to see that the principle of 'equality of sacrifice' was carried out.[40]

Snowden had misled the Cabinet by omission although it may be questionable whether such knowledge would have made much difference to the almost supine acceptance of Snowden's views by some ministers.

It is also maintained that Snowden deceived the Cabinet on the issue of suspending the £50-odd million payments to the Sinking Fund. The Cabinet had shown interest in this suggestion on the 21 August largely because such a decision could have averted the need to cut unemployment benefit. Snowden had informed the Cabinet at 9.30 am on 22 August that Conservative leaders and the City bankers had advised against it and that it was of 'paramount importance that the Budget should be balanced in an honest fashion'.[41] Later that day the Cabinet gave MacDonald and Snowden permission to discuss the crisis with the head of the Federal Reserve Bank in New York. On their behalf, the acting Governor of the Bank of England informed his New York counterpart of the details of the Budget package and noted that 'the balance was to be economized out of the sinking fund'.[42] Although the details are difficult to reconstruct, it appears that the City bankers had informed Snowden that, if all other measures were satisfactory, there would be no objection to some suspension of the payment to the Sinking Fund. The Cabinet was never informed of this possibility, even at the crucial meeting on 23 August when a vote was taken on the cut in unemployment benefit.

The detailed events of the financial crisis are complex and confusing. Nevertheless, it would appear that Snowden could have advised a smaller cut in unemployment benefit than the 10 per cent which was voted upon and offset this by suspending part, or the whole, of the Sinking Fund payment. In addition, it is now clear that the tax increases would be less than the Cabinet had been led to believe and that the 'equality of sacrifice' argument was not going to be applied in the way which the Cabinet expected. Whatever the precise pattern of events, Snowden's role was crucial in the decision-making which led to the collapse of the second Labour Government. At the least he was guilty of withholding vital information on the options which were available to the Cabinet. It was he who effectively decided that the vital Cabinet meeting on 23 August would have only two options – to reduce or not to reduce unemployment benefit by 10 per cent.

Snowden was also less than candid in his dealings with the TUC and the Labour Party. When he and MacDonald met the NEC of the Labour Party and the General Council of the TUC on 20 August 1931 they offered only the most general outline of their intentions. Snowden suggested that unemployment insurance might be modified in a number of ways to make it self-financing but would give no details on this matter or on the new sources of taxation which he proposed. The TUC minutes record Snowden as saying that 'They had not made any proposals for a reduction with regard to benefit.'[43] Snowden clarified the point later, arguing that 'I put before the meeting a statement of economies on which the Cabinet had already agreed but pointed out that at the present they had not decided upon a reduction in the unemployment allowance.... That statement however was not my intention.'[44] However, the General Council understood this to mean that there would be no reduction in unemployment benefit.

The General Council went away to consider the position and rejected the need for public sector cuts or any worsening of the position of the unemployed. They also discussed the need for tariffs, though this was referred to Congress, due to meet in September. At 8.15 pm, later that day, the General Council contacted MacDonald, who was in a Cabinet meeting, and arranged to send a deputation to see Snowden, MacDonald and the rest of the Cabinet Economy Committee. This was a heated encounter in which the General Council stressed its opposition to Snowden's ideas and, amongst other suggestions, argued the need to suspend the Sinking Fund. Snowden implied that the General Council was unwilling to recognize the seriousness of the economic situation and MacDonald later recorded that the TUC's stance was 'practically a declaration of war'.[45]

It is now clear that the Labour Party would be divided if the Labour Cabinet accepted Snowden's cuts in unemployment benefit. The General Council's opposition inspired Henderson and others to oppose the cuts. In a desperate attempt to unite his Cabinet, MacDonald asked for the opinions of the opposition leaders, the Bank of England and the City, and the New York bankers between 21 and 23 August.

On the 21 August the opposition leaders were informed by Snowden that the Cabinet had reduced the Economy Committee proposals from £78 million to £56 million and that if these economies did not restore confidence they would be followed by 'the deluge'. The opposition leaders, and particularly Neville Chamberlain, were not satisfied and later that day Chamberlain expressed to MacDonald, and possibly Snowden, that the economies were not sufficient and that they would have to overthrow the Labour Government – though they expected

MacDonald to avoid the financial crisis and would help him to do so as best they could.

The opposition leaders looked to economies of £80 or £85 million, not to those offered by the Cabinet and MacDonald and Snowden informed the full Cabinet of this position at 9.30 am on Saturday 22 August. Effectively there had to be a cut in unemployment benefits. Without this action Parliament would be summoned and the two opposition parties would defeat the Labour Government. Snowden and MacDonald were putting the vital decision to the Cabinet, and Snowden made no bones where his sympathies lay.

> So far as he was concerned he had no doubt whatever that, if he was compelled to choose between retaining the Labour Movement in its present form and reducing the standard of living of the workmen by 50% which would be the effect of departing from the Gold Standard, he knew where his duty would be.[46]

The Cabinet agreed to ask the opposition parties whether or not they would accept economy figures of £76 million rather than their original £56 million, without formally indicating their decision to accept such cuts. It appears that the opposition leaders agreed to this as long as it was sufficient to raise a foreign loan to defend the pound. Snowden wrote:

> we received the impression that if this could be done [ie secure the confidence of the bankers] they would regard the total of our economies as satisfactory. But they urged that this was a matter upon which the bankers should be consulted and, if they were satisfied the Opposition leaders would raise no further objection.[47]

This view was carried back to the Cabinet and MacDonald and Snowden began a bewildering round of discussions with the foreign bankers.

Eventually MacDonald made a last appeal and then put the final list of economies to the vote at a Cabinet meeting on the evening of Sunday 23 August. Eleven ministers supported MacDonald and eight opposed him, with one absent, on the 10 per cent cut in standard unemployment benefit.[48] It was agreed that the Cabinet could not continue and that MacDonald would offer their resignation to the King and meet the opposition party leaders the next morning.

The second Labour Government was dead, destroyed by the cost of unemployment – the only issue which Snowden allowed it to discuss. Snowden had suppressed all other alternatives – tariffs, the suspension of the Sinking Fund and enormous increases in taxation – and had sought to justify reducing the income of the unemployed by supporting the dubious demand for 'equality of sacrifice'. His upbringing and early political career helped to ensure that the events of 1931 would make him a prisoner of his own economic orthodoxy. If he wished to maintain Britain as a free trade nation operating the gold standard at a pre-First World War parity then he had no other alternative than to obtain foreign loans by inspiring international confidence in the ability of the government to balance the budget. In the end, despite the fact that some leeway was offered by the City bankers on the issue of suspending the Sinking Fund, that meant one thing – a reduction in the unemployment costs which had brought about government overspending. Such a course of action had the additional advantage that it was supported by the Gregory Report and the May Report. It also commanded the respect of the opposition parties who always had the capacity to overthrow the minority Labour Government. Snowden was in a powerful position, and able to count upon significant economic and political support in the policies he pursued. By 1931 he was a representative of the economic establishment and was prepared to put its views, which he shared, above the survival of a Labour Government.

Having defined the parameters of discussion within the Labour Government, what part did Snowden play in the subsequent formation of the National Government? And, why did he join such a Government?

There is no evidence that Snowden was anything other than an interested bystander in the events which led MacDonald to form a National Government. Nevertheless, he was obviously aware that such a development was a possibility for Beatrice Webb's diary records that, according to her husband, the issue had been raised at the Cabinet Meeting on the 22 August.

> J.R.M. raised the question of a Coalition Government: some of the Labour Cabinet Ministers remaining in office. This he intimated was what the King desired and might propose. This proposal Henderson and other members hotly rejected. The impression left on S.W.'s [Sydney Webb] mind was that J. R.M., Snowden and Jimmy MIGHT CONSIDER IT.[49]

Yet the final meetings between MacDonald and the opposition leaders and the meetings with the King were all events from which Snowden was excluded. It appears that he was invited to join the new Government at, or just after, the last meeting of the full Labour Cabinet on 24 August, along with Jimmy Thomas and Lord Sankey. Although he had been largely responsible for the economic context of the events which had brought about the formation of this Government at least one author suggests that it was an 'almost unwilling Philip Snowden' who accepted the commission.[50]

He continued as Chancellor of the Exchequer in the new government for a couple of months, before being raised to the Lords. But, for a variety of reasons, the experience was not one which he wished to remember with pride – especially due to the fact that he was forced to take Britain off his much-beloved gold standard in September 1931. And, significantly, in his *An Autobiography*, he took the opportunity to defame MacDonald:

> He neither showed nor expressed any grief at this regrettable development. On the contrary, he set about the formation of the National Government with an enthusiasm which showed that the adventure was highly agreeable to him.[51]

It was, indeed, Snowden who fuelled the speculation that MacDonald had deliberately planned the whole episode, a view which was taken up by later writers and historians who were anxious to distance the Labour Party from MacDonald. Snowden was particularly vituperative, and unfair given his own views, when he wrote that

> Taking all these things together, I think they give ground for the suspicion expressed by Mr. Henderson and other Labour ministers that Mr. MacDonald had deliberately planned the scheme of a National Government, which would at the same time enable him to retain the position of Prime Minister and to associate with the political colleagues with whom he was more in sympathy than he had ever been with his Labour colleagues. He had always entertained a feeling of something like contempt for the Trade Union leaders. His mind for a long time before this crisis arose had been turning to the idea of a new party orientation and government by what he called a Council of State.[52]

The contempt for trade unionism was not confined to MacDonald and the accusation that he schemed was based upon rumour, not evidence. Given Snowden's own attempts to create a new party, his criticism of MacDonald was hardly fitting. MacDonald rightly felt aggrieved and wrote in his diary:

> Have looked back in this book to refreshing memory on incident[s] referred to by S. Not many are even mentioned, those which are show how spite rarely requires to invent facts but only to change their relations & (relative) meaning.[53]

Given Snowden's misgivings, why did he join this government? He ascribed to himself the purest of motives. He had deluded himself into believing that his separation from the Labour Party, on a 'comparatively minor matter', would be a temporary one and that relations would be restored once the crisis was over.[54] It was his sense of duty which drove him on. It was, he argued, only the misrepresentation of facts by the TUC and the Labour Party which made the break permanent.

The message is clear – three years after the events of 1931 Snowden was distancing himself from MacDonald. His parting shot against MacDonald ran as follows:

> As I have already said, I do not think that Mr. MacDonald felt any regret that the break with his Labour colleagues had come to pass; and later developments have only confirmed this belief. The day after the National Government was formed he came into my room at Downing Street in very high spirits. I remarked to him that he would now find himself popular in strange quarters. He replied, gleefully rubbing his hands: 'Yes, tomorrow every Duchess in London will be wanting to kiss me!'[55]

Of course, it could have been that MacDonald was making light of the situation in which he now found himself.

Snowden certainly defamed others for the events of August 1931: his role was that of the faithful public servant and unlike that of the opportunist MacDonald and the irresponsible, and unrealistic, trade-union dominated Labour Party. Yet his efforts to expunge his own part in these events could not remove two main charges. The first is that it was his economic policies which helped to intensify the economic crisis between 1929 and 1931. There were alternative strategies being discussed but he dismissed them out of hand. Secondly, it is clear that he did mislead the Cabinet on the issues of the possible suspension of the Sinking Fund and the true meaning of the 'equality of sacrifice' principle which he endorsed. He may not have been personally involved in the decision to form a National Government but his pursuance of economic orthodoxy and his determination to reduce unemployment benefit always made that outcome a realistic possibility. Also, in the final analysis he was prepared to betray the Labour Party and join the National Government. But one should not be surprised at this outcome, for Snowden was a highly predictable man who bore the stamp of Gladstonian Liberalism which had been impressed during his early years at Cowling, Keighley and Blackburn. His fixity of purpose, like that of his modern Grantham equivalent, was legend.

Notes

1 Snowden, *An Autobiography*, p. 754.
2 Marquand, op. cit., p. 490.
3 *Election Address of the Right Hon. Philip Snowden, Colne Valley Parliamentary Division, 1929 General Election.* Copy in the Snowden Collection, Reference Department, Keighley

Public Library.
4 Labour Party, *Annual Report*, 1929, p. 304.
5 Marquand, op. cit., pp. 477–9.
6 Ibid., p. 477.
7 Ibid., p. 479.
8 Ibid., p. 480.
9 H. Berkeley, *The myth that will not die: The Formation of the National Government 1931* (Croom Helm, London, 1978), p. 23.
10 T. Jones, *Whitehall Diary, Vol. II 1926/1930*, ed. by K. Middlemass (OUP, London, 1969), p. 196.
11 PRO, Cab. 23, report of Cab 24(29), 26 June 1929, 11 am.
12 Jones, op. cit., p. 259, 20 May 1930.
13 Trades Union Congress, *Annual Report, 1930*, p. 69.
14 PRO, 30/69, item 1753, MacDonald Diaries 1910–1937, 8 March 1931.
15 Ibid., 10 March 1931.
16 Ibid., 11 and 14 June 1931.
17 Ibid., 27 April 1931.
18 Quoted in Marquand, op. cit., p. 559.
19 Marquand, op. cit., p. 562.
20 Ibid.
21 PRO, MacDonald Diary, 9 October 1930.
22 Ibid., 16 October 1930.
23 PRO, Cab. 23, report of meetings 4, 11 March 1931.
24 Snowden, *An Autobiography*, p. 879.
25 Ibid., p. 908.
26 Ibid., p. 909.
27 PRO, MacDonald Diary, 9 June 1931.
28 Ibid., 16 June 1931.
29 Snowden, *An Autobiography*, p. 910.
30 Marquand, op. cit., p. 601.
31 PRO, MacDonald Diary, 16 June 1931.
32 Marquand, op. cit., p. 608.
33 PRO, MacDonald Diaries, 13 August 1931.
34 Berkeley, op. cit., p. 48.
35 PRO, Cab. 23, report of meeting 19 August 1931.
36 *Daily Express*, 20 August 1931.
37 Quoted in Berkeley, op. cit., p. 52.
38 PRO, Cab. 23, report of meeting 19 August 1931.
39 PRO, MacDonald Diaries, 22 August 1931.
40 B. C. Malament, 'Philip Snowden and the Cabinet Deliberations of August 1931', *Society for the Study of Labour History*, Bulletin, 41, autumn 1980, p. 32.
41 PRO, Cab. 23, report of meeting 22 August, 9.30 am.
42 Ibid.
43 Quoted in A. Bullock, *The Life and Times of Ernest Bevin, 1881–1940*, vol. 1 (Heinemann, London, 1960, 1969), p. 482. The Archives of the Labour Party, National Executive Committee, Minutes, 20 August 1931 are less precise.
44 Snowden, *An Autobiography*, p. 941.
45 PRO, MacDonald Diaries, 21 August 1931. Also Berkeley, op. cit., 60.
46 Berkeley, op. cit., pp. 70–1.
47 Snowden, *An Autobiography*, p. 945. Incorrectly quoted in Berkeley, op. cit., p. 73.
48 Berkeley, op. cit., p. 83. He suggests that there was one vote unaccounted for and that Lord Parmoor was the only absentee. Marquand, op. cit., p. 634 suggests that the voting was 11 to 9.

49 Berkeley, op. cit., p. 71.
50 H. Nicolson, *King George* (London, 1952), p. 467, quoted in Berkeley, op. cit., p. 92.
51 Snowden, *An Autobiography*, p. 953.
52 Ibid., p. 954.
53 PRO, MacDonald Diaries, 20 October 1934.
54 Snowden, *An Autobiography*, p. 955.
55 Ibid., p. 957.

13 'Bolshevism Run Mad': Snowden, the National Governments and his Declining Years, 1931–7

Snowden's association with the first two National Governments was brief and unhappy, lasting for little more than a year. During this period he was forced to abandon his support for the gold standard, though he fell short of supporting protectionism. Such unfortunate aberrations were blamed upon the Labour Party, whose unreasonable attitude had, according to Snowden, intensified the financial crisis. Indeed, Snowden regarded the Labour Party's opposition to his economic policies as giving him leave to ignore his initial declaration that he would only enter a National Government in order to deal with the crisis and would not support that government when it went to the electorate. He not only supported the National Government during the election of October 1931 but declared that the Labour Party's policy was 'Bolshevism Run Mad'.[1]

As Chancellor of the Exchequer of a hastily contrived National Government, Snowden was given free reign to put forward the type of budget he had envisaged whilst in the Labour administration. On 3 September 1931 he emphasized to his Cabinet colleagues 'the importance of preparing the public mind in a general way for a considerable increase in taxation'.[2] On 10 September he introduced his emergency budget in which he announced tax increases of about £81 million, a package of £56 million in cuts which had been approved by the Labour Cabinet plus a reduction of £13 million on unemployment benefits. But there was one respect in which he moved from his earlier economic stand. Faced with an extremely deflationary budget he finally relented on the Sinking Fund contribution, reducing the debt remission from £50 million to £32,500,000. If Snowden had been prepared to accept that strategy in mid-August 1931 it is possible that the second Labour Government would not have needed to divide on the issue of unemployment benefits.

It looked as though Snowden's emergency budget had done the trick and MacDonald considered it a 'Great triumph'.[3] Snowden recorded the great sense of achievement he felt, reporting that one political commentator had acknowledged that

> Mr. Snowden has had his hour, and has bidden such a farewell to politics as is given to few men for their retrospect. He could take the memories of his last Budget into retirement and live in content.[4]

It looked as though the budget had restored confidence in the pound. But a mutiny of naval ratings at Invergordon on 16 September, directed against the government's pay cuts, destroyed economic confidence: the run on the pound could not be halted and Snowden took Britain off the gold standard on 21 September 1931. The unthinkable had happened: the defence of a key element of the nineteenth-century economic philosophy, which Snowden had strongly supported, came to an end. Instead the British Government and other governments moved inexorably towards managed currencies, and the prospect of protectionism was revived. Just a month before, Snowden had been strongly defending the fixed parity and the gold standard. Now he accepted the need to allow the pound to decline, although he wished for a regulated fall. Snowden's justification for his action was that things had changed since August. The government had put forward a balanced budget, which meant that it would not have to print money and thus generate inflation. The suspension of gold was purely to deal with the excessive withdrawal of foreign deposits from London. Nevertheless, he did later claim that he saw no durable alternative to the gold standard, stating that 'I believe the countries will return to an improved Gold Standard'.[5]

Within a month of leaving the Labour Government and joining the National Government, Snowden had thus delivered two broadsides against the economic policies which he had staunchly advocated to the Labour Cabinet. To many Labour politicians it seemed that Snowden had compounded the deceptions he had practised in August 1931. By the end of September 1932, Snowden felt free to break his promise to the Colne Valley Labour Party not to fight against the Labour Party at any future election. His defence for supporting the National Government in the October 1931 General Election was that the Labour Party had been feckless and irresponsible throughout the financial crisis and that part of the crisis still remained to be tackled.

Yet there may have been other factors at play. On 28 September 1931 the National Executive of the Labour Party decided to expel Snowden, and all the other Labour ministers in the National Government, from the Party: 'it decided that Members of Parliament and others who are associated or in future associate themselves with the present Government thereby cease to be members of the Labour

Party'.[6] There was now considerable pressure on Snowden and MacDonald to give the new government a more permanent character and reluctantly, though almost inevitably, he was drawn into supporting the Conservative Party's decision to force a general election. He must have feared that a general election at this stage would produce an overwhelming Conservative majority in the National Government which would be strongly supportive of the protectionist measures which he so abhorred. But sucked into a political situation there appeared to be no escape route available except to support the National Government and the Conservative demand for an election. Snowden appears to have accepted this situation more readily than MacDonald who noted:

> I saw Snowden after it [the decision to call a general election] was over walking (crawling) down the corridor to the Ladies' Gallery – his last [visit]. He was unmoved apparently. It is all too terrible, but what else can be done? The people I care for in my heart suspect me & are confused. Will old relations & affections return? I shall try, but the machine Labour men will stand in the way.[7]

As Snowden made ready for his final departure from the Commons, the *Daily News* reported upon the scene. After the other MPs had departed, Snowden sat alone for fifteen minutes on the Treasury bench, his arms folded. 'He sat there like an image carved out of stone.'[8] He then hobbled out of the House of Commons for the last time.

Snowden was at his most vitriolic during the general election campaign. On 16 October he circulated an election letter to National Labour candidates, being too ill to tour the constituencies, attacking the irresponsibility of the Labour Party. The following day he broadcast through the BBC and condemned the Labour Party manifesto:

> I hope you have read the election programme of the Labour Party. It is the most fantastic and impracticable document ever put before the electors. All the derelict industries are to be taken over by the State and the taxpayer is to shoulder the losses. The banks and the financial houses are to be placed under the national ownership and control, which means, I suppose, that they are to be run by a joint committee of the Labour Party and the Trades Union Council. Your investments are to be ordered by some board, and your foreign investments are to be mobilised to finance this madcap policy.
>
> This is not Socialism. It is Bolshevism run mad.[9]

He also contrasted the Labour Party's 'revolutionary' policies with his own 'sane and evolutionary Socialism', justifying his support of the National Government in terms of the temporary need to carry through the national retrenchment policies which he saw as vital to the economic well-being of the country. He was offering the 'doctor's mandate' to the nation, a compromise measure which united the National Government in its election campaign which would otherwise have been fragmented between Conservatives who supported tariffs and Liberals who favoured free trade.[10]

Colin Cross has argued that it is generally accepted that this speech swung 'tens of thousands, possibly hundreds of thousands, of votes', presumably from Labour to the National Government.[11] It is impossible to calculate whether or not that was so. The fact is that the financial crisis and the British electoral system ensured that Labour alone would be penalized, not advantaged by an election. Snowden's position as the Chancellor of the Exchequer and an ex-Labour minister was probably of marginal significance.

The National Government won its expected victory. It had 554 supporters in the Commons – though 473 of them were in fact Conservatives. But Snowden was not one of the victors. In June 1931 he had decided not to contest any future parliamentary contests. It appeared that he might finally retire from politics but, in the wake of the National Government's election victory, MacDonald persuaded him to accept the post of Lord Privy Seal. This ranked high in status but involved no departmental duties. Also, on 17 November 1931, he accepted the offer of a peerage and, on 26 November, formally assumed the title of Lord Snowden of Ickornshaw, after his birthplace. The *Daily Express* cartoonist had a field day, depicting Snowden in all his robes passing by a mixed group of onlookers, whose comments included 'Hi! Come Orf It!!!, 'Now Ain't That Pretty', 'Blimey! Look Wot 'E's Got Out O The National Sweep!' and 'Pity He Missed the Lord Mayor's Show!'[12] The Labour press was more critical of a man who had once declared the necessity of abolishing the Lords. Snowden simply explained his action in terms of appeasing Ethel's demands: 'Ah! Snowden! Snowden! It's just Dead Sea Fruit – Dead Sea Fruit. But it's Mrs. Snowden, Mrs. Snowden.'[13]

In the House of Lords, Snowden was now on the periphery of political affairs, though he continued to exert some limited influence on MacDonald's National Government. He had advised MacDonald to appoint Walter Runciman, a free trader, to the Board of Trade and, in December 1931, joined the Cabinet Trade Committee set up to examine the trade balance. But he soon found himself at odds with the National Government's economic strategy. The Trade Committee, which met on five occasions between 16 December 1931 and 18 January, reported on 19 January in favour of reducing imports by imposing a general tariff of 10 per cent combined with a variable surtax on non-essential goods. The necessary legislation was enacted in March 1932.

Snowden protested at these moves. As early as December 1931, he informed MacDonald that

Some of us are perturbed about the rapidity with which we are drifting into a full Protectionist policy. We have accepted the doses which have been given up to now with reluctance, but it seems clear from what happened at the Cabinet this morning that a large section of the Cabinet are going to force the full Protectionist and Preference policy, including food taxes on practically every staple article of food. I feel that by making concessions in one direction and another to the Protectionists we are getting into a compromised position.

I feel that it is necessary that you should know how I am feeling about these matters. I cannot go on sacrificing beliefs and principles bit by bit until there are none left.[14]

Snowden then joined with Runciman, Sir David Maclean, Sir Herbert Samuel and Sir Archibald Sinclair to meet the Prime Minister in a deputation. But, according to Snowden, the meeting was unproductive and MacDonald appeared evasive and unwilling to resist Tory policy.

Pressure was later applied to Snowden to accept the proposed 10 per cent revenue tariff, but he would not relent. Having failed to deflect the Cabinet from its protectionist course he opposed the measure in the House of Lords. At the end of February 1932 he reminded the Lords that 'Free Trade is not dead. The generation which knew from experience the horror of starvation from Protection is gone. The new generation must learn what Protection means from its own experience and sufferings.'[15]

Snowden became even more frustrated when the government moved towards extending a measure of permanent tariffs and Imperial preference to the Empire through the Ottawa Conference of August 1932. Unable to compromise on free trade, there was every possibility that he would resign.

MacDonald noted the tensions which were developing within his Cabinet. He was worried by the opposition of free traders and, following the afternoon meeting of the Cabinet on 22 January 1932, wrote that there was

hopeless deadlock. Snowden, Samuel, Maclean & Sinclair intimated resignation. Not quite prepared for this although I knew that there had not been complete agreement, I had been led to understand that the minority would not go so far as to resign & end this Govt. 8.30 Saw them at Snowden's (72 Carlisle Mansions). Put their responsibility for the Nat. Govt; for the result of election; the issues national & internation [al], the position in which I was left. No avail. They admitted everything but would not budge. Maclean & Sinclair simple political minds; Samuel pettifogging . . .: Snowden just as stiff necked & unaccommodating as ever he has been.[16]

In the complicated in-fighting within the National Government,

Snowden remained convinced that he would not give way on free trade. He campaigned outside government, as well as inside, to maintain this vital principle. On 2 April 1932 he addressed an international conference to promote free trade among nations, held at the Victoria Hotel, Northumberland Avenue, Westminster. But this type of action was an irrelevancy to a government which was overwhelmingly supported by protectionists.

On 29 August Snowden wrote a letter to MacDonald informing him that the free-trade members would not acquiesce on the Ottawa agreement. To do so 'they would be justly objects of contempt and derision'.[17] On 17 September 1932 he wrote another letter to MacDonald about Ottawa 'which was plainly resignation'.[18] MacDonald saw him on 8 September at Carlisle Mansions:

> He had not read the Ottawa agreements as they were handed to him only as I sat there, but said he could not remain in office. The Tories had let us down: they could not respct other people's opinions; they could not work in a mixed term: they were IT; they were destroying our work & steadily insinuating their views everywhere; he pitied those who had come with us & had isolated themselves. I did not argue with him nor press him. He had too much truth on his side, though I should look at the landscape from a Different angle.[19]

Snowden was clearly determined to go, and on 28 September 1932 in a 'cold, repelling and vindictive' mood he announced his resignation to the Cabinet.[20]

> The Lord Privy Seal said he spoke for no Party but only for himself.... The reasons which led him to resign had already been fully and admirably expressed by the Home Secretary.... It was not only on the Ottawa agreement that he disagreed with his colleagues. In all these financial matters his own position had been very difficult and irksome, during the last many months. He had accepted the agreement to differ with reluctance. At that time Protection had not gone very far. Now the cumulative effect of the various measures amounted to a full system of Protection.... There was one point he wanted to maintain in advance, in case there was any misunderstanding hereafter. This was the pledge made at the last Election by the Prime Minister and himself had not been maintained and had certainly been violated. He did not think that on its Election pledges, the Government had any mandate for protective measures.[21]

In his book, *An Autobiography*, he noted that he could no longer remain a member of the government 'without a loss of self-respect'.[22]

The free trade principles was Snowden's final sticking point. Perhaps more than MacDonald, Snowden had entered the National Government in order to apply the distinctively Liberal solutions of 'Gladstonian' finance to the national crisis. By 1932 most of that strategy had been abandoned. Once free trade had been abandoned there was little reason for Snowden to remain in government.

Without party or political attachment Snowden now assumed the role of elder statesman. Now that his political importance was diminished he was free, a redundant and largely ignored figure, to indulge himself in the whims of a lifetime. His political outbursts and campaigning attracted very little serious consideration and his views on free trade and temperance were regarded as idiosyncratic by the mid-1930s and sparked only residual interest. During these years he was as driftwood in the stream of politics. Yet some sort of shape was given to his declining years through his hostility to MacDonald, the exigent need to earn a living and the blossoming of his personal and political relationship with David Lloyd George.

His dislike of MacDonald drew most attention. Snowden and MacDonald had clashed frequently throughout their political careers, and Snowden had practically accused him of lying to the 1914 'Coming of Age' Conference of the ILP. Yet the fine detail of their economic and social views had differed little up until 1932. Indeed, when Snowden resigned MacDonald stated that 'He and the Lord Privy Seal were old colleagues. Sometimes they disagreed, but generally they found themselves on the same platform.'[23] Both shared similar aspirations for the Labour Party and were doubtful and distrustful of the role of trade unions. But similar views and similar ambitions eschewed respect between these two politically ambitious politicians. Working closely together, their personal hostility was kept in check. However, after 1932 Snowden felt at liberty to criticize MacDonald openly.

His campaign against MacDonald began in earnest in May 1933 when he stunned the House of Lords with his 'Ferocious Attack on the Prime Minister'. One parliamentary correspondent reflected that he 'delivered what was hardly less than an impeachment of the Prime Minister'.[24] Snowden continued in the same vein when he spoke to the House of Lords on 3 July 1934. He mocked MacDonald's sincerity and maintained that the National Government was a fraud since 'Tories have got power for Tory purposes.' He said of MacDonald that 'Every time he speaks he exposes his ignorance or incapacity.'[25] And, in 1933, he was most critical of MacDonald's policy for unemployment.

> The Prime Minister's most recent statements on the subject show that he has frankly abandoned the task of providing employment by government help. With the gift of £10,000 to private charity he has suggested that the unemployed may be dealt with by teaching men how they may be able to furnish their homes, to make mats out of bits of old

> rope for a few pence. Such complacency in the face of such a terrible problem is driving millions to despair.[26]

Soon afterwards Snowden published *An Autobiography* in which he accused MacDonald of deliberately scheming to end the life of the second Labour Government. Politicians took note of his criticisms and those in the Labour Party enjoyed the spectacle of traitor number two attacking traitor number one. To the National Government, however, it was an embarrassment made all the more touchy by the fact that Snowden's attacks were so personal and vindictive. They listened but tried not to hear.

When Snowden resigned from the National Government he had not served long enough to receive a ministerial pension. This fact forced him to earn his living, once again, from journalism. As an ex-minister his services were much in demand and he wrote for a variety of papers, including the *Sunday Express*, the *Sunday Chronicle*, the *Daily Express*, the *Daily Mail* and the *Sunday Dispatch*. Colin Cross estimates that he earned about £2,000 per year from such work. He was, indeed, a prolific and wide-ranging columnist. He wrote extensively on financial matters, offered advice and criticism on successive budgets, was concerned to prevent another war with Germany, waxed lyrical about the virtues of temperance and advised parents not to send their children into 'dead-end' jobs.

Many of Snowden's views were idiosyncratic and anachronistic. For instance, his pre-war Radical attitudes had led him to oppose the First World War and, like many other Radicals of his type, he preferred Germany to France. In the inter-war period he had expressed his hostility to the Treaty of Versailles and was supportive of Germany when she reclaimed the Rhineland. Although he did attack Hitler's anti-semitism and the use of torture in German concentration camps, he was prepared to accept at face value Hitler's protestation of peace: 'There is no reason to suppose Hitler is not sincere in his pacific declarations. He realises that he needs peace for his work of internal reconstruction.'[27] These were views which he shared with David Lloyd George. But by the mid-1930s such views were very much out of touch with the political currents of the day. Public opinion was gradually moving against Hitler and the events in Germany, and most Labour Party branches were no longer willing to support the 'No More War' movement. Even the ILP had renounced its pacifism over the Spanish Civil War. Snowden was still shaping his attitudes on the basis of pre-1914 Radical sentiments and prejudices.

This was also evident in the attention he gave to the drink problem. In 1936 he wrote a pamphlet entitled *End This Colossal Waste: A Neglected Palliative for Unemployment*. Despite the numerous social surveys of the inter-war years which indicated that unemployment, old age and ill health were the major causes of poverty, Snowden believed that alcohol consumption was a major contributory factor to poverty. His argument was that the expansion of the British home market out of slump depended upon three factors – efficient production, effective purchasing power and the elimination of waste in production and consumption. He was particularly concerned with the last of these and related how drink brought about the dissipation of the workforce and a reduction in working efficiency. He ended with an appeal:

> If we do recognise the tremendous economic waste of the expenditure on Drink; if we are anxious to do something to stimulate useful trade and employment; and beyond that to raise the moral tone of the nation, to improve the physical condition of our people, and to give a better chance to the children, so that when they are grown to be men and women they may be better fitted to take an intelligent interest in and to solve the other grave social problems which perplex us today, we should take a deeper interest than in the past in this most important question of the National Waste in our Expenditure on Drink.[28]

Snowden's views were clearly anachronistic in the more informed social environment of the 1930s.

Snowden also expressed interest in the American New Deal but was particularly critical of President Roosevelt's inclination to force up prices by destroying output. He felt that the artificial creation of higher prices could never be successful in the long term. In addition, he maintained that large-scale government expenditure could only be feasible if it were the result of a budget surplus. It was within this context that he supported Lloyd George's New Deal in 1935.

Lloyd George had launched his programme at a lecture delivered at Bangor on 17 January 1935. In effect he offered a revised and updated version of his 1929 manifesto *We Can Conquer Unemployment*, which had advocated a policy of government intervention which would be self-financing and which would generate employment and the better use of resources. He also drew inspiration from Roosevelt's New Deal.

Snowden and Lloyd George had become close friends in the 1920s. They lived near each other, did not see class as the basis for Radicalism and so cherished the idea of some type of alliance between the forces of the centre, and both were out of date by 1935. These elder statesmen of British politics shared many views, among them the belief that Hitler wanted peace and the conviction of the need to control drink. Lloyd George had been as adamant as Snowden about the temperance issue during the First World War. It was one of the few issues on which he was consistent throughout his political career. Indeed, he wrote the introduction to Snowden's temperance pamphlet, *End This Colossal Waste*.

Snowden was supportive of Lloyd Geoge's 1935 programme. He

approved of the boldness of the proposal and admired the sensible and modest approach it entailed. Writing to Lloyd George he stated that

> The crusade you are beginning for a great and united national effort to revive industry and to rescue the mass of our population from hardship and suffering of unnecessary poverty deserves, and I believe will receive, the support of earnest and sympathetic men and women of all parties and of that large and increasing number of electors who have no party affiliations. This is a time for action ... the country is waiting for an inspiring lead on a programme of courageous national reconstruction.[29]

Like Lloyd George, he did not see class as the base for Radicalism. He also disliked the way in which national resources were wasted, and maintained that they should be organized so as to improve output, reduce unemployment and to provide higher living standards.

Soon afterwards Snowden published his own pamphlet on Lloyd George's ideas entitled *Mr. Lloyd George's New Deal*. The main thrust of his argument was that he had supported a programme of public works as the Chancellor of the Exchequer in the second Labour Government, and was willing to do so now, since his own financial actions in September 1931 now permitted the National Government the latitude with which to pursue such a policy. He stressed that

> Now the financial position is quite different. A policy which was temporarily inadvisable 4 years ago has become a national necessity today. The fact is realised by men of outstanding position who, at the time of the crisis in 1931, demanded retrenchment in national expenditure.[30]

The passage is revealing for it is clear that Snowden was still committed to balancing the budget and that his approval of state intervention could only be contemplated within the confines of such a budget. Snowden's vision of the New Deal was thus not that of printing money, nor of increasing government borrowing and financing activity through a deficit budget. His subsequent comments look advanced until one realizes the constraints which he had set. Nevertheless, he was willing to contemplate a degree of state intervention which he would not have accepted in 1929. Before the second Labour Government came to power he had constantly stressed that state schemes which were not self-financing would only divert funds away from equally productive private activity. He now seemed to accept that the state might become involved in more activities without necessarily damaging private industry:

> a vast amount of useful and necessary work waiting to be done which lies outside the sphere of private enterprise. If the State undertook this

work it would not depress capital industry, but on the contrary . . . would stimulate such interest.[31]

In addition he supported Lloyd George's proposal to increase British exports to the Empire and approved of the proposal to set up a National Investment and Development Board drawn from industry, finance, workers and consumers. It was envisaged that such a board would be a substitute for the Cabinet, which provided no effective leadership on finance. Snowden's only objection was that, unlike Lloyd George, he did not feel that the Bank of England was in need of reform.

Both men were also drawn together in the activities of the Council of Action for Peace and Reconstruction. This body, which appears to have been dominated by Anglican priests and Nonconformist ministers, had Lloyd George as its President and Chairman and Philip Snowden as one of its Council members. The Viscountess Snowden was chairman of the Executive Committee of the Women's Council. Its main policies were close to Philip's heart, being the pursuit of disarmament and social and economic reconstruction in Britain. It supported the League of Nations, believing that it should call a world conference to bring about a general reduction of tariffs and the promotion of free trade, which it was felt would improve the prospects of world peace. It was also concerned to find work for and feed the unemployed: 'The Nation's energies should be directed to seeing that the people get the right kind of food for sound health.'[32] The Council captured the mood of Liberal, progressive and Christian sentiments in the mid-1930s and was dominated by the Christian conscience – with half the twelve area organizations being run by priests or ministers and priests, the most important being W. Coggan MA, filling the two posts of honorary secretary. Snowden obviously joined this body because it represented the type of policies which he had pursued throughout his life and fulfilled his sense of being needed.

Snowden's 'wilderness years' came to an end with his death, due to a heart attack and after a long illness, in the early hours of 15 May 1937. He was cremated at Woking and a week later his ashes were scattered on the open moor at Ickornshaw, about one mile from his birthplace of Cowling, at a ceremony presided over by Rev. Alfred Booth of Cowling Methodist Church and attended by between 2,000 and 3,000 people.

His death provoked an instant outpouring of emotive recollections. Lloyd George declared Snowden to have been one of the most able Labour politicians ever returned to Parliament. Those who attended the burial service at which his ashes were scattered were similarly effusive. Sir Ben Turner, an old ILP colleague, one-time MP for Dewsbury and former president of the Trades Union Congress, asserted, in a rhetorical flourish, 'He is not dead: his work is living and his deeds are living with us today. The work he has done during the last 40 years cannot die.'[33] Ben Riley, Labour MP for Dewsbury, added 'He was certainly the most outstanding figure in the public life of our part of the country for the past 150 years.'[34] But it was Willie Leach, though he was not present at the service, who perhaps best expressed the mood of Snowden's old colleagues:

> We were very close friends for a period extending over 40 years, and I always felt a very high appreciation of his powers as a Socialist propagandist. He earned the affection and trust of millions of working people and it was a source of great grief to us that he should sever the relationship with the Socialist movement as he did in 1931.[35]

Leach had known Snowden from his early ILP days and had been with him in Parliament and government during the inter-war years.

It is perhaps a sad, though revealing, reflection that neither the Labour Party nor the Independent Labour Party sent any official representatives to Snowden's burial service, nor the memorial service which was held at St Margaret's, Westminster on 26 May. Those Labour politicians who did attend did so on a personal basis. Indeed, it is even sadder to reflect that the Labour Party's National Executive Committee, which had a practice of announcing the deaths of local Labour worthies at its meetings, should not have noted the more substantial, if erratic, contribution of Snowden to the Labour movement. His death goes unrecorded in their minutes. Even MacDonald, whose personal relations with Snowden were never very good, acknowledged his work.

> First news of the day that Snowden has died. Sent sympathies to Lady Snowden & at once received a gratifying message. Sent tribute to the morning papers which rang up. His bitterness concealed his heart. When I last saw him about a year ago I told him that nothing he would do (I had heard that he was to turn some of his squirt upon me) would ever make me forget the long friendship ... & even then he seemed as though he would like to bite my hand. It was disappointing.... Deeply do I feel Snowden's passing.[36]

A year later, in the summer of 1938, a nine-foot cairn was unveiled by Lord Sankey on Ickornshaw moor to mark the spot where Snowden's ashes had been scattered. On the plate of the cairn was written the following inscription:

IN THIS PLACE
MINGLED WITH THE SOIL
AND NEAR THE FRIENDS HE LOVED
ARE THE ASHES OF
PHILIP SNOWDEN

FIRST VISCOUNT OF ICKORNSHAW
WHO LIVED HIS WHOLE LIFE IN THE
SERVICE OF THE COMMON PEOPLE
AND DIED IN LOVE OF
HIS NATIVE LAND
ON MAY 15 1937

Notes

1 *Daily Telegraph*, 19 October 1931.
2 PRO, Cab. 23, meeting 3 September 1931.
3 PRO, 30/69, 1753, MacDonald Diaries, 11 September 1931.
4 Snowden, *An Autobiography*, p. 971.
5 Ibid., p. 977.
6 Ibid., p. 987.
7 PRO, MacDonald Diaries, 7 October 1931.
8 Cross, op. cit., p. 314.
9 *Daily Telegraph*, 19 October 1931.
10 Cross, op. cit., p. 311.
11 Ibid., p. 320.
12 *Daily Express*, 19 November 1931.
13 Cross, op. cit., p. 324.
14 Snowden, *An Autobiography*, p. 1006.
15 Cross, op. cit., p. 328.
16 PRO, MacDonald Diaries, 22 January 1932.
17 Marquand, op. cit., p. 725.
18 PRO, MacDonald Diaries, 9 September 1932.
19 Ibid.
20 Ibid., 28 September 1932.
21 PRO, Cab. 23, meeting 28 September 1932.
22 Snowden, *An Autobiography*, p. 1081.
23 PRO, Cab. 23, meeting 28 September 1932.
24 *Daily Telegraph*, 25 May 1933.
25 Cross, op. cit., p. 333.
26 *Sunday Express*, 5 February 1933.
27 Ibid., 4 February 1934.
28 P. Snowden, *End this Colossal Waste: A Neglected palliative for Unemployment by The Rt. Hon. Viscount Snowden and a foreword by The Rt. Hon. David Lloyd George, OM, MP* (United Kingdom Alliance, London, 1936), p. 16.
29 Lloyd George Papers, G 18/7/11, 14 January 1935.
30 Loc. cit., p. 26.
31 Ibid., p. 6.
32 *Peace and Social Justice: Being a Statement of the Policy of the Council of Action for Peace and Reconstruction* (n.d., n.p.), p. 14.
33 *Keighley News*, 29 May 1937.
34 Ibid.
35 Ibid., 22 May 1937.
36 PRO, MacDonald Diaries, 15 May 1937.

14 Verdict

Philip Snowden remains an immensely fascinating and controversial figure. Rather like MacDonald he has been enveloped in a cloud of criticism and consigned to the 'traitor's grave' by the Labour Party and its historians. The epithets have flowed fast and furious. He has been described as visionless, venomous, narrow-minded, spiteful and bitter. Many have seen him as a grudging and unfeeling man. Yet even in the mid-1930s he was not entirely forgotten by his old colleagues and still communicated on friendly terms with Fred Jowett, Ben Riley and other members of the pre-1914 ILP. Yet, underpinning all these views has been one enduring question – why did Philip do it?

There were clearly many reasons for his actions in 1931. One vital factor is the way in which the Labour Party changed between 1900 and 1951. Snowden's generation of ILP members, influenced by nonconformist and Liberal Radical views had grown out of touch with the new more trade union-orientated policies of the Labour Party and were bound to come into conflict in their approach to matters such as unemployment benefit. A new generation of Labour politicians had emerged and Snowden noted this in a letter to Fred Jowett, who, for different reasons, was also out of the mainstream of Labour politics by the mid-1930s.

> A few former comrades and colleagues keep in touch with me but the younger generation are strangers. It is in a way sad that we should have been alienated from the movement we have served so long and so deeply.[1]

Snowden probably deserved the obloquy which was heaped upon him. He had helped to hand over power to Labour's political enemies. He has been openly hostile to his former colleagues and his reference to Labour's electoral programme of 1931 as 'Bolshevism run mad' aggrieved many of his former supporters. Of the one major charge levelled against him – that he betrayed the Labour Party in 1931 – there is no doubt. Nevertheless, it must be emphasized that the course of action he took on 1931 was perfectly consistent with his previously declared views. He remained faithful to the Liberal Radical shibboleths of his youth and invariably advocated a set of economic policies which focused upon the need to balance the budget, to maintain free trade and to operate the gold standard. It was the demands of his economic philosophy which led him to advocate a reduction of unemployment benefits in 1931.

In many respects he was typical of one section of the Party – the Liberal Radical/ILP group – which had become ensconced in the policy making of the Labour Party well before the successful 1906 General Election. Along with MacDonald, who was of the same school of thought, he believed that the Labour Party would achieve its mandate for socialism through the growth and development of capitalism. It speaks volumes for the intellectual poverty of the Labour Party that Snowden's views should carry such weight and support up to the crisis of 1931. It is true that trade union support for the First World War had isolated Snowden from the bulk of Labour opinion and that his Liberal Radical emphasis upon peace was rejected. But his commitment to economic retrenchment was not seriously challenged by Labour politicians until the trade unions were inevitably forced to defend the living standards of their members. It was a gut reaction against the economic implications of Snowden's deflationary policies which forced the split rather than some sophisticated and coherent economic thought. In 1931 it was not so much that the class of 1906 defected, for practically all the 1906 and 1910 entrants were no longer MPs, so much as the fact that the leading advocates of Liberal Radical ideas moved into the National Government.

Although Snowden was both consistent in the views he expressed and typical of a particular genre of Labour politicians, he must personally take some responsibility for the events of 1931. His upbringing had stifled his vision and left him uncritical of the economic institutions – the Treasury, the Bank of England and the City – which were heavily influencing the responses to the financial crisis. He was an outsider who could sustain no alternative and durable cultural and political vision – when there were alternatives. The ILP, Mosley, the Lloyd George section of the Liberal Party and Ernest Bevin had suggested a number of diverse expansionary strategies to deal with unemployment and bring about economic recovery. Snowden was able to ignore these, helped partly by the fact that his advocacy of the need for free trade did evoke some responses from the expansionist camp, some members of whom also feared the impact of protection as much as he did. Robert Skidelsky has noted that the unusual situation of 1931 demanded that the government should risk a new strategy. Snowden was not the man to rise to that challenge. He could not jettison the economic policies of his youth. Instead, he helped to create a National Government specifically formed to endorse the deflationary policies which he advocated.

There is obviously a sense in which Snowden was incidental to the events – and was presiding over matters over which he had limited control. Nevertheless, it was his fixity of purpose and lack of vision which helped to limit the government's responses and force the split in the second Labour Government. But if he is to be held culpable for the events of 1931 then so must the Labour Party for allowing his views, first fixed in the 1890s, to govern its economic approach for so long.

Throughout the 1930s, and indeed ever since, the Labour Party has attempted to distance itself from the events of 1931 by disowning those leaders who deserted. This scapegoat approach may comfort the Labour Party but, given its earlier compliance with Snowden's views, is something of an indecency. Yet it would appear that the Party was kinder to Snowden than it was to MacDonald, recognizing that some of the principles which had led him to split with Labour in 1931 led him to resign from the National Government in September 1932. In even the most critical of studies there has been at least a recognition of his work within the Labour Party – though often accompanied with some barbed comment. This was also true of his obituaries. For instance, one noted that

> Philip Snowden was a man of rare and distinguished gifts, and for one great service he will ever be remembered in the Socialist movement: he was in the forefront of those who created so powerful a movement that when he tried to destroy his work he failed in the attempt and went into oblivion.[2]

And it should never be forgotten that he did contribute to the events which saw the Labour Party hand over political power to the Conservative-dominated National Government. For this reason, if no other, he will continue to deserve the epithet of 'political blackleg'.

Notes

1 Cross, op. cit., p. 339.
2 *Leeds Weekly Citizen*, 21 May 1937.

Epilogue

Philip Snowden was survived by his wife, Ethel, who was just as idiosyncratic as Philip and spent the remaining years of her life cultivating respect for her husband, condemning the Labour leadership, campaigning to be returned to the board of the BBC, and reflecting upon the trustworthiness of Hitler. Indeed, she attended the Nuremburg Rally and reflected that Hitler was a 'simple man of great personal integrity'.[1]

Subsequently she revised her views and supported Britain in the war effort, and during the Second World War became a great defender of public and personal morality. She believed that there was too much drunkenness amongst service women and that moral standards were declining.

In the immediate post-war years she was critical of the Attlee Labour governments, which she felt were remote from Philip's vision of socialism. Indeed, in February 1930 she gave her political support to Cyril Black, a militant teetotaller, who stood as Conservative candidate for Wimbledon. She called him 'a tried man of progressive outlook' and wished him 'overwhelming victory'.[2]

Ethel's active life was circumscribed in 1947, when she suffered a stroke. From then onwards she was confined to a nursing home, where she died of a second stroke on 22 February 1951. She was 69 years of age. Her remains were cremated and her ashes were scattered over the moorland which had received Philip's ashes in 1937. A plaque was later attached to the cairn on Ickornshaw Moor, just below that honouring Philip. It reads:

HERE ALSO ARE THE ASHES OF ETHEL
HIS BELOVED AND DEVOTED WIFE
WHO SHARED HIS LABOURS FOR
SO MANY YEARS AND DIED
ON FEBRUARY 22ND 1951

Notes

1 Cross, op. cit., p. 343.
2 Ibid., p. 344.

Extracts from the Writings and Speeches of Philip Snowden

'The Teetotal Paradox of the Country', 1 January 1895

This was the first substantial piece of writing that Snowden ever undertook as a socialist. It was a 3,000-word letter to the editor of the *Keighley News*, which was published on 12 January 1895. It was reproduced on 10 January 1920, in a small pamphlet which was issued in honour of Philip Snowden's twenty-five years as a socialist. Much of it has also appeared in Colin Cross, *Philip Snowden* (1966), pp. 25–28.The main argument is that no matter how thrifty the 203 families in Cowling were, no matter how temperate, there would be many families still living in poverty. Utopia would not come from adopting temperance and teetotalism but from ethical socialism and the moral values of Christianity.

★ ★ ★

> But my purpose is to prove by a few facts and figures that the vampire of capitalism and landlordism on the one hand, and on the other hand acquaintance of the thrifty teetotaller, and the competition of labour in a lesser degree, have brought about in Cowling, prematurely, a condition of things, which would follow everywhere by the national adoption of temperance, unless the present inexorable laws of political economy ceased to operate, and some innovative ... principle of protecting the labourer against the microbes of commercialism, and securing to him the fruits of his labour could be established.

The letter then goes on to discuss the questions raised by Mr. Horner, a Keighley Labour leader, of a Mr Pickles, enquiring into the standard of living of the people of Cowling over the last fifteen years when they had embraced teetotalism and saved money through savings banks. In answer to the question 'do not the men in Cowling earn sufficient to support a family without wife and child labour?', Snowden continued in the following manner:

In 142 cases, or 70 per cent, the wives have to work in the factory. In these families 90 per cent of the children over eleven are factory operatives. In the remaining 61 families the wives are mostly aged women who would gladly be in the mill if they could get, but they have been driven out by the competition of younger hands, or their family of workers is so large as to compel the mother to be confined to her domestic duties. In the extremely few cases where younger married women are kept at home, they take in children to nurse, or do some other work to 'addle a bit o' summat'. It is a reproach for a young married woman with only a house to follow, and herself, a husband and one or two children to wait upon to stay away from the mill. The gospel of thrift as taught here tells her it would seem her better to be trying to do her share towards putting something by for a rainy day.

[Snowden then examined what had happened to Cowling in the previous ten years, a period of hard work and thift.] In Cowling, at least, it is capitalism, not capitalists, which is responsible for the results I will now summarise.

(1) Wages have gone down 50 per cent. (2) Rents have gone up 50 per cent. (3) Population has gone down by 5 per cent in ten years. (4) A married man cannot keep up a house without wife and child labour.

This is the result of the 'almost total adoption of temperance principles'. This is the teetotal solution of the social problem. An isolated community of practical, hard-headed, thrifty, teetotal factory operatives have solved the complex social problem, banished poverty, established brotherhood by the simple expedient of closing three beershops and building in their place a public house with double the aggregate drinking facilities. Could anything be simpler? Utopia-founders note!

I ... will now, if you will permit me, give my version of a fact which Mr. Pickles is particularly proud. The factory people of Cowling have £22,000 in the Penny Bank (£10 a head). They have. To somebody's shame be it said. If I were to quote the fact that this country spends £130 million a year on drink as proof of the wealth and prosperity of the nation, what would Mr. Pickles say? 'The maddest nonsense ever talked outside Bedlam.' And that would be the truth, but not half as true as the fact that the £22,000 in Cowling Penny Bank represents the moral, physical and intellectual degradation of a community of the best brain and muscle to be found in 'Merrie' England; the unsexing and condemning to slavery of what should have been pure and cultured womanhood; the withholding from boys and girls of every advantage which, as God's creatures and heirs to all the ages, they have a right to demand. It represents our money valuation of the sacrifice involved in little babies being torn from their mothers' breasts for twelve hours a day; of schoolchildren shivering in the snow on winter nights, homeless till the mill stops; ... It represents, in short, every charge ever brought against the established order by every agitator, from the maddest street-corner orator to the arch-agitator Christ Himself; it represents injustice doubly damned, because inflicted on those whose virtues are made instruments to scourge them. It is this sturdy spirit of independence, that desire to be self-respecting and respected, the inherent trait of emulation, which we as Socialists expect to be such powerful forces in social regeneration; it is these virtues which, struggling for material embodiment and yet being too weak and ignorant to make a fitting environment, sacrifice everything to the hope of being able, by incessant toil, to preserve in some measure that same independence and self-respect when physically unable to provide for it from day to day. They are heroes, these despised factory men and women. They are resigned to their lot; scarce ever a murmer is heard....

... Mr. Pickles is interested in Cowling. He may be pleased to know that even here we have a younger generation of thinking men who refuse to accept this 'teetotal paradise' as a State Utopia. Their unregenerate hearts refuse to accept as eternal a Divine order which punishes the innocent and rewards the guilty, which knows no higher ideal of life than a sordid struggle for material existence, and where Christian virtues shine with divinest lustre in calm resignation to oppression and undeserved poverty. And they, too, are inspired by faith and hope. By faith in God and His humanity; by hope that the coming change is nigh when a nation's wealth shall be estimated, not in silver and gold, but in the realised aspirations of an enlightened people, and in the merchandise which is better than the merchandise of silver and the gain thereof than fine gold.

'The Two Salvations'

This extract is taken from an article which Philip Snowden wrote for the *Labour Prophet* in April 1898. A section from this article, dealing with Snowden's religious experiences in childhood, has already been quoted extensively in Chapter 2. This extract follows on from that and indicates Snowden's view that personal salvation was not sufficient to regenerate the world from social chaos. Those who had found personal salvation had a duty to examine the social problems of society in order to lessen individual suffering, which was not the result of individual fault, and to realize the 'New Jerusalem' on earth.

★ ★ ★

Most of us who are grown to men and women have at one time or another had experience of this method of obtaining salvation [referring to his juvenile experiences of hell and damnation in the Methodist Church]. But this is not one of the two salvations of which I wish to write. For salvation from hell for original sin is getting out of date. With another generation of School Board education it will disappear altogether. I now know that my inability to obtain salvation was not due to the outraged justice to a loving Father, but because I was unfortunately less imaginative and less emotional, but not less sincere, than my fellow penitents.

But among those who are agreed that the object of salvation should be, not to save us from the consequences of sin, but from the committal of sin, there is a grave difference of opinion as to the means by which this agreed object is to be attained. We are all familiar with the man who tells us that he agrees with Socialism at every point but we are going the wrong way to secure it. We must begin with the individual; get the individual heart all right and then I suppose a perfect society will be spontaneously added unto it. It is a striking commentary on the limited capacity of average intelligence that such a charge as this can be urged against us, when all our missionary efforts are directed to the individual, are appeals to him to realise his individual power and his individual responsibility. We are entirely at one with those who see the necessity for individual regeneration, but we recognise that social evils are of such a character as to be altogether beyond the power of even the regenerated individual to remove. The man who believes that personal salvation, improvement in personal character, is sufficient, stops short with the discovery of half the truth. The individual possesses the power, within certain limits, to mould his environment; the environment influences the character, though not wholly, yet to a very considerable extent. Here and there we have an individual whose strength of character is so powerful that he is able to rise above adverse circumstances, but the majority are crushed by the weight of social oppression which, strive as they may, they have not the power to overcome.... It is the conditions under which the people are compelled by our industrial system to live which inevitably breed the class of people whose character we so much deplore. To change these conditions, which are preventing the individual regeneration of the masses, is the social salvation which it is necessary to preach and put into practice as the complement to the preaching of individual salvation. And by improving the condition under which the people live we make the work of individual regeneration easier and possible. We all know that it is the poorest and most ignorant who are the least conscious of the horror of their condition and who are most difficult to be impressed. It seems as though deepening poverty were an opiate numbing the powers of self-reliance and producing the feeling of indifference and contentment. The appetite grows by what it feeds upon; by giving improved conditions we create a discontent with anything less and a desire for something better.

That personal religion alone is not sufficient to regenerate the world our social chaos is a standing witness; and this failure applies not to one only but to all the religions of the world. Such teaching has failed to recognise the necessity for a congenial soil and atmosphere in which the new-born aspirations of the individual might grow and flourish. The Christian Church of our country, especially since it became a victim to the Individualistic revival following the economic changes of three hundred years, has confined itself exclusively to the preaching of personal regeneration as the cure for all worldly ills, and it has therefore done nothing, unless by accident, for the social amelioration of the people. And it is not possible that it could be otherwise; for if we believe in Individualism, we believe that the individual is an all-powerful and independent being, and that he has within himself, or by individual help of God, the power to mould his own condition; and thinking this we must believe also that individual fault. Holding this opinion the Christian

Church has seen no necessity for teaching anything but the importance of the individual making his own private arrangements with his Creator. But in saying that the Christian Church has done nothing for the social amelioration of the people I am not denying that it has done much by way of charity for individual sufferers. For when a man gets the love of God into his heart, the sufferings of others begin to appeal to his sympathies. He feels a desire to do something to help them; but as no amount of changed heart can give a man greater practical knowledge, he can discern no way to help the suffering but by charity. This alone is sufficient reason why the personal salvation of churches can never regenerate the world. We want something more than sympathy or love. This the personal salvation will supply. We want the knowledge of how we can best help others. The affections should be the motive power, but the intellect must be the guiding hand. But we who have given some consideration to the cause of individual suffering, are convinced that such suffering need not be eternal, but that the remedy is at hand if we would but apply it; and knowing this, what we ask for is not charity but justice; not shortsighted benevolence but a cure for the disease. It is the duty of all who claim to have found personal salvation to seek out the causes of these social evils and irregularities, and to try to obtain full salvation by making for themselves and for all humanity a material habitation where all that is best may have every encouragement to grow. The greatest efforts to attain a high individual character and yet to be indifferent to the conditions of others – if we could imagine such a thing – will never save a man, no more than earnest efforts for Social Reform if accompanied by an inconsistent private character; for to use an Eastern simile, Personal Salvation and Social Salvation are like two palm trees which bear no fruit unless they grow side by side.

And I think we who are engaged in preaching the necessity of dual salvation have much reason to be satisfied with the success of our humble efforts. On every hand there are signs that the need for full salvation – salvation from violation of all law and order – is becoming increasingly recognised. I have found everywhere men upon whom the principles of Socialism have had a remarkable effect in the raising of their personal character. Socialism has regenerated them in the truest sense. They have become better fathers, better husbands, better citizens; more sympathetic, more earnest, more self-denying men. And this same spirit is everywhere at work throughout the world. This is the Spirit of Truth come to lead us unto all Truth. Under the spell of its power the old men are dreaming dreams and the young men are seeing visions; under its influence all oppression and wrong must fall, for it will still go forward, conquering and to conquer, until it has brought down the New Jerusalem on the cities of the earth.

The Christ that is to be

This pamphlet was originally published by the ILP, London, in 1903, and is perhaps the best example of Snowden's faith in the ethical and individual basis of socialism. It was frequently republished and was the basis of a lecture which Snowden regularly performed in his early years. The ethical socialism which he preached asserted the equality of man, an equality based upon the intrinsic value of human beings. But he believed that the objectives of ethical Socialism could only be achieved if the capitalist economic system was replaced by a socialist one, where land and industry came under public ownership. He also provided a utopian vision of a world where poverty, hatred, bitterness and strife have ceased to exist. He united politics with religion to produce the socialist crusade of righteousness.

★ ★ ★

> The life of Christ is the great example of human perfection. His precepts are widely accepted as the supreme guide to the attainment and practice of personal righteousness.... To-day the nominal, if not the real, worship of Christ is acknowledged in a million temples, and men of every nation and colour are joined outwardly at least in acknowledging that without distinction of race or tongue, they are all one in the sonship of Christ Jesus.... Never were the Churches more materialised than today. Never was the Church more the slave of rich men, who look upon the Church, aye, and its ministers too, as a valuable commercial asset. Never did the Church cling more tenaciously to its pagan creeds, for never did its priesthood realise more clearly that the final death-struggle between reason and superstition is close at hand. The recent bitter struggle over the education question proves that the Church realises that it holds its power by the influence it is able to exercise through ignorance and superstition on weak and unreasoning minds.

He goes on to argue that despite its faults, Christianity obviously appealed to eternal human needs.

> But the recognition of the fact that there is in Christian teaching certain vital eternal truths in no way involved acceptance of everything which Christ taught or is said to have taught. The rejection even of the belief in the personal Christ does not diminish, indeed to the highly cultured mind it increases, the value of the teaching attributed to Christ, because it is probable that much of the teaching attributed to Christ represents rather the highest collective moral ideas of his time.
>
> ... But Christ has lived and conquered because His teachings have appealed to the eternal needs of humanity, because His life is the promise of the human life which is yet to be. The growth of human knowledge ... may tend to change or to modify the meaning of certain New Testament texts, or to reject certain statements attributed to Christ, yet human experience, the growth of knowledge and social and industrial development, all go to emphasise the vital truth of the fundamental principle of the New Testament teaching. The law of sacrifice, the saving of the individual life by losing the individual life in the common life, which is the

foundation of Christ's teaching, is indeed proved by scientific discovery and by all human experience to be the fundamental law of life, the law by which the mother rears her child, the law which holds and binds men together in society. And with this knowledge a new conception of the meaning and purpose of the sacrifice on the Cross is dawning upon an enlightened world. In view of this, the sacrifice of Christ is not regarded in the pagan light of the laying down of an innocent life to satisfy the vengeance of an outraged Deity. Salvation by the blood of Christ in the light of this knowledge means, not that that sacrifice is a substitute for sacrifice by others, but it is an example that only by such sacrifice can others be saved. And with this knowledge the individual consciousness is passing into a consciousness of the social life.

This law of sacrifice, this law of love, of association, of co-operation, is not only the foundation of Christian teaching, but it is the basis of all the great ethical religions of the world and of all schools of morality. Not by individual selfishness or national selfishness has the progress of the human race been advanced. Men who have sacrificed themselves for the sake of what they believed to be the truth, have been instruments by which succeeding generations have been raised to a higher morality and to a higher civilisation. Just as the arisen Christ is the symbol of the triumph of sacrifice over death, so men have ever risen to higher things "on stepping-stones of their dead selves." And the religion of the future is to be this religion of the common life, this religion of salvation by losing one's life by finding salvation in the common life. The religion of the future will recognise the unity of all men. It will have for its ideal the complete organic unity of the whole human race. And this religion will be a political religion. It will be a religion which will seek to realise its ideal in our industrial and social affairs by the application and use of political methods. If Christianity is to be of any use it must be applied to our everyday life, and the only way in which principles, either Christian or otherwise, can be applied to social and industrial conditions is through the agency of political means. The popular conception of politics as something apart from religion, that politics is a thing too profane to be mentioned on the Lord's Day or in the House of God, that idea, so sedulously fostered in some quarters, is a cunning device of the devil to serve his own ends; just in the same way as the popular impression that politics is something apart from bread and butter, and shorter hours and better homes and better industrial conditions, just as the idea is fostered by the possessing class who use and control political power in order to maintain and strengthen their own unjust monopoly. There can be no separation between politics and religion. Law makers and administrators are inspired by certain ideas, and if these ideas be not moral then the law and its administration will be immoral. We cannot have a healthy religious life side by side with a corrupt political system. The two things are inseparable, each will partake of the character of the other, and the religion of the future will be an application of the moral truths of religion through politics to our industrial and social conditions.

This ideal of religion as saving one's life in the common life; this new conception of politics as a means of realizing this religion; all this to-day may seem far away, but it is the only way in which individual and social salvation can be attained. And in spite of so much around us opposed to the coming of this kingdom of righteousness, there are signs on every hand of a great and righteous power at work in the world.... There are signs on every hand that this social spirit is being awakened. The individual is feeling the throbbing of a new social consciousness; the Sun of Righteousness is rising with healing in its wings. The Christ that is to be appears. And this spirit of Christ, of love, of sacrifice, is taking possession of men's minds, and under its inspiration, old forms, old institutions, old passions will disappear, and a new brighter social order will arise. It is the promised New Jerusalem. The horrible social conditions existing to-day – poverty on the one hand and riches on the other – arduous toil on the one hand, luxurious idleness on the other, these will give way before this divine impulse, and the poverty of the many and the luxury of the few will join hands in a union of contented happiness for all. The horrible social conditions of to-day cannot continue before the diffusion of this social spirit. And this awakened social consciousness believed that hidden somewhere in the destiny of the human race is a social order in which it shall not be necessary for millions to toil hard and long for a miserable pittance that denies the opportunity for a happy, a healthy, and a cultured life. It believes in the possibility of our increased power over nature, and increased capacity for producing wealth being used not as now to add to the poverty and degradation of the many to increase the enormous riches of the few, but rather than the spread of knowledge and the increase of human power ought to be used to lighten men's toil and liberate their intellectual faculties, now enslaved by a gross materialism....

This social ideal, the ideal of co-operation and association, in the future is to be the dominating ideal, dominating not only industry, but every sphere of social activity, politics, religion, and philosophy. We have, by historical development, reached the stage when we are entering on a new historical era, when the dominating ideal shall not be individualism, but the social ideal, not the idea of man as an independent individual, but the idea of the individual as a member of the social body. Legislation under individual has been to give liberty to the individual to do as he liked, or to protect him against his fellows, but legislation in the era on which we are entering will be to give liberty to the individual, not to do as he likes, but liberty to associate and co-operate with his fellows for the mutual advantage of all. The work of the political democracy will be to discover the laws which require our obedience, and to translate them into Acts of Parliament, and to make our industrial and social conditions conform with the precept of the Golden Rule. The political democracy dominated by the social ideal will be the coming of Christ to rule the nations in righteousness.

And when this social ideal shall be universally accepted, when it shall dominate all men, what a change there will be in the face of the land! I do sometimes dream dreams, and I see a vision of what the world will be when this spirit of love and sacrifice which has actuated some noble spirits in all ages, and which shone with the glory of full perfection in the life and example of Jesus of Nazareth – I sometimes see 'as through the glass darkly,' a vision of what the world will be when the spirit of love and sacrifice shall animate all men. I see that old things have passed away, and all things have become new; I see this sordid struggle for material existence superseded by a social order in which men seek the gratification of their natural ambitions, not by the amount of tribute they levy on their fellows, but by the greatness of the service they can render to them; ... I see an industrial order where every man for a fair day's work has a bountiful harvest, and abundant leisure when his necessary work is done.... But the only way to regain the earthly paradise is by the old, hard road to Calvary – through persecution, through poverty, through temptation, by the agony and bloody sweet, by the crown of thorns, by the agonising death. And then the resurrection to the New Humanity – purified by suffering, triumphant through Sacrifice.

The Individual Under Socialism

This was a famous lecture by Snowden (ILP, London, 1905), which was produced in pamphlet form. In this he made it clear that individualism in the conventional sense was a direct contradiction to the basic tenets of socialism. Drawing heavily upon Carlyle and Ruskin he argued that man was naturally good as an individual and it was only capitalist society which made him bad. Thus the aim of socialism must be to work towards a society which would allow the conditions in which man could be naturally good once more. In order to achieve this moral objective there had to be changes in the economic system of production. Land and industry had to be taken into public ownership. Through this economic transformation of society there would also be an improvement in moral attitudes. Unlike the attitude of many Fabians, socialism was asserted in the name of social justice and not in terms of increased efficiency.

★ ★ ★

A common objection against Socialism is that a Socialist State would involve the sacrifice of individual liberty, and that there would be no opportunity for the satisfaction of individual ambition.

Socialism, it is urged by these opponents, considers only the satisfaction of mere physical needs. Socialism they tell us, lacks the moral element, it ignores human nature, it is meat and drink and nothing more. Such an objection as this betrays an ignorance of Socialism and the Socialist movement which would be irritating if it were not amusing. 'Socialism merely meat and drink and material conditions and nothing more!' And were it so, surely is there not need enough to-day for a movement which seeks to provide these things for the millions who are lacking meat and clothing, and homes? With, according to the latest investigation made in an industrial English town, about 80 per cent of the working class living in houses which do not fulfil the basic needs of health and decency; with 52 per cent of the working class families unable, by long hours of toil, to gain income sufficient to obtain enough food to satisfy the needs of the body; . . .

But it is further urged that if such an organisation of industry could be established as would ensure work for all willing workers, and satisfy the physical requirements of all, that such an organisation would be obtained at the cost of all that makes life worth living. Remove the incentive of gain, and we are told the motive force of all progress would be destroyed. Socialism would reduce all to one dead level of mediocrity. The individual would lose his identity in a cast iron State. Men would be converted into mere machines, life would be an intolerable servitude, the nation would be converted into one huge prisonhouse. The great principle of Socialism, these objectors remind us, is Equality; and to ensure a condition of perfect equality would be the work and function of the State. Aye, the State – a monster more terrible in its strength and more tyrannical in its despotism than ever the genius of Frankenstein created. To ensure this condition of perfect equality, the State will allot to each individual his appointed task, and the whip of the State taskmaster will enforce its full discharge. Intellectual equality would be secured by depriving superior ability of all encouragement to excel, the mental condition of the lowest would be the standard to which all would be degraded to maintain a condition of perfect equality. The State would decide and direct the minutest details of each individual life. The work, the place of abode, the dress, the food, the home, the amusement, the recreation – all would be directed by the State, leaving the individual no freedom but to obey. For the certainty of being fed and clothed, we are to sacrifice the glorious privilege of individual liberty and the blessings of a civilisation won for us by the efforts of gifted free individuals in all past ages. But in the end, it is further predicted, this dead mass of equality would sink into a condition of squalid animalism spurred on to effort only by the whip of the State taskmaster. Socialism, which promised liberty, equality, and plenty, will end in a cataclysm, and want.

. . . This picture of the Individual under Socialism, drawn by our opponents, is an illustration of the difficulty of getting away from the familiar ideas, for it is a very faithful representation of the condition of the individual of to-day under a system of boasted individualism. What to-day, under our much vaunted individual freedom, is the type of the developed individual? If you would see the works of Competition, and the play of the Incentive of Gain, look around! You will find their monuments everywhere. Surely but it must be in grim irony we are told that Socialism will destroy individual liberty and close the avenues for intellectual development. Let those who fear that Socialism will destroy individual liberty and hinder her intellectual development go with their talk to the machine workers of our great northern towns, who are chained for eleven hours a day to a monotonous toil with the eye of the overseer and the fear of dismissal spurring them on to an exertion which leaves them at the end of their day's work physical wrecks, with no ambition but to restore their wasted energies at the nearest public house. Let them go with their talk. Let them go with their talk of the blessings of civilisation to the pottery and chemical workers, whose systems are poisoned, whose sight is destroyed, where through the bodies of the parents being saturated with poison, half the children are born dead . . . – tell them to hold fast to their share of the blessings of our glorious civilisation . . . – talk to them of individual liberty and warn them of the tyranny of the coming Socialism. ... Why not talk of individual freedom and equality of opportunity, under a system of cannabalistic competition like this, is like the mocking laughter of a raving maniac gloating over the torture of the victim it holds in its murderous grip.

There can be no individual liberty where land, the absolute essential to a man's existence, is the property of a few, and is used by this few to dictate to the many the terms on which they shall be permitted to live. There can be no individual liberty so long as machinery which has been made by the associated labour of all workers become the property of a class, and is used by that class to keep themselves in idleness and to pay the workers wages by wealth taken from them. Under such a system, where the common needs of life are the object of a competitive struggle in which all goes to the victors, leaving nothing to the vanquished; in which the sole object in life is to secure a monopoly of what all need so that by this monopoly one may get his fellows into his power to use them for his own selfish ends – under such a system there can be no individuality....

... Look where we will in our life to-day and we find everywhere this lack of individuality, a slavery to fashion, to conventional ideas....

Our ideal of individual liberty is freedom to develop those qualities which will enable a man to get rich. It is true that Socialism will destroy such individual liberty as that – the liberty of brute force and cunning wit to crush the weak and rob the innocent.

Socialism means the elevation of the struggle for existence from the material to the intellectual plane. Competition for material things – which are limited in supply – must result in extremes of poverty and riches.... But Socialism will raise the struggle for existence into a sphere where competition shall be emulation, where the treasures are boundless and eternal, and where the abundant wealth of one does not cause the poverty of another. The time has passed when men need to struggle against each other for their physical needs. We have a command over natural forces capable of supplying every need without the necessity for arduous toil – a command which increases more rapidly than our capacity for its rational use. By the sensible organisation of industry all might be provided with the needs of a comfortable existence with the expenditure of a little time and labour. The struggle for existence, instead of being a struggle by individuals against each other, should be a struggle by men united together to subdue the external forces of nature for the service of humanity.

Socialism will justify God's way to man. That divine instinct of affection in human nature has through all the ages rebelled against the merciless slaughter of the weak, for tho'

Nature red in tooth and claw with ravine
Shrieked against our creed....
We felt that God is love indeed
And love Creation's final law.

And now Socialism comes as the Angel of Light bearing to mankind the message of truth....

Socialism, by making land and machinery the common property of all, and using these instruments to supply material needs, will completely change the business and object of life. Socialism will change human nature. The opportunity makes the man. Socialism will take away the desire for accumulating riches ... under Socialism, the possession of riches will cease to be a ruling passion, for honest labour will be a guarantee against want, and riches will no longer be the passport to social position. Under such condition the possession of riches will be a superfluous burden which no sane man will wish to bear....

When the acquiring of riches has ceased to be the object of life; when men's minds are free from the carking care of providing for the morrow, when the perpetual fear of poverty is removed; then men will seek for fresh avenues for the satisfaction of their individual desires. When men have leisure, and they are not enervated by exhausting toil, or demoralised by superfluous riches, they cannot help themselves from following their natural instincts. Man, under natural, that is under favourable, material conditions, is an intellectual being, and his intellectual aspirations will manifest themselves when his material needs are satisfied....

And Socialism will create a condition of things favourable to the development of the higher type of individuality. The organisation of industry, the saving of the present waste of competition, will reduce the labour of supplying the physical needs to the narrowest limits, leaving abundant leisure for the satisfaction of individual desires. And the conditions under which this necessary work will be done will be healthy, pleasant, and elevating. Men and women will be educated to take an intelligent interest in their work. Society will have discovered that it is best for society and for the individual to put him to the work he can best do, and this will transform his labour from a drudgery to a perpetual joy. John Ruskin truly says: 'When a man is rightfully employed his amusement grows out of his work as the colour petals out of a fruitful flower.' Socialism will realise that desirable condition.

Socialism will provide all the conditions which are necessary for the gratification of every reasonable desire.... Under Socialism, nineteen-twentieths of the people will be better off materially than they are to-day, for they will be equal partners in all the productive and distributive wealth of the community.

Socialism will establish the moral conditions which are necessary for the development of true individuality, and the exercise of true liberty. The moral basis of Socialism is the recognition of the eternal moral law, that the individual as a member of society is limited in his development by the development of the society in which he is a member. Herbert Spencer puts it in this form: 'The individual development in a given period is determined by the corresponding development of the social organism.' In other words, the civilisation of the mass determines the condition of the individual....

Socialism is something more than meat and drink, and food and clothing. It attaches so much importance to industrial reform, because we must first establish the material base of life on a moral foundation before we can raise up a society of moral and intellectual men and women. Material conditions are the soil out of which the intellectual life of the people grows. Socialism seeks first the kingdom of industrial righteousness, and then all else shall be added unto it.

Instead of Socialism being merely a material movement, seeking only the satisfaction of physical needs, it is a movement which is seeking to subordinate materialism to the intellectual life, and Socialists are working for the industrial commonwealth because they realise that only by such an industrial organisation can there be individual liberty and opportunity for true individual development....

And in conclusion may we point out that the moral spirit which Socialism will generate will not be confined within the selfish limits of nationality. Socialism is brotherhood; and brotherhood is as wide as the heaven and as broad as humanity. The growth of international Socialism is the promise of the realisation of the angel's natal song: 'On Earth peace; Goodwill towards men.'

A Plea for Peace

This pamphlet, published by the Blackburn Labour Party, was based upon Snowden's speech to the House of Commons on 23 February 1916, the first major wartime speech to demand a negotiated settlement to the First World War. There is little to suggest that Snowden's appeal punctured the desire of the British Government or the British people for a military victory. Nevertheless, the demand for a negotiated peace settlement assumed increased importance in May 1916 when President Wilson, of the United States, spoke in favour of a negotiated peace settlement.

★ ★ ★

The Bill we are now asked to read a second time authorises a further expenditure of over £400,000,000 on the War, making a total of Votes of Credit of over £2,000,000,000. I do not propose this afternoon to deal with the grave financial problems involved in these colossal figures. There will be other and early opportunities for doing this. But I think when the House of Commons is asked to vote such an enormous sum as this we are justified in asking whether there be no alternative to this continual expenditure, and whether it be not possible by some other means to bring this War to an end on terms and conditions which will realise the objects for which we are fighting. The Secretary of State for the Colonies, speaking in this House three months ago, in reply to a speech made by my Hon. Friend the Member for Elland Division, said it was absurd to say that any Member of the Government would not jump at a chance of bringing this War to an end, provided that it could be brought to an end on such terms as would realise our object. He said that everybody is anxious to bring the War to an end on conditions consistent with our national honour and security.

The Appalling Horror

That precisely explains my position this afternoon, and it is the justification for the proposal which we are putting forward. We make this proposal with a deep sense of the seriousness and importance of the action we are taking. I am well aware that I speak to an audience which, in one respect, is out of sympathy with the proposal I make, but I am confident that the House of Commons will extend to me the courtesy and consideration to which all views honestly and reasonably stated are entitled when they are put forward with an earnest hope of doing something to bring this awful tragedy to an end....

The Time is Ripe

... I think it would be true to say that this country desires no other conclusion to this War than one that will give us reparation for the wrong that has been done, and, as far as human judgement can secure it, guarantees and conditions against its repetition. The only difference between those of us who are opposed to it, is that while all are equally anxious to see a speedy and successful termination of the War, we believe that this is more possible now than by the prolongation of the War in the hope that a decisive military victory will enable us to dictate terms to a vanquished foe....

The Military Situation

... The prolongation of the War can only be justified by the reasonable expectation that, by its continuance, we shall be placed in a position to dictate such terms to the enemy as will secure the future of European peace. I know there have been some wars in the past in which the fortunes of battle for long seemed to go against that side which eventually emerged more or less successfully. The fact that after eighteen months of war the military situation is so unsatisfactory to the Allies is no evidence in itself that a decisive military victory may not yet come to the Allied Forces. But in a matter like this, where so much is at stake, where millions of lives are in peril, and where the fate of Europe is involved, we must be honest with ourselves and it is criminal to encourage self-deception.

'Unconquered and Unconquerable'

I am sure that there are few men who, taking an intelligent and dispassionate view of the military situation and of the new experiences which this War has brought, would say that there is any reasonable ground for the hope that a decisive and crushing military victory can come to either of the contending parties....

A War of Attrition

... War by attrition will be long and costly and it will leave every one of the belligerent nations financially and commercially ruined, and it will be the very worst form of inconclusive peace, for it will endanger chronic hate and revenge, and it will unite in a common determination to re-establish in their national position the liberal and democratic forces and the military party in the German nation....

To Make Another War Certain

The settlement of this War will depend upon the frame of mind and spirit in which the cessation of hostilities finds the various nations. No victory in the field can establish the conditions of a permanent peace unless there be the willingness, and the disposition, to accept that superior right which recognises that the real interest of a nation lies in respecting and safeguarding the interests of all. The ruthless subjugation of Germany would be the very worst preparation for a just and lasting peace in Europe....

The Great Lessons of the War

The outstanding lesson of this War is that militarism stands discredited. It is now proved to be a futile method of serving aggressive designs. No great modern nation can conquer or be conquered, and that fact has a most vital relation to the conditions of peace.... If it now be the fact that military power is useless for the purpose of aggrandisement and aggression, then these conditions and the future relations of Europe must be governed by that fact. An inconclusive ending of this War, in the sense that all the belligerent Powers realise the futility of military power would be surest guarantee against a repetition of war. ...

Our Government's Responsibility

I submit that the facts I have adduced prove that there is reasonable ground for believing that the present is a favourable opportunity for holding out the hand of negotiation. I am sure that such an effort coming from this Government, speaking with all the authority that this Government could do, would be heartily welcomed, and it would find a hearty response from the sorely stricken people of other countries, and would be regarded by German Socialists as an encouragement to them to increase their efforts to secure a peace as I am quite sure all parties might regard as an honourable and satisfactory end to this War. I am fully aware of the difficulty, but I was especially gratified by the tone and terms of a reply to a question which I addressed to the Prime Minister last December, in which he said the Allied Governments would be willing to consider any serious proposals for peace which might come from belligerent or neutral countries.

One Step Further

The Prime Minister only needs to go one step further. He can give encouragement to offers of peace.... There are many channels open to the Government through which negotiations may be opened up, and we have the right to demand that the Government shall state in much more definite and precise language the terms upon which they would be willing to consider peace.

War or Peace?

This is an extract from a speech delivered by Snowden to the House of Commons on 13 February 1918. At this time the Peace Campaign which Snowden had launched was faltering, very largely due to the fact that the United States, which had once encouraged moves for a negotiated peace had now entered the War against Germany. Snowden's speech was a meticulous analysis of the contradictions of Government policy and reiterated the demand for a negotiated settlement. The main thrust of Snowden's attack upon the Government was that there were no clear Allied War Aims and that there had been secret diplomacy about the carve up of Europe and particularly, the Balkan states and Central Europe, in the wake of War. He then referred back to the national demand for peace.

★ ★ ★

I know something of the state of feeling in the country. There is no enthusiasm for the war. There is an almost universal desire for peace. In a certain town in this country not long ago a rumour spread that peace had been declared. The population went wild for two or three hours, and then the rumour was found to be untrue. It occurred to somebody afterwards that never during the time of jubilation had a single person asked upon what terms the war had been settled. The people want peace; the soldiers want peace. One cannot travel in a railway train without knowing that. I was going down to South Wales about a fortnight ago, and in the compartment were an Australian soldier, a Canadian soldier, and two British soldiers. They talked freely. They were all, to use a very common expression, 'fed up.' I do not know if the Government know the state of feeling amongst the soldiers. It is not confined to the soldiers of our own army. We know it is the same in Germany; indeed it is in all the armies ... and I repeat it here, as bearing upon this point, that about three weeks or a month ago a soldier called to see me one evening. He had just returned from the front and he said he had been sent by his comrades to ask me how Alsace-Lorraine had come into the war. He said they had volunteered to fight for the liberation of Belgium and not to try to redress the result of a fifty-year-old quarrel. I warn the Government, as the late President of the Board of Trade warned them, of this change in public opinion. The chairman of the Labour Party said that there was a real danger of revolution. There may be; there will be if the Government do not realise the state of feeling in the country and take steps to prevent it.

This amendment asks that the Government shall not rely merely upon the military weapon, that they should keep open the door of diplomacy, and that they should encourage instead of throwing cold water upon every promising chance of promoting peace.... The military situation to-day is no more hopeful than it was twelve months ago. If we go on another twelve months it will be less hopeful than it is to-day. The Government could have made better peace terms six months ago, twelve months ago, two years ago than they can make to-day. The longer the war continues, the less prospect there is that they will be able to enforce their unreasonable terms. During the last twelve months, for no military advantage whatever, we have sacrificed in killed and wounded, according to the returns of the War Office, a million men.... I am looking for the conclusion of this war by a union of the democracies of all belligerent nations. They have learned that lesson in common affliction and although one can hardly say that any good which may result from this war would be anything of a compensation for the stupendous evil which it has created, still it would be something if, as a result of this war, we had for ever a sweeping away of the power of those who have misused their powers in the past and have used them, not for the good of the people, but in order to satisfy their own Imperialist and selfish aims.

Prospect and Retrospect

This extract is taken from the full report of the Presidential Address delivered by Snowden to the Twenty-Seventh Annual ILP Conference held at Easter, 1919. It was reproduced, under Snowden's name, by the ILP, London, 1919. It is an interesting address for it came at a time when Snowden had just lost his seat in Parliament, was still frustrated with the Labour Party and infectiously hopeful of the ILP's future political prospects. He was, nevertheless, pessimistic about the Versailles peace terms promising future peace.

★ ★ ★

Twelve months ago I was able to congratulate the Conference upon a record of progress during the previous twelve months unparalleled in the history of our Party. During the past year that progress has been maintained. One hundred and thirty-nine new branches have been formed during the year, and the membership has increased by over 11,000. The Party is daily gaining recruits, mainly from the working classes, but also from men and women of influence and reputation, who have lost all faith in the old political parties, and who recognise in the Independent Labour

Party a movement which expresses the economic, political, and international ideals and needs of the age....

The Labour Party in Parliament

In industrial matters, the Labour Party in the House of Commons is doing well, but it is very disappointing in regard to such fundamental questions as civil liberty and economic and international policy. It has remained silent while conscientious objectors have been tortured in prison.... The Labour Party will never become a great political party, and it will never deserve success unless it champions, in season and out of season, the cause of those who are oppressed, and fights for a high standard of national morality in home and foreign affairs. There is no place in the future for a political party whose vision is limited by considerations of mere material improvement for one class of the community. The results of the recent bye-elections have shown that unless the Labour Party can rise to the greatness of the present need, the electors will turn in disappointment from it, and in despair will trust once more the old Liberal Party, which failed them so pitiably in the past.

The Labour Unrest and its Cure

The country is seething with industrial unrest.... The governing classes appear to be living in the realm of pre-war conditions and ideas, and their proposals for dealing with Labour unrest do not go beyond offers of some slight palliation of working conditions in the capitalist system. They fail to realise that the old economic order has broken down, and is no longer capable of satisfying the workers' demand for a higher standard of living, and for partnership as intelligent human being(s) in the ownership and direction of industry. No palliatives will permanently settle Labour unrest.... The War has hastened the break-up of the capitalist system, and the only solution of the Labour and Social problem is the establishment of the Socialist Commonwealth in which the workers engaged in the respective industries and services will be allowed full participation in the control of the factory and workshop, and the ordering of their own lives....

The Delayed and Secret Peace

... The proceedings at Paris, and the terms of the Treaty which are to be submitted to the German Republic, confirm every fear which has been entertained of the character of the peace which would follow a military victory, and justify every statement we have made during the war about its capitalistic character and its imperialistic aims....

'The World is the New Nation.'

The League of Nations, which had captured the idealism and enthusiasm of the democracies, has not been, and is not likely to be established by governments who are still under the spell of the old and wicked conception of the conditions of national security. No League of Nations which is a league of capitalist government can ever be more than an aggravation of the old system of groupings and alliances maintained by armed force. There is only one cement that can bind the nations of the earth together in a League of Peace, and that is the spirit of internationalism and fraternity. The only permanent security for a nation lies in internationalism. The statesmen who, for three months at Paris, have been trying to settle the affairs of Europe, live still in a world which is passing away, and they are blind to the new forces and new ideas which are animating the new democracy. To Socialism and Internationalism these old problems of national boundaries and national securities are out of date. The world, and not a geographical area, is the new nation. That is the idea that is inspiring the world revolutionary movement, and all arrangements made under the old conception of geographical areas, with special and selfish interests to be maintained against others, will be swept away by the force of the international ideal.

The I.L.P. Fully Justified

Let me examine for a moment the attitude of the Independent Labour Party to the war, and let us see how far that attitude is justified by events up to the present moment. In the Manifesto issued by the Party at the outbreak of war it was pointed out that we had long maintained that the diplomatic policy pursued by European rulers, and supported by the force of murderous armaments, would inevitably lead to universal war or universal bankruptcy, or both. The outbreak of war, and the course of the war which has dragged the whole world into the conflict, and has left practically every belligerent nation in a state of famine and economic exhaustion and bankruptcy, have tragically fulfilled that prediction. While not attempting to apportion the exact measure of responsibility and blame which the various countries must share for the war, it was pointed out that the policy of encirclement and groupings and the pursuit of Imperialistic ambitions and capitalist interests were the cause of the war, for which every European Power must share the responsibility. We have maintained during the war that a decisive military victory by the one side or the other was improbable, and that if the war were continued it would end by the collapse of one side through economic exhaustion, leaving the victorious Powers themselves near the point of economic ruin. The facts which have come to light since the signing of the Armistice as to the utter exhaustion of the Central Powers prove the truth of this prediction. . . .

The Price of the Knock-out Blow

. . . In every respect the attitude of the Independent Labour Party towards the war, its analysis of the causes and character of the war, its prediction as to the course of the war . . . its contention that not by military force, but by the renunciation of all aggressive aims, could peace be achieved, are completely justified. We have nothing to excuse, we have nothing to withdraw. The state of Europe to-day, the proceedings of the Paris Conference, the inconclusive and provocative terms to be imposed upon the enemy, are the condemnation of the Knock-out Blow policy, and the justification of all we have maintained.

The New War has Begun

The terms to be submitted to Germany are not peace terms. They will not end the war. The new war has already begun. The Armageddon has not yet been fought. The final struggle has yet to be decided.

The Big Business Budget

This was a pamphlet produced by the Labour Party and the TUC in 1923, based upon the House of Commons speeches of Snowden made at the time of the 1923 Budget. This brief extract reflects Snowden's commitment to economic orthodoxy. There is a copy of this pamphlet in the Snowden Collection, Keighley Library, and a copy in the Archives of the British Labour Party, Series Two, 1923/64.

★ ★ ★

... you cannot have a tax reduction on sound economic lines so long as the National Debt exists....

One might think from the criticism made against the Labour Party during these debates that we are not in favour of lower taxation. We are in favour of lower taxation. What is the object of the proposal we put forward for a levy on capital, except to reduce the amount of debt and thus to reduce the amount of debt and thus to reduce the amount of taxation necessary to pay the interest on the debt? The only difference, if we would only understand each other, between those who are demanding a reduction of taxation without regard to the debt and ourselves, is that we realise that you cannot reduce taxation till you have reduced the debt, and therefore the first thing is to reduce the debt in a thorough manner.

The Housewife's Budget

This pamphlet was produced in 1924 by the Labour Party and was a verbatim report of the speech delivered by Snowden on the occasion of his first Budget speech on 29 April 1924. In this speech Snowden reiterated his concern to pay off the National Debt and to maintain sound, orthodox, financial policies.

★ ★ ★

Meanwhile, it is clear that we must take every opportunity and devote as much of our resources as possible to the redemption of Debt (Cheers). Some people seem to think that Debt reduction is something which confers no public advantage. I know a reduction of 1s. in Income Tax is much more spectacular than paying off £50,000,000 of Debt. In the first case the relief is obvious, in the second, it is indirect, but none the less real, and in fact is more widespread and penetrating in its benefits. Improvement in national credit in its turn regulates the rates at which money can be borrowed for industrial purposes.

Colne Valley Parliamentary Division: General Election 1929. Election Address of The Right Hon. Philip Snowden, 1 May 1929

A full copy of this is to be found in the Snowden Collection, Keighley Reference Library.

★ ★ ★

LABOUR'S TAXATION POLICY

The Labour Government will remove all taxes from necessaries. It will revise the Income Tax laws so as to give relief to the smaller incomes. It will look for its revenues to the Death Duties, a graduated Surtax, and Taxation of Land Values.

The Labour Government will aim at re-establishing National Credit so that the intolerable burden of the War Debt Charges may be reduced. It will endeavour to settle the reparations and the Inter-Allied Debts problems in a way which will do justice to all concerned and relieve Britain from the unfair burdens which the actions of the Tory Government has imposed upon us.

AN APPEAL TO THE WOMEN

I make a special appeal to women. It is they who suffer most from Industrial and Social evils. Unemployment, Low Wages, Bad Housing, Heavy Taxes and War, cause the greatest burden of misery to fall on them.

NO PLEDGES WE CANNOT FULFIL

We shall not deceive the people by saying that the task of National Reconstruction is easy, or that it can be accomplished in a twelve month [period].

But we do pledge ourselves to undertake this great task with energy and determination, confident that in the full life-time of one Parliament we can make a great advance in industrial prosperity, in social well-being, and in a juster distribution of the fruits of Labour.

The Labour Party is a Socialist Party. It is opposed to force, revolution and confiscation as a means of establishing the New Social Order. It believes in ordered progress and in democratic methods.

WHY I ASK FOR YOUR SUPPORT

You have already elected me as your member three times. The record of my work in Parliament and in the country is before you. On that record I again confidently ask for your continued confidence.

I do that only that I may take my part in the great task of making this country of ours a happier land for all men, women and children. I want to help remove poverty and social injustice, and to banish war and establish perpetual Peace.

I look with the fullest confidence to the result of the Election which, I am sure, will show that this Constituency stands firm in its democratic faith and in its desire to do its part in bringing in the new era of Prosperity and Peace.

An Autobiography

This book gives reflections on the end of the second Labour Government and the formation of the National Government. Extensive comment has been made about the events of August 1931 and Snowden's views on MacDonald's actions have already been quoted in the text. Nevertheless, it is worth reflecting upon the reasons which Snowden gave for his decision to join the National Government and his incredulous belief that his split with the Labour Party would be temporary since it was based upon a comparatively minor matter. It reveals a degree of insensitivity to the Labour Party's structure and support that he could have ever entertained such views given that he had committed the cardinal sin of attacking the living standards of the unemployed.

★ ★ ★

When the members of the Labour Cabinet were leaving after the Prime Minister announced that we had agreed to form a National Government, he asked me and Mr. Thomas and Lord Sankey to remain behind. We then had a frank conversation about the new situation which had so unexpectedly arisen. He asked us if we were prepared to join him in the Government which was to be formed. In view of my position as Chancellor of the Exchequer, and the exceptional responsibility I had for helping to get the country out of its difficulties, I felt that there was no other course open to me than to assist the new Government provided I could get certain assurances as to its character and its purpose. The definite assurances which were given to me were:

(1) That the new Administration would not exist for a longer period than to dispose of the emergency, and that when that was achieved the political parties would assume their respective positions.
(2) That the Administration would not be a Coalition Government in the general sense of the term, but a National Government for one purpose only.
(3) That as soon as the financial crisis had been settled there should be a General Election, and at that Election there would be no merging of political parties and no 'Coupon' or other party arrangements.
(4) That the Administration which was being formed would not pro-

pose any party legislation of a controversial character, but would confine itself to the one purpose for which it was being formed.

I had not the least expectation then of the developments which followed later. It never entered my mind that this meant the permanent separation from my former colleagues in the Labour Party. I expected that, though we had differed on what, after all, was a comparatively trivial matter, we should be able to resume our former cooperation in the Labour Party when the emergency legislation had been passed.

Attack upon MacDonald in the House of Lords, 24 May 1933

This attack upon MacDonald, widely reported in most newspapers on 25 May 1933, was made within the context of the impending World Economic Conference. Snowden was critical of the National Government's failure to offer clear economic policies which might help Britain to return to free trade. This report is taken from the *Yorkshire Post*, 25 May 1933.

★ ★ ★

Whether the reason for that [the National Government's failure to offer a clear economic policy] is that the Government have no policy or whether it is due to the constitutional inability of the Prime Minister to make a clear statement I do not know.... I have referred to that speech [a recent speech by MacDonald] and there is not from the beginning to end a word about the Government's policy at the World Economic Conference. There is no reference to the Conference, except the expression of a wish that it might be held as soon as possible....

I would suggest to the Cabinet that they should look into the case of the Prime Minister, not only in his own interests, but in the interests of the country for it is a positive danger to the country that its affairs should be in the hands of a man who, every time he speaks, exposes his ignorance and incapacity.

[He then attacked MacDonald's visit to Washington and his joint statement with President Roosevelt.] He might just as well have saved the country the expense for the joint statement is nothing except a repetition of platitudes....

I have had experience of the last four international economic conferences and the weakness of all of them has been the lack of adequate preparation and lack of genuine agreement before the conference meets, resulting in an enormous waste of time and open differences in the conference which might otherwise be avoided....

[He then went on to attack particular parts of the joint statement, particularly that which referred to credit arrangements.] I have never favoured the squandering of public money for public works, but I have always supported sound schemes of national work which would be remunerative in their character. The condition was that they should be remunerative and not merely relief works. Finding work for the sake of it – that has never been part of any programme.

[Snowden then went on to examine the suggestions that there ought to be a tariff truce whilst the World Economic Conference was in progress, a proposal made by the Expert Conference.] What reception did this proposal get from the British Government? As soon as the proposal was made the Prime Minister made a statement to the effect that it could only be accepted with certain reservations. These reservations have been made, and they amount to a practical rejection of any tariff truce during the sitting of the Economic Conference. The Tariff Advisory Committee are not to discontinue their work, and all the time the Conference is sitting are to be actively at work considering cases for increased tariffs.

The World Economic Conference will begin denouncing tariffs, will declare how prejudicial they are to international trade, and at the same time the British Government will be actively engaged in making preparations for a further increase in tariffs.

So far as the Prime Minister is capable of making a definite statement, or one which is not capable of half-a-dozen different interpretations we have a statement that the tariff truce was not intended to prevent us from continuing our work, work we have now begun and which we are now developing.

What is the work? The work is the establishment of a system of high protection in their country. He talks about a low-tariff country. But we are not a low-tariff country. Surely nobody is going to pretend that a duty of 33 1/3 per cent can be regarded as either moderate or low.

'Attack upon MacDonald, and the Government's protectionist policy, and the Government's decision, in the Finance Bill, Snowden's Land Tax, which had been announced in his 1931'

This speech was made in the House of Lords, 3 July 1934 and reported in *The Times*, and other newspapers, on the 4 July 1934. In this speech. Snowden recalled how MacDonald had pleaded with him not to resign over the Land Tax conflict with the Liberals in June 1931. He argued that MacDonald no longer seemed interested in the policy of taxing land values, as he had once been, and that he was no longer prepared to defend free trade.

★ ★ ★

At the last General Election millions of Labour, Liberal and free trade votes were given to the National Government candidates – because the electors believed Mr. Baldwin's statement that free trade and protection were not the issue at the election. Now the Government were boasting that they had killed free trade and established tariffs for generations to come. . . . 'He had been betrayed.' That mattered little, but the country had been betrayed, and millions of electors who trusted to the statements of the party leaders had lost their confidence in the faith and honesty of their political leaders. . . .

When the House of Commons were discussing this question [the suspension of the taxation of Land Values] there were demands that the Prime Minister should be present, but he was spending his time in Downing Street listening to a concert. The Prime Minister had broken his silence once in regard to the subject in a letter which he had written to the Committee for the Taxation of Land Values. That letter was described by a Liberal member of the House of Commons as a piece of nauseating hypocrisy. He [Lord Snowden] thought that was an apt description and he could not improve upon it. . . .

The truth is that the Tories have got the power, and they mean to use it. At the next election the slogan will be National Government or Socialist Government. At that election the Tories will have no use for the Prime Minister except as an exhibition on Tory platforms . . . as a one-time Socialist who has seen the error of his ways, and has found salvation and his spiritual home in the Tory Party. He will be used for the same purpose as the reformed drunkard is used at the temperance meeting. (Laughter) The Prime Minister told us at a recent meeting that he stood by everything he has said as a Socialist. Let him act upon that, and then he will see what use his Tory colleagues will have for him. He told us in the same speech that what the country needs is honest political leadership. I quite agree.

Appendix 1 The major events occurring throughout Snowden's life

Year	General political events	Labour developments	Snowden's life
1864	American Civil War 1861–65	International Working Men's Conference, London, 1864	Born 18 July 1864 at Cowling, near Keighley, Yorkshire.
1879–86	Irish Affairs and Home Rule Question. 1884: Third Reform Act extends household suffrage to county seats.	1881: Democratic Federation formed. 1883: D.F. becomes Social Democratic Federation. 1883–4: Fabian Society formed. 1884: Socialist League formed.	1879: moved to Nelson, Lancashire. Employed as an insurance clerk. 1880–86: Nonconformist activist and attended meetings of Nelson Liberation Society which was attempting to disestablish the Church of England. Liberal in politics.
1886	Home Rule split within Liberal Party	TUC decides to set up a Labour Representation Committee to get more working-class political representation.	Joins the civil service as a junior exciseman and leaves Nelson.
1887–92	1888: Local Government Act creates county councils. Irish Question still dominant. 1890: Irish Nationalists split after Parnell cited in O'Shea's	13 November 1887: 'Bloody Sunday' demonstration when Irish, Socialists, Radicals and unemployed dispersed at Trafalgar Square.	1891: Snowden injured in cycling accident which was possibly the reason for his retirement from the civil service. 1892: he returns to Cowling.

	divorce action. October 1891: Gladstone endorses Newcastle Programme. 6 October 1891: Parnell dies. 1892: General Election sees return of Liberal Government.	August 1889: London Dock Strike. 1890–91: Manningham Mills strike, Bradford. May 1891: Bradford Labour Union (ILP) formed. 21 July 1891: Colne Valley Labour Union formed. 14 May 1892: Manchester and Salford ILP formed. July 1892: Halifax Labour Union formed. July 1892: J. Keir Hardie wins West Ham South in General Election and Ben Tillett narrowly defeated in Bradford West. October 1892: Keighley Labour Union formed. November 1892. Leeds ILP formed.	
1893–95	8 September 1893: Second Home Rule Bill defeated in the Lords. March 1894: Gladstone resigns and Rosebery becomes Liberal Prime Minister. June 1895: Rosebery Government defeated and	Hull dock strike and widespread industrial action. 14–16 January 1893: Inaugural ILP Conference at Bradford. ILP activity in many areas and John Lister third, with 3,028 votes in Halifax by-election.	November 1893: speaks of Socialism, in glowing terms, to Craven Liberal Party. 19 June 1894: listens to E. R. Hartley's lecture, given in Cowling, on 'The Need for a Labour Party'. 12 January 1895: letter in *Keighley News* announces Snowden's full conversion to socialism.

Appendix I–continued

Year	General political events	Labour developments	Snowden's life
	July General Election sees the return of a Conservative Government under Lord Salisbury.	1893: Hardie's *Labour Leader* published. 1894: Manchester ILP sees National Administrative Council streamlined. 1895 General Election saw the ILP defeated in 29 seats and Keir Hardie loses his West Ham South seat.	Joins Keighley ILP. 1894: returned to Cowling Parish Council as parish clerk. 17 February 1895: lectures to Keighley Labour Church on 'The Religion of Socialism'. 1895: returned to Cowling School Board. Contests Keighley for the ILP in the 1895 General Election but withdraws when ILP runs out of funds.
1896–97	1896: Rosebery resigns as Liberal leader. Workmen's Compensation Act 1897.	November 1896: Bradford East by-election where Keir Hardie obtains 1,953 votes. March 1897: Tom Mann third in the Halifax by-election.	
1898	May 1898 death of Gladstone.	ILP rejects fusion with the SDF at April Conference.	Becomes a member of the NAC of the ILP. Editor of *Keighley Labour Journal* (to 1902).
1899	Campbell-Bannerman becomes Liberal leader. South African War (Boer War) begins.	ILP criticizes the South African War.	Returned to Keighley Town Council and Keighley School Board.

1900	Khaki Election at which Conservatives returned to power.	Labour Representation Committee formed. Keir Hardie wins Merthyr seat in General Election.	Defeated at Blackburn in the General Election.
1901		SDF leaves the LRC. July, 1901: Taff Vale Judgement.	
1902	Lord Salisbury replaced by Balfour as Prime Minister.	H. Quelch defeated in Dewsbury by-election after row over his selection between SDF and LRC.	Comes second in Wakefield by-election in a straight fight with the Conservatives.
1903	Chamberlain's Protectionist Programme launched.	LRC wins by-elections at Woolwich and Barnard Castle. Gladstone–MacDonald secret pact finalized.	Becomes Chairman of the ILP for three years.
1904	Licencing Act offends temperance lobby.	February, *Labour Leader* becomes official ILP paper.	
1905	Unemployed Workmans Act passed.		Marries Ethel Annakin, 13 March.
1906	Liberals win massive victory in general election.	29 LRC candidates successful in general election, only those opposed by Liberals. LRC becomes Labour Party.	Wins one of the two Blackburn seats.

Appendix I–continued

Year	General political events	Labour developments	Snowden's life
1907–8	School Feeding Act implemented, School Medical Bill passed and old-age pensions introduced by Liberal Government.	Labour Party/ILP active in promoting social legislation. Victor Grayson returned in Colne Valley by-election of 1907.	Involved in the selection and examination procedure which led to Grayson's candidature for Colne Valley, 1907.
1909	'People's Budget' presented by David Lloyd George.	Grayson 'affair' at ILP Conference.	Retires from NAC of the ILP with Hardie, MacDonald and Glasier.
1910	General elections in January and December.	Increasing internal criticism of the 'failures' of the Labour Party.	Returned for Blackburn in two general elections.
1911–13	Liberal reforms continue. National Insurance Act passed in 1911.	British Socialist Party formed 1911–12 to organize and unite all socialists.	
1914–18	First World War Asquith's administration until 1916. Lloyd George Coalition from 1916. 1918 Franchise Act widens the franchise and brings constituency changes. 1918 General Election brings	Socialist groups divided over war. The Labour Party supports the Coalition Government. 1918 Labour Constitution passed, strengthening the control of the trade unions within the Labour Party and	Philip and Ethel tour Canada, USA and New Zealand, July 1914 to February 1915. 1915: on Liquor Control Board. 1916: on NAC of ILP. 1917: Chairman of ILP (until 1920). Constantly opposes the war in the House of Commons. Defeated at Blackburn in 1918 General Election.

	a landslide victory for Lloyd George's Coalition Government.	introducing clause four, with its commitment to common ownership of the means of production.	
1919	Numerous small army and navy mutinies	Pressure on socialist groups to form a Communist Party.	Active as Chairman of the ILP. Ethel goes to Russia.
1920		Communist Party of Great Britain formed.	Becomes Treasurer of the ILP and disturbed by ILP 'Bolshevik' hostility to Ethel.
1921		Labour Party rejects CPGB application to join.	Retires as Treasurer of the ILP and leaves the NAC of the ILP.
1922	Lloyd George Coalition ends, Bonar Law becomes Conservative Prime Minister in October 1922. General Election.	Labour Party wins 142 seats in General Election, almost tripling its previous election performance. James Ramsay MacDonald becomes leader of the Parliamentary Labour Party.	Returned as MP for Colne Valley. Becomes Shadow Chancellor despite voting against MacDonald in the leadership election.
1923	Stanley Baldwin becomes Conservative Prime Minister in May, General Election held in December. Baldwin goes on to electorate on a Protectionist platform.	Labour Party wins 191 seats to Liberals 159 and Conservative Party's 259. Labour, as the largest free trade party forms the new government.	Returned as Labour MP for Colne Valley.

Appendix I–continued

Year	General political events	Labour developments	Snowden's life
1924	Labour Government formed in January. October General Election. Conservative Government formed under Baldwin in November.	Labour Government formed under MacDonald. Its short duration in office was highlighted by the opening up of relations with Russia, the Campbell case and the Zinoviev letter.	Becomes Chancellor of the Exchequer and introduces the first Labour Budget, 'The Housewife's Budget'. Returned for Colne Valley.
1925–28	Coal crisis in 1925 followed by the General Strike in 1926. 1927 Trades Dispute and Trade Union Bill passed to ban sympathetic strike action.	Attacks upon MacDonald's leadership and Labour leadership keep quiet through the General Strike.	1925 made a freeman of Keighley. Keeps as 'mum as a mouse' during the General Strike, May 1926. 1927: makes dramatic speech against the Trades Dispute and Trade Union Bill.
1929	Second Labour Government formed under MacDonald, following General Election in May. Wall Street Crash.	Labour Government formed and faces rapidly rising unemployment.	Returned as MP for Colne Valley and becomes Chancellor of the Exchequer for the second time. Wins prestige at The Hague Conference which was dealing with the reparation issue.
1930	Government introduces Coal Mines Act to help rationalize the industry. Unemployment continues to rise.	Labour Government faces discontent over unemployment problems. Oswald Mosley protests about the economic policies of the Labour Government.	Introduces his second budget.

1931	August 1931: collapse of second Labour Government and formation of a National Government under MacDonald. General Election, October. Landslide victory for the National Government.	Labour Party and Labour Government divided over the reduction of unemployment benefits. The Labour Party opposes the National Government. Labour Party reduced to 46 MPs.	Avoids censure by agreeing to formation of May Committee which was set up to examine finances. Financial crisis looms in July and August and he insists upon the reduction of unemployment benefits. Joins the National Government in August 1931 and remains Chancellor of the Exchequer, taking Britain off the gold standard in September. Does not contest the 1931 General Election but raised to the House of Lords in November and becomes Lord Privy Seal. Takes the title of Lord Snowden of Ickornshaw.
1932	National Government moves towards production and imperial preference, which is discussed at the Ottawa.	Labour Party tightens its controls over its members. ILP leaves the Labour Party.	Objects to threat to free trade and resigns from the National Government, September.
1933–37	National Government continues under MacDonald until Baldwin takes over in June 1935. General Election in November. Oswald Mosley and Fascist threat emerges. July 1936: Spanish Civil War.	Labour Party becomes involved in improving its organization and membership and increases its representation to 154 MPs in 1935 General Election Labour Party rejects the Communist Party objective of forming a United Front against Fascism.	Attacks MacDonald in the House of Lords, 1933 and 1934. Publishes his *An Autobiography*, 1934. Supports Lloyd George's New Deal in 1935. 15 May 1937: dies of a heart attack. 22 May 1937: his ashes are scattered on Ickornshaw Moor.

Appendix 2 Snowden's Parliamentary Election Performances

Blackburn (two seats) 1900 General Election

Sir W. H. Hornby, Bt.	Conservative	11,247	40.5% of vote
Sir W. Coddington, Bt.	Conservative	9,415	33.9% of vote
P. Snowden	Labour	7,096	25.6% of vote
		2,319	8.3%

Wakefield Parliamentary By-Election, 25 March 1902

E. A. Brotherton	Conservative	2,960	59.9% of vote
P. Snowden	Labour	1,979	40.1% of vote
		981	19.8%

Blackburn (two seats) 1906 General Election

Sir W. H. Hornby, Bt.	Conservative	10,291	26.8% of vote
P. Snowden	Labour	10,282	26.7% of vote
G. Drage	Conservative	8,932	23.3% of vote
E. Hamer	Liberal	8,892	23.2% of vote
		1,399	3.6%
		1,350	3.4%

Blackburn (two seats) January 1910 General Election

Sir T. Barclay	Liberal	12,064	28.4% of vote
P. Snowden	Labour	11,916	28.1% of vote
Lord Robert Cecil	Conservative	9,307	22.0% of vote
G. F. S. Bowles	Conservative	9,112	21.5% of vote
		2,757	6.4%
		2,609	6.1%

Blackburn (two seats) December 1910 General Election

P. Snowden	Labour	10,762	26.4% of vote
Sir H. Norman	Liberal	10,754	26.3% of vote
W. B. Boyd-Carpenter	Conservative	9,814	24.0% of vote
H. L. Riley	Conservative	9,500	23.3% of vote
		948	2.4%
		940	2.3%

Blackburn (two seats) 1918 General Election

Sir Henry Norman	Liberal-Coalition	32,078
Lt.-Col. P. Dean	Unionist-Coalition	30,158
P. Snowden	Labour	15,274
		16,804

Colne Valley 1922 General Election

P. Snowden	Labour	12,614	39.5% of vote
T. Brooke	Conservative	11,332	35.4% of vote
F. W. Mallalieu	Liberal	8,042	25.1% of vote
		1,282	4.1%

Colne Valley 1923 General Election

P. Snowden	Labour	13,136	40.4% of vote
T. Brooke	Conservative	11,215	34.4% of vote
P. H. Heffer	Liberal	8,223	25.2% of vote
		1,921	6.0%

Colne Valley 1924 General Election

Rt. Hon. P. Snowden	Labour	14,215	43.3% of vote
F. Thorpe	Conservative	10,972	33.4% of vote
R. F. Walker	Liberal	7,651	23.3% of vote
		3,232	9.9%

Colne Valley 1929 General Election

Rt. Hon. P. Snowden	Labour	21,667	48.3% of vote
R. B. Carrow	Conservative	12,532	28.0% of vote
F. Brook	Liberal	10,630	23.7% of vote
		9,135	20.3%

Bibliography and Bibliographical Essay

Philip Snowden left no private collection of correspondence for he expressly instructed Ethel to destroy his personal records upon his death. As a result of this action, the Snowden Collection in Keighley Public Library is composed almost entirely of published material – the *Labour Leader*, the *Labour Prophet*, reports of ILP conferences, books, pamphlets and collections of newscuttings. He also pre-empted his later biographers by publishing his *An Autobiography* (1934), some of which was quite clearly based upon letters and general correspondence which no longer survive. It is thus difficult to obtain a fully three-dimensional image of Snowden: there are no diaries or personal correspondence of a substantial nature which indicate his personal views on matters or help to explain his relationship with his wife. His *An Autobiography* is a plaited narrative of his life but is shallow on his personal life and pawky and partial on more public matters.

To reconstruct Snowden's life I have had to rely heavily upon his printed statements, which are voluminous, and the collections of manuscripts and records of the Independent Labour Party and the Labour Party. In this area, Labour records have become more readily available through the work of Harvester Microform Ltd., who have in recent years published, on microfilm and microfiche, the Francis Johnson Collection of Independent Labour Party correspondence, the correspondence of the Labour Representation Committee and an extensive collection of Labour Party material, including the National Executive Committee minutes and the pamphlets of the Labour Party. These records do vary in the light they throw on Snowden but are essential reading for those who wish to gain an insight into Snowden's position within Labour politics.

Of all the early Labour leaders, Snowden has been the least examined. Keir Hardie has been the subject of at least half a dozen serious biographical studies and Ramsay MacDonald, so frequently analysed before his death, has been examined by L. MacNeill Weir and David Marquand in two monumental works which move in opposite directions. Snowden has been paid scant attention in comparison with his two great contemporaries. The relative lack of interest in him may be due to the opprobrious reaction of the Labour movement to his political defection in 1931 but is more likely due to the lack of a central source of reference for the study of his life. In fact there have only been three biographical studies of Snowden. Two were admiring studies, published in 1929 – one by 'Ephesian' (C. E. Bechofer Roberts) entitled *Philip Snowden: An Impartial Portrait* and the other by A. Andreades (translated by Dorothy Bolton), simply entitled *Philip Snowden*. Both have obvious limitations for they outline Snowden's career before the cataclysmic change it underwent in 1931. Since then there has been only one detailed biographical study by Colin Cross, who wrote his book *Philip Snowden* in 1966, apart from a brief recent collection produced by Bradford Library services.

Notwithstanding such slight interest, Snowden has been the subject of criticism and examination in many other studies. The bibliography produced below attempts to provide a reasonably full list of primary and secondary sources which deal with aspects of Snowden's life.

Primary Sources

Books and Pamphlets by Philip Snowden

Individual under Socialism (Keighley ILP Pamphlet), 1903.

The Christ that is to be (ILP) 1903. This pamphlet is perhaps the best example of Snowden's faith in the ethical and individual basis of socialism. It was frequently republished and was the basis of a lecture which Snowden regularly performed in his early years.

The Chamberlain Bubble (Pamphlet), 1903.

Labour Politics (ILP, Pamphlet with J. Keir Hardie and David Shackleton), 1903.

The Industrial Muddle and the Way Out (Yeadon and Guiseley District Factory Workers' Union Pamphlet), Union, c. 1901–c. 1905.

Protection, Free Trade and Monopoly (ILP, London), 1904.

Facts for the Workers (Pamphlet), 1904.

A Straight Talk to Ratepayers (ILP, London, Pamphlet), 1906.

The Socialist Budget (George Allen, London, Pamphlet), 1907.

The New Workmen's Compensation Act Made Plain (ILP, London, Pamphlet), 1907.

Old Age Pensions, This Year (ILP, London, Pamphlet), 1907.

Socialism and the Drink Lobby (ILP, London, Book), 1908.

How to Get an Old Age Pension (Pamphlet), 1908.

Socialism and Teetotalism (ILP, London, Pamphlet), 1909.

Where is the Money to Come From: The Question Answered (ILP, London, Pamphlet), 1909.

A Few Hints to Lloyd George (Pamphlet), 1909.

In Defence of the Conciliation Bill (Wadsworth & Co., Keighley and Women's Press, London, Pamphlet), 1911.
The Living Wage (Book), 1912.
The Dominant Issue (Pamphlet), 1913.
Socialism and Syndicalism (Collins, London, Book), 1913.
A Plea for Peace (Blackburn Labour Party, Pamphlet), 1916.
Labour in Chains (National Labour Press, London, Pamphlet), 1917.
How to Pay for the War – Tax the Unearned Incomes of the Rich (Pamphlet), 1916.
War and Peace (National Labour Publications, London, Pamphlet), 1918.
Prospect and Retrospect (ILP, London, Pamphlet), 1919.
Labour and National Finance (Leonard Parsons, London, Book), 1920.
Twenty Objections to Socialism (ILP, London, Pamphlet), 1920.
Wages and Prices (Faith Press, London, Pamphlet), 1920.
Labour and the New World (Cassell & Co. Ltd., Book), 1921, revised 1924.
If Labour Rules (Labour Publishing Company, London, Pamphlet), 1923.
The Big Business Budget (Labour Party, London, Pamphlet), 1923. This attacks the Conservative Budget of 1923 and is based upon Snowden's speech to the House of Commons.
20 Objections to Socialism Answered by Philip Snowden (ILP, London, Pamphlet), 1920 and reissued throughout the 1920s.
The Housewife's Budget (Labour Party, London, Pamphlet), 1924. This was Snowden's 1924 Budget speech to the House of Commons.
The Rich Man's Budget (Labour Party, London, Pamphlet), 1925. This was Snowden's House of Commons speech attacking Winston Churchill's 1925 Budget.
Tory Government's Pitiable Confession of Incapacity: Labour's Rising Challenge (Labour Party, London, Pamphlet), 1926.
Rising Challenge (Labour Party, London, Pamphlet), 1926.
The Way to Industrial Peace (John Clifford Lecture, London, Pamphlet), 1927.
The Faith of a Democrat (Ernest Benn, London, Pamphlet), 1928.
An Autobiography (Ivor Nicholson & Watson, London, Book: 2 vols.), 1934. This book outlines Snowden's career.
Mr. Lloyd George's New Deal (Ivor Nicholson & Watson, Pamphlet), 1935.
The General Election (Liberal Publication Department, London, Pamphlet), 1935.
End this Colossal Waste: A Neglected Palliative to Unemployment (Ivor Nicholson & Watson, Pamphlet), 1936. This pamphlet discusses the waste of spending on drink and argues that it contributes considerably to the problem of poverty and unemployment.

Books and Pamphlets of Ethel Snowden

Women: A Few Shrieks (E.S., Pamphlet), 1907.

Women and the State (Pamphlet), 1907.
The Woman Socialist (ILP, London, Book, in The Labour Ideal series), 1907.
The Feminist Movement (National Library, London, Book), 1913.
Through Bolshevik Russia (Cassell & Co., London, Book), 1920.
A Political Pilgrim in Europe (Cassell & Co. Ltd., London, Book), 1920.
British Standards of Child Welfare (Pamphlet drawn from a lecture), 1926.
Welfare as Tested by 'The Declaration of Geneva' (Shaftesbury Society & Ragged School Union, London, Pamphlet), 1926.

Manuscript Collections

Archives of the British Labour Party: National Executive Committee Minutes, Labour Party pamphlet collection and the Labour Representation Committee, Correspondence 1900–1907. (Recently published by Harvester Microform).
Cabinet Papers, (Public Record Office).
Colne Valley Divisional Labour Party, Minutes. (Polytechnic Library, Huddersfield).
Francis Johnson Collection: Correspondence of the Independent Labour Party (British Library of Political and Economic Science).
J. B. Glasier Collection (University of Liverpool Library).
Lloyd George Papers (House of Lords Library).
J. R. MacDonald Diary and Papers (Public Record Office).
Symington Collection (West Yorkshire Archives Service, Sheepscar Library, Leeds).

Printed Collection

Snowden Collection (Keighley Public Library).

Newspapers and Journals

Snowden wrote extensively for the *Daily Express*, the *Daily Mail*, the *Sunday Dispatch* and the *Star*.
He also wrote in the
Blackburn Labour Journal (became the *Workers' Tribune* in 1909).
Blackburn Times
Bradford Pioneer
Christian Commonwealth
Huddersfield Citizen
Keighley Echo
Keighley Labour Journal. Snowden edited this paper between 1898 and 1902.
Keighley News. This was the paper in which Snowden's first published

socialist contribution, a letter, appeared in January 1895.
Labour Leader. This was the official organ of the ILP.

Secondary Sources

Biographies

Andreades, A. (translated by Dorothy Bolton), *Philip Snowden* (P. S. King, London), 1930.
Cross, C. *Philip Snowden* (Barrie & Rockliffe, London), 1966.
'Ephesian' (C. E. Bechofer Roberts), *Philip Snowden* (Cassell & Co. Ltd., London), 1929.
Laybourn, K. and James, D. (eds.) *Philip Snowden* (Bradford Metro), 1987.

Secondary Books and Pamphlets

Bealey, F. and Pelling, H., *Labour and Politics, 1900–1906* (Macmillan, London), 1958.
Brockway, F., *Towards Tomorrow* (Granada, London and Manchester), 1977.
Brockway, F., *Inside the Left* (Allen and Unwin, London), 1942.
Brockway, F., *Socialism over Sixty Years: The Life of Jowett of Bradford, 1864–1944* (Allen and Unwin, London), 1946.
Carston, F. L., *War Against War* (Batsford, London), 1982.
Clark, D., *Colne Valley: Radicalism to Socialism* (Longman, London), 1981.
Clarke, P. F., *Lancashire and the New Liberalism* (Cambridge UP, London), 1971.
Craig, F. W. S., *British Parliamentary Election Results 1885–1918* (Macmillan, London), 1974.
Craig, F. W. S., *British Parliamentary Election Results 1918–1949* (Macmillan, London), 1977.
Clay, Sir H., *Lord Norman* (Macmillan, London), 1957.
Clynes, J. R., *Memoirs* (Hutchinson, London), 1977.
Cole, M., *Growing up into Revolution* (Longman Green, London), 1949.
Cowling, M., *The Impact of Labour 1920–1924* (Cambridge University Press), 1971.
Dowse, R. E., *Left in the Centre* (Longman, London), 1966.
Graham, T., *Willie Graham* (Hutchinson & Co., London), 1948.
Hamilton, M. A., *Arthur Henderson* (Heinemann, London) 1938.
Hamilton, M. A., *Remembering My Good Friends* (Jonathan Cape, London), 1944.
Howell, D. *The British Workers and the Independent Labour Party, 1888–1906* (Manchester University Press, Manchester), 1983. This is very useful on Snowden's early career with the ILP.

Jones, Thomas, *Whitehall Diary*, edited by Keith Middlemass, vol. I 1916–1925 and vol. II 1926–1930 (Oxford University Press, London), 1969.

Joyce, P., *Work, Society, Politics* (Harvester Press, Brighton and London), 1980.

Laybourn, K. and Reynolds, J., *Liberalism and The Rise of Labour 1890–1918* (Croom Helm, London), 1984.

Liddington, J. and Norris, J., *One Hand Tied Behind Us* (Virago, London), 1978.

Liddington, J., *The Life and Times of a Respectable Rebel: Selina Cooper 1864–1946* (Virago, London), 1984.

Marquand, D., *Ramsay MacDonald* (Jonathan Cape, London), 1977. This is a very detailed, though much attacked, biography of Snowden. It confirms the view that Snowden had little to do with the political decision to form a National Government in 1931, even though his policies shaped the contours of the crisis.

Marwick, A., *Clifford Allen: The Open Conspirator* (Oliver & Boyd, Edinburgh and London), 1964.

Miliband, R., *Parliamentary Socialism* (Allen and Unwin, London), 1961.

Moore, R., *The Emergence of the Labour Party 1880–1924* (Hodder and Stoughton, London), 1979.

Morgan, K. O., *Keir Hardie, Radical and Socialist* (Weidenfeld and Nicolson, London), 1975. This is the best book on Hardie and contains some references to his relations with Snowden.

McKibbin, R., *The Evolution of the Labour Party 1910–1924* (Oxford UP, London), 1974. This is still the best book on British Labour history for the period it covers.

McLean, I., *Keir Hardie* (Allen Lane, London), 1975.

Pelling, H., *The Origins of the Labour Party 1880–1900* (Macmillan, London), 1954. This is a pioneer study on the early history of the Labour movement and has remained the principal book on this area for thirty years.

Poirier, P., *The Advent of the Labour Party* (Allen and Unwin, London), 1958.

Pierson, S., *Marxism and the Origins of British Socialism* (Cornell UP, Ithaca), 1973.

Pierson, S., *British Socialists* (Harvard UP, Harvard), 1979. This is very good on the ethical side of the movement, which Snowden represented.

Reid, F., *Keir Hardie: The Making of a Socialist* (Croom Helm, London), 1978.

Skidelsky, R., *Politicians and the Slump: The Labour Government of 1929–1931* (Macmillan, London), 1967. This is easily the best outline of the economic philosophy of Snowden and those who supported deflationary policies in the 1920s and early 1930s. It is excellent on the 1931 financial crisis.

Thompson, L., *The Enthusiasts* (Gollancz, London), 1971. This is about the Glasiers but is useful in that it emphasizes the ethical aspect of the Labour movement and does discuss Snowden, Keir Hardie and other Labour leaders.

Weir, L. M., *The Tragedy of Ramsay MacDonald* (Secker & Warburg, London), 1938. This is a vitriolic biography of MacDonald which uses Snowden's dislike of MacDonald as evidence of his treachery.

Articles

Barker, B., 'Anatomy of Reformism: The social and political ideas of the Labour leadership in Yorkshire', *International Review of Social History*, XVIII(1), 1973.

Bealey, F., 'Negotiations between the Liberal Party and the Labour Representation Committee before the General Election of 1906', *Bulletin of Historical Research*, XXIX, 1956.

Bealey, F., 'The Northern Weavers, Independent Labour Representation and Clitheroe, 1902', *Manchester School*, 25, 1957.

Clarke, P. F., 'British Politics and Blackburn Politics 1900–1910', *Historical Journal*, 1969.

Duffy, A. E. P., 'Differing Policies and Personal Rivalries in The Origins of the ILP', *Victorian Studies*, VI, 1962–63.

Jowitt, J. A. and Laybourn, K., 'The Wool Textile Dispute of 1925', *The Journal of Local (now Local and Regional) Studies*, vol. 2, no. 1, Spring 1982. This refers to Snowden's role as a Labour representative on the Court of Inquiry which was set up to settle the dispute.

Malament, Barbara C., 'Philip Snowden and the Cabinet Deliberations of August 1931', *Society for the Study of Labour History*, Bulletin, 41, Autumn 1980.

McKibbin, R., 'The Economic Policy and the Second Labour Government, 1929–1931, *Past and Present*, no. 68, August 1978.

Reynolds, J. and Laybourn, K., 'The Emergence of the Independent Labour Party in Bradford', *International Review of Social History*, XX, (3), 1975.

Thompson, E. P., 'Homage to Tom Maguire' in Briggs, A. and Saville, J. (eds) *Essays in Labour History* (Macmillan, London), 1960. This is the seminal article on the growth of the Labour movement in Yorkshire and Lancashire during the 1890s.

Yeo, S., 'A New Life: The Religion of Socialism in Britain 1883–1896', *History Workshop*, (4), Autumn 1977. This substantial article recaptures the ethical and religious aspect on the Labour movement out of which Snowden emerged.

Unpublished Theses

Clark, D. G., 'The Origins and Development of the Labour Party in Colne Valley 1891–1907', unpublished PhD thesis, University of Sheffield, 1978.

James, D., 'The Emergence of the Keighley Independent Labour Party', unpublished MA dissertation, The Polytechnic, Huddersfield, 1980.
Walton, R. L., 'The Labour Movement in Blackburn 1880–1914', unpublished MA dissertation, The Polytechnic, Huddersfield, 1982.

Index